The Fed and Lehman Brothers

The bankruptcy of the investment bank Lehman Brothers was the pivotal event of the 2008 financial crisis and the Great Recession that followed. Ever since the bankruptcy, there has been heated debate about why the Federal Reserve did not rescue Lehman in the same way it rescued other financial institutions, such as Bear Stearns and AIG. The Fed's leaders from that time, especially former Chairman Ben Bernanke, have strongly asserted that they lacked the legal authority to save Lehman because it did not have adequate collateral for the loan it needed to survive. Based on a meticulous four-year study of the Lehman case, *The Fed and Lehman Brothers* debunks the official narrative of the crisis. Ball argues that in reality, the Fed could have rescued Lehman but officials chose not to because of political pressures and because they underestimated the damage that the bankruptcy would do to the economy. The compelling story of the Lehman collapse will interest anyone who cares about what caused the financial crisis, whether the leaders of the Federal Reserve have given accurate accounts of their actions, and how the Fed can prevent future financial disasters.

LAURENCE M. BALL is Professor of Economics and Department Chair at Johns Hopkins University and a Research Associate at the National Bureau of Economic Research. He has been a Visiting Scholar at the Board of Governors of the Federal Reserve System, the Federal Reserve Banks of Boston, Kansas City, and Philadelphia, foreign central banks, and the International Monetary Fund. His research topics include inflation, unemployment, and monetary and fiscal policy.

STUDIES IN MACROECONOMIC HISTORY

Series Editor: Michael D. Bordo, *Rutgers University*

Editors: Owen F. Humpage, *Federal Reserve Bank of Cleveland*
Christopher M. Meissner, *University of California, Davis*
Kris James Mitchener, *Santa Clara University*
David C. Wheelock, *Federal Reserve Bank of St. Louis*

The titles in this series investigate themes of interest to economists and economic historians in the rapidly developing field of macroeconomic history. The four areas covered include the application of monetary and finance theory, international economics, and quantitative methods to historical problems; the historical application of growth and development theory and theories of business fluctuations; the history of domestic and international monetary, financial, and other macroeconomic institutions; and the history of international monetary and financial systems. The series amalgamates the former Cambridge University Press series *Studies in Monetary and Financial History* and *Studies in Quantitative Economic History*.

Other Books in the Series

Continued after Index

The Fed and Lehman Brothers

Setting the Record Straight on a Financial Disaster

LAURENCE M. BALL

Johns Hopkins University

CAMBRIDGE
UNIVERSITY PRESS

CAMBRIDGE
UNIVERSITY PRESS

University Printing House, Cambridge CB2 8BS, United Kingdom

One Liberty Plaza, 20th Floor, New York, NY 10006, USA

477 Williamstown Road, Port Melbourne, VIC 3207, Australia

314–321, 3rd Floor, Plot 3, Splendor Forum, Jasola District Centre, New Delhi – 110025, India

79 Anson Road, #06–04/06, Singapore 079906

Cambridge University Press is part of the University of Cambridge.

It furthers the University's mission by disseminating knowledge in the pursuit of education, learning, and research at the highest international levels of excellence.

www.cambridge.org
Information on this title: www.cambridge.org/9781108420969
DOI: 10.1017/9781108355742

© Cambridge University Press 2018

First published 2018
Reprinted 2018

Printed in the United States of America by Sheridan Books, Inc.

A catalogue record for this publication is available from the British Library.

ISBN 978-1-108-42096-9 Hardback

Contents

    The Fed and the Treasury in 2008
    Henry Paulson's Role in the Lehman Crisis
    Ben Bernanke's Role in the Lehman Crisis
    Why Was Paulson in Charge?

12 Explaining the Lehman Decision   209
    Fear of Political Backlash
    Expectations about the Costs of Lehman's Failure
    The Fed's Shift on AIG

13 Conclusion   225

    Notes   229
    References   250
    Index   255

Preface

On September 10, 2008, economists at the Federal Reserve prepared one of their regular analyses of the US economy for the senior policymakers setting interest rates. Falling real estate prices and rising defaults on home mortgages had caused stresses in financial markets and the economy, and the unemployment rate had drifted up from 5.0 percent at the end of 2007 to 6.1 percent in August 2008. The Fed's economists believed, however, that these problems would be contained. They forecasted that the unemployment rate would average 6.2 percent over the last three months of 2008, remain at that level in 2009, and then start falling.[1]

Five days after these forecasts were made, the US financial system was hit with a disaster: the bankruptcy of Lehman Brothers. Founded in 1850, Lehman was the country's fourth largest investment bank and a pillar of Wall Street. In 2007, it had ranked number one on *Fortune* magazine's list of "Most Admired Securities Firms." With $600 billion in assets, it was by far the largest US corporation in any industry to file a bankruptcy petition (the previous record holder, the communications giant WorldCom, had only about $100 billion of assets when it failed in 2002).

The bankruptcy ushered in a six-month period that many have called a "financial tsunami."[2] With Lehman destroyed, confidence in the remaining Wall Street firms quickly collapsed, and many of them, from Citigroup to Goldman Sachs to Morgan Stanley, had trouble raising the funds they needed to make investments and provide credit to other companies. Across the country, banks cut back sharply on lending and corporations had to pay pathologically high interest rates to issue bonds. The Dow Jones stock index, which had been near 13,000 at the start of 2008, fell to about 6,500 in March 2009.

The crisis in the financial system quickly spread to the rest of the economy. As wealth was destroyed and flows of credit broke down, consumers and firms cut their spending sharply, producing the Great Recession of 2008–2009. Total US employment fell by almost 500,000 in October 2008, and then by 700,000–800,000 in each of the following six months. In April 2009, the unemployment rate was 9 percent and rising rapidly. Princeton economist Alan Blinder summarizes these events with a vivid metaphor: the economy was hit by a truck, and "the license plate of that truck read: *L-E-H-M-A-N*."[3]

At the height of the crisis, many people feared that the financial system and economy would collapse as profoundly as they did in the 1930s. In January 2009, Nobel Prize winner Paul Krugman said, "This looks an awful lot like the beginnings of a second Great Depression." Henry Paulson, the Secretary of the Treasury in 2008, later wrote, "The economic damage . . . could easily have equaled or even exceeded that of the Great Depression, with 25 percent unemployment, or worse."[4]

A catastrophe of that magnitude did not come to pass. In the Spring of 2009, stability began to return to Wall Street and stock prices began to recover. The financial crisis was arrested in large part because of extraordinary actions by economic policymakers, including more than a trillion dollars of loans from the Federal Reserve to financial institutions. These loans saved a number of firms from near-certain failure, including the investment bank Bear Stearns and the insurance company AIG. Other policy actions included purchases of the stock of financial institutions by the US Treasury under the Troubled Asset Relief Program, and the new Obama administration's fiscal stimulus program.

Yet the financial crisis was contained only after the economy had sustained severe damage. The Great Recession was not as bad as the 1930s Depression, but it was the worst downturn since then and it was followed by a painfully slow recovery. Employment fell through the end of 2009, and the unemployment rate reached 10 percent. Employment started to recover in 2010, but it took until

September 2015, seven years after Lehman's bankruptcy, for the unemployment rate to fall back to 5 percent, roughly what economists consider a normal level for the long term.

Behind these unemployment statistics, there is terrible damage to people's lives. Social scientists have found that a period of unemployment leaves long-term scars by reducing a worker's earnings for decades. People with the bad luck to finish school during a recession have trouble starting a career, thus hurting their lifetime prospects. The experience of unemployment increases the risk of depression, substance abuse, suicide, and death from heart disease. For children, having an unemployed parent increases the risk of repeating a year in school and the risk of health problems such as obesity.[5]

The Lehman Brothers bankruptcy was a shocking event in part because it was unique. Many Wall Street firms reached the brink of failure during 2008, but Lehman was the only one that was *not* rescued by a loan from the Federal Reserve, and had to file for bankruptcy. Why didn't the Fed rescue Lehman? That question has been hotly debated from the firm's bankruptcy filing until today, and it is the primary subject of this book.

The question has been asked of Federal Reserve officials on many, many occasions, and they have given a consistent answer: they did not rescue Lehman because they lacked the legal authority to do so. The Fed couldn't lend to Lehman because the firm could not post enough collateral to secure the loan that it needed, as required by Section 13(3) of the Federal Reserve Act. As Fed Chair Ben Bernanke said in 2010, "The only way we could have saved Lehman would have been by breaking the law."[6]

Lehman executives have bitterly disputed the Fed's position, saying their firm could have survived if the Fed had treated it the same way it treated other firms both before and after the bankruptcy. Among disinterested students of the financial crisis, some have supported the Fed's position and others have not. In 2013, William Cline and Joseph Gagnon of the Peterson Institute for International

Economics said that, because of Lehman's inadequate collateral, "saving Lehman would have required an outright deception on the part of the Fed that was not required for other loans." But in 2014, Ryan Avent of the *Economist* magazine said, "There was no reason Lehman had to fail" and "the decision to let Lehman fail was political."[7]

As this controversy developed, I, like many people, wondered which side was right. In the summer of 2012, I started to look for evidence about Lehman's finances and the feasibility and legality of a Fed rescue of the firm. I soon discovered something that is not widely appreciated: there is a huge amount of hard evidence on these topics that is easily available to anyone. The sources of this evidence include Federal Reserve records, the financial statements that Lehman filed with the Securities and Exchange Commission, research by journalists, and, most important, investigations performed by the Examiner for the Lehman bankruptcy court and by the Congressionally appointed Financial Crisis Inquiry Commission.

I spent four years analyzing these records and found that they support some firm conclusions about the Lehman episode. The central conclusions in this book concern the claim of Fed officials that they did not rescue Lehman because the firm lacked the collateral needed to make a loan legal. This claim is wrong: the evidence shows clearly that issues of collateral and legality were *not* important factors in the decisions of Fed officials. In addition, Lehman actually *did* have ample collateral for a loan that would have averted its sudden bankruptcy.

Why, then, didn't the Fed rescue Lehman? The available evidence supports the view that policymakers were deterred by the strong political and public opposition to a rescue. The evidence also shows that Fed officials underestimated the damage that the Lehman failure would do to the economy.

Economists have long understood that banks can experience runs, or liquidity crises, that can damage or destroy otherwise healthy institutions. Fears that a bank may fail, whether warranted or not, can lead to a cutoff of funding that causes the failure to occur. The traditional version of a run is one in which people rush to a bank to withdraw their money and the bank runs out of cash. An example, fictional but realistic, is the run on Jimmy Stewart's bank in the 1946 classic *It's a Wonderful Life*.

The 2008 crises on Wall Street were twenty-first century versions of bank runs. They originated with bad investments in real estate, but losses from these investments were not the direct cause of Lehman's sudden collapse or of the near-collapses of the institutions that the Fed chose to rescue. Instead, the fatal development was a loss of confidence by other financial institutions, which led them to suddenly refuse to renew short-term loans that Lehman and the other distressed firms needed to operate. Without the cash from such loans, Lehman could not pay the debts it had coming due on September 15.

A run need not doom a financial institution to a bankruptcy like Lehman's. An economy's central bank can save an institution from a run by serving as the "lender of last resort," a concept introduced by British businessman and journalist Walter Bagehot in his 1873 book *Lombard Street*. Bagehot's basic idea was that a central bank can lend to a bank when a run has disrupted its usual sources of cash, thereby enabling the bank to stay in business. Bagehot emphasized that such a loan must be made "against good collateral" to ensure that the central bank is eventually repaid – essentially the same condition that US law imposed on Fed loans in 2008. In the late nineteenth and early twentieth centuries, Bagehot's principles were used to quell financial panics in the United Kingdom, France, and Canada.[8]

In the United States, the Federal Reserve was created in 1914 to serve as a lender of last resort. The greatest mistake in the Fed's history was its failure to fulfill that role in the 1930s. Its failure to lend as panic-induced runs destroyed banks across the country ushered in the Great Depression. After World War II, a consensus grew that the Fed should avoid repeating its mistake if another crisis struck. This view was advocated by Milton Friedman and Anna Schwartz in their 1963 *Monetary History of the United States,* and the position was strengthened in the 1980s by research on the Depression by a young academic named Ben Bernanke.[9]

As Fed Chairman, Bernanke explicitly invoked Bagehot's principles to explain the 2008 rescues of financial institutions such as AIG.[10] These principles would also have justified a loan to rescue Lehman, because Lehman faced a run and it had the collateral required by Bagehot and by the law governing the Fed. But Fed policymakers chose not to rescue Lehman. In making this decision, as in the 1930s, the Fed failed to perform its role as lender of last resort.

We can hope that the Fed does not make a similar mistake in the next financial crisis, but there is reason for pessimism: bank regulation since the 2008 crisis has taken a wrong turn. In response to widespread condemnation of "bailouts," Congress included stringent new restrictions on Fed lending in the Dodd-Frank Wall Street Reform Act of 2010. The details are complex, but the effect is that some of the Fed's 2008 rescues of financial institutions – and the Lehman rescue that *could* have occurred – might truly be illegal during the next crisis. As I emphasize in the conclusion of this book, it is vital to the future safety of the financial system that Congress correct its 2010 mistake.

Many excellent books discuss the 2008 financial crisis. Authors such as Alan Blinder, David Wessel of the Brookings Institution, and Martin Wolf of the *Financial Times*, to name just a few, provide insights into the many causes and effects of the crisis, the deeper flaws in the economy and financial regulation that the crisis reflected, and the pros and cons of the policies pursued by the Fed and the Treasury department.[11]

What distinguishes this book from all the others on the financial crisis is the level of detail in which it examines the crisis's pivotal event, the Lehman Brothers failure, and the amount of evidence it analyzes to get to the bottom of what happened and why. This evidence allows me to cut through the competing claims of previous authors and set the record straight on why the Fed did not rescue Lehman. My research establishes that Fed officials' claims about their actions are not credible, no matter how often and how strongly these claims are repeated.

Acknowledgments

In July 2016 I completed a monograph on the Federal Reserve's role in the Lehman Brothers bankruptcy, which I have presented to audiences of academics and central bankers. Through discussions of my work, I came to believe that a wider audience might want to understand the Lehman episode, and as a result I have written this book. I have maintained the rigor of my academic piece but have sought to make my analysis more accessible by adding background on some topics and, wherever possible, using plainer English to supplement more technical language.

I am deeply grateful to the people who have helped with this project. Michael Bordo of Rutgers University offered to include my work in the series on monetary history that he edits for Cambridge University Press, and editors Stephen Accera and Karen Maloney of Cambridge University Press have expertly overseen the process of planning and publishing the book.

Most important, development editor Jane Tufts guided me in expositing my research for a broad audience. Jane is widely known as the best development editor working in the field of economics, and her writing talent and her dedication to this book have truly been extraordinary. I was able to hire Jane thanks to generous financial support from the Smith Richardson Foundation.

I am also deeply grateful to all those who helped with my 2016 monograph.

- David Romer and Markham Ball gave me detailed comments that improved every part of that work.
- The following people offered comments and suggestions: Stephen Cecchetti, William English, Jacob Goldfield, Patrick Honohan, Joanne Im, Edward Nelson, Athanasios Orphanides, Julio Rotemberg, Jeffrey Sachs,

Andrei Shleifer, Charles Steindel, Lawrence Summers, John Taylor, and my colleagues at Johns Hopkins University.

- The participants in many seminars provided helpful feedback. These seminars were held at the following: Rutgers University, the University of Mississippi, the Graduate Institute in Geneva, Harvard Business School, the University of Chicago Booth School of Business, the University of Michigan Law School, the Federal Reserve Bank of Boston, the Riksbank (central bank of Sweden), and the National Bureau of Economic Research.
- Edmund Crawley provided outstanding research assistance.
- Half a dozen people with first-hand knowledge of the Lehman episode spoke to me off the record and gave me deeper insight into what happened in 2008.

Not everyone who commented on my work agrees with my conclusions. All opinions expressed in this book are strictly my own.

A Chronology of the Lehman Disaster

[All dates are in 2008][*]

THE GROWING CRISIS

February 29	After increases in risky investments, Lehman's total assets peak at $786 billion.
March 11	The Fed creates the Term Securities Lending Facility (TSLF).
March 14	The Fed lends Bear Stearns $13 billion to meet its obligations that day.
March 16	The Fed creates Maiden Lane LLC to purchase $30 billion of real estate assets from Bear Stearns, facilitating the acquisition of Bear by JPMorgan Chase.
March 16	The Fed creates the Primary Dealer Credit Facility (PDCF).
March 18	Lehman reports better-than-expected earnings for 2008 Q1.
March	Lehman begins efforts to sell illiquid assets and to find a strategic partner.
March–April	In the wake of Bear Stearns's near-failure, bond rating agencies announce negative changes in their outlooks for Lehman.
May 21	In a prominent speech, hedge fund manager David Einhorn argues that Lehman's real estate assets are overvalued.

---

[*] This chronology draws on previous chronologies of the Lehman episode from the Bankruptcy Examiner, the Financial Crisis Inquiry Commission, and the UK Financial Services Authority, along with other sources cited in this book.

May–June	The NY Fed performs liquidity stress tests for Lehman.
June 9	Lehman reports a $2.8 billion loss for 2008 Q2, its first ever quarterly loss.
June 9	Lehman raises $6 billion by issuing new stock.
June 12	Lehman replaces its President and Chief Financial Officer.
June	JPMorgan Chase begins to demand collateral to clear Lehman's tri-party repos.
June–July	Rating agencies downgrade Lehman's bonds. Media suggest that Lehman is endangered.
June–August	Lehman has difficulty issuing unsecured debt and loses some repo financing.
July 11	NY Fed staff prepare a plan for replacing the repo funding of a broker-dealer, focusing on Lehman.
July 15	The NY Fed's William Dudley circulates a plan for a "Maiden Lane type vehicle" to buy illiquid assets from Lehman.
August 31	The Korean Development Bank proposes a $6 billion investment in Lehman.
September 7	The Treasury department places Fannie Mae and Freddie Mac into conservatorship.

LEHMAN'S FINAL WEEK

Tuesday, September 9

The Korean Development Bank ends negotiations about a Lehman investment.

The Investment Bank of Dubai says it needs a "time out" in negotiations about an investment.

S&P and Fitch place Lehman's bond rating on a negative watch.

JPMorgan Chase demands an additional $5 billion of collateral from Lehman.

Bank of America begins due diligence for a possible acquisition of Lehman.

Lehman's stock price falls from $14 to $8.

Lehman's liquidity pool (by author's calculations) stands at $23 billion, down from $48 billion on May 31.

Wednesday, September 10

Lehman announces a $3.9 billion loss for 2008 Q3. It also announces plans to create REI Global and to sell a majority stake in its Investment Management Division.

Moody's puts Lehman's bond rating on a negative watch, threatening a two-notch downgrade if the firm does not find a strategic partner by September 15.

NY Fed President Geithner leads a conference call on options for aiding Lehman, including "a Fed take out of tri-party lenders" and "a Fed-assisted BoA acquisition."

A "liquidity consortium gameplan" for rescuing Lehman circulates within the Federal Reserve.

Wednesday–Friday, September 10–12

Lehman experiences an acute liquidity crisis. Cash drains include losses of repos, collateral calls from derivatives counterparties, and withdrawals from prime brokerage accounts.

Thursday, September 11

JPMorgan Chase and Citi threaten to stop clearing transactions for Lehman if it is not acquired by another firm by September 15.

In a conference call with Geithner and Fed Chairman Bernanke, Treasury Secretary Paulson says "there would be no public assistance for a Lehman bailout."

Friday, September 12, morning and afternoon

Paulson has breakfast with Bernanke in Washington, DC and then travels to New York.

Barclays begins due diligence for a possible acquisition of Lehman.

Bank of America loses interest in acquiring Lehman.

Fed Vice Chair Kohn reports that Fed and Treasury oppose "involvement [with Lehman] beyond liquidity provision."

Emails among Fed staff discuss options if Lehman loses repo funding on September 15.

Lehman's liquidity pool is $1.4 billion at the close of business.

LEHMAN'S FINAL WEEKEND *

Friday, September 12, evening

7:00 PM   Paulson convenes a meeting about Lehman with Wall Street CEOs at the New York Fed. He says "there would be no public money to support Lehman."

Saturday–Sunday, September 13–14

Analyses by Lehman and its advisors determine that the firm will quickly run out of cash if it opens for business on Monday, the 15th.

Saturday, September 13

Fed staff continue to discuss options if Lehman loses repo funding.

7:00 AM   Paulson arrives at the NY Fed to try to broker an acquisition of Lehman.

Morning   Bernanke receives "discouraging reports" on Lehman from Geithner.

Morning   Lehman executives meet at the NY Fed to discuss a wind-down plan for the firm, but then officials tell them to concentrate on a Barclays transaction.

Afternoon   A tentative deal is reached: Barclays will purchase all of Lehman except for $40 billion of assets that will be financed by a consortium of Wall Street firms.

Afternoon   NY Fed tells Barclays that, to receive Fed approval of the deal, Barclays must immediately guarantee all of Lehman's obligations.

* Many of the times listed here are approximate.

7:00 PM	Bernanke receives a briefing on Lehman in a conference call with other Fed officials.
9:00 PM	Paulson leaves the NY Fed, feeling "optimistic about the prospects for a deal."

Sunday, September 14

8:00 AM	Callum McCarthy, head of the United Kingdom's Financial Services Authority, calls Geithner and says the FSA will not allow Barclays to immediately guarantee Lehman's obligations.
9:00 AM	Paulson's chief of staff reports on a call to the White House: "government is united behind no money" for Lehman.
10:00 AM	SEC Chair Christopher Cox calls McCarthy but cannot resolve the impasse over the guarantee issue.
10:00 AM	Paulson calls President Bush's chief of staff, who says Paulson does not have Presidential approval to "commit Federal resources" to a Lehman rescue.
11:00 AM	Paulson calls Alistair Darling, the UK's Chancellor of the Exchequer, but is unable to rescue the Barclays deal.
Midday	Paulson and Geithner tell the Wall Street CEOs that the Barclays deal is dead and Lehman will file for bankruptcy.
Midday	Geithner calls Bernanke to report the failure of the Barclays deal and the plan for Lehman's bankruptcy.
1:00 PM	At a meeting with Lehman executives, NY Fed General Counsel Baxter directs the firm to file for bankruptcy. He says that the PDCF will assist Lehman's New York broker-dealer, LBI, to keep it in operation, but the PDCF will only lend against

	collateral that was on LBI's balance sheet on Friday, September 12.
1:22 PM	The Fed announces expansion of the acceptable collateral for the PDCF and TSLF. There is confusion about whether the expansion applies to Lehman.
2:00 PM	The NY Fed hosts a special session of derivatives trading, allowing some financial institutions to reduce their exposure to Lehman.
2:55 PM	Bernanke emails Fed Governor Kevin Warsh, who is at the NY Fed, to ask for news.
3:03 PM	Vice Chair Kohn emails Bernanke to report news from Warsh: an announcement of Lehman's bankruptcy is planned for 4:30.
4:12 PM	Lehman prepares a plan for LBI to borrow from the PDCF on behalf of other parts of Lehman.
4:16 PM	Bernanke again emails Warsh to ask for news.
Midafternoon	Paulson tells Geithner and Cox, "Lehman's got to file immediately."
Midafternoon	The Fed tells Lehman that the PDCF is not open to Lehman's London broker-dealer, LBIE.
Midafternoon	Lehman CEO Richard Fuld appeals unsuccessfully for help from Morgan Stanley CEO John Mack.
Midafternoon	George Walker, a Lehman executive who is a second cousin of President Bush, calls the White House but does not reach the President.
Midafternoon	Lehman executives begin work on an "orderly liquidation plan" for the firm, but abandon the effort when they learn that the government insists on an immediate bankruptcy.
Midafternoon	Bank of America agrees to acquire Merrill Lynch.
5:00 PM	Lehman's board of directors meets and learns that LBIE, the firm's London broker-dealer, is out of cash

	and will file for administration in the United Kingdom.
5:00 PM	In a conference call, Paulson, Bernanke, and others "review the day's dreadful events."
6:55 PM	Lehman's board convenes again.
8:00 PM	At Paulson's insistence, Cox calls Lehman's board and tells them to "make a decision quickly."
Late evening	Lehman's board votes to declare bankruptcy.

Monday, September 15, early morning

1:45 AM	Lehman's law firm, Weil Gotshal, files a bankruptcy petition for Lehman.
2:24 AM	Lehman receives a letter from the NY Fed saying the firm is eligible for the PDCF collateral expansion.

AFTER LEHMAN'S BANKRUPTCY

September 15–17	The PDCF makes overnight loans to LBI.
September 16	The Federal Open Market Committee meets and votes to keep its interest rate target unchanged, citing a balance between "downside risks to growth" and "upside risks to inflation."
	The Fed establishes an $85 billion line of credit for AIG.
	The Reserve Primary Fund "breaks the buck" due to losses on Lehman's commercial paper.
September 17–18	Money market mutual funds experience a run.
September 19	Barclays purchases part of LBI from the Lehman bankruptcy estate.
	The rest of LBI enters liquidation under the Securities Investors Protection Act.
	The Treasury temporarily guarantees shares in money market funds.

The Fed creates a facility to finance banks' purchases of commercial paper from money market funds.

September 21   Goldman Sachs and Morgan Stanley become bank holding companies.

The Fed opens the PDCF to the London broker-dealers of Goldman Sachs, Morgan Stanley, and Merrill Lynch.

September 23   In Congressional testimony, Bernanke says that the Fed "declined to assist Lehman" because markets were prepared for its failure.

Goldman Sachs raises $5 billion of capital from Berkshire Hathaway.

September 29   Morgan Stanley's total borrowing from Fed facilities reaches $107 billion.

Morgan Stanley raises $9 billion of capital from Mitsubishi UFJ.

October 3   President Bush signs legislation creating the Troubled Asset Relief Program.

October 6   The Fed grants AIG an additional credit line of $38 billion.

October 7   Bernanke says for the first time that rescuing Lehman would have been illegal because the firm lacked adequate collateral.

The Fed establishes the Commercial Paper Funding Facility.

November 10   The Fed creates Maiden Lane II and Maiden Lane III to assist AIG.

December 31   Goldman Sachs's total borrowing from Fed facilities reaches $69 billion.

I   Introduction

On Monday, September 15, 2008, at 1:45 AM, Lehman Brothers Holdings Inc. filed a bankruptcy petition in the United States Bankruptcy Court for the Southern District of New York. This action was the most dramatic event of the financial crisis of 2007–2009, and many economists believe it greatly worsened the crisis and the Great Recession that followed.

Why did Lehman Brothers fail? At one level, the answer is clear. Lehman suffered large losses on real estate investments in 2007–2008, which threatened its solvency. Other financial institutions lost confidence in Lehman, precipitating a liquidity crisis: the firm could not roll over the short-term debt that funded its illiquid assets. Lehman declared bankruptcy in the early hours of September 15 because it did not have enough cash to open for business that morning and pay debts that were due immediately.

At another level the Lehman story is less clear. Lehman was the only large financial institution that had to file for bankruptcy during the financial crisis. Others, such as Bear Stearns and AIG, also experienced liquidity crises and surely *would* have gone bankrupt if not for emergency loans from the Federal Reserve. Why didn't the Fed make a loan to rescue Lehman?

This question is controversial among students of the financial crisis. Some say that Fed officials bowed to political opposition to a Lehman "bailout." Others say that policymakers were concerned about moral hazard: they feared that rescuing Lehman would encourage excessive risk-taking by other firms. Yet another factor, according to many, is that policymakers underestimated the damage that Lehman's bankruptcy would do to the financial system and economy.

Fed officials insist, however, that none of these views is correct. The people in charge in 2008, from Federal Reserve Chairman Ben Bernanke on down, have said repeatedly that they wanted to save Lehman, but could not do so because they lacked the legal authority. When the Fed lends to a financial institution, Section 13(3) of the Federal Reserve Act requires that the Fed receive "satisfactory" collateral to protect it if the borrower defaults. In a speech at the Fed's Jackson Hole conference in 2009, Bernanke said of Lehman:[1]

> [T]he company's available collateral fell well short of the amount needed to secure a Federal Reserve loan of sufficient size to meet its funding needs. As the Federal Reserve cannot make an unsecured loan ... the firm's failure was, unfortunately, unavoidable.

Bernanke reiterated this point in 2010 in his testimony before the Congressionally appointed Financial Crisis Inquiry Commission (FCIC):[2]

> [T]he only way we could have saved Lehman would have been by breaking the law, and I'm not sure I'm willing to accept those consequences for the Federal Reserve and for our systems of laws. I just don't think that would be appropriate.

In his 2015 memoir, *The Courage to Act*, Bernanke states again that Lehman did not have "sufficient collateral to back a loan of the size needed to prevent its collapse."[3]

This book sets the record straight on why the Fed did not rescue Lehman Brothers by presenting evidence that clearly supports two related conclusions. First, Fed officials' beliefs about their legal authority were not the real reason that they chose not to rescue Lehman. Second, the Fed did, in fact, have the authority to rescue the firm.

The following findings support these conclusions:

- A substantial record of policymakers' deliberations before the Lehman bankruptcy contains no evidence that legal barriers deterred them from assisting Lehman or that they examined the adequacy of the firm's collateral.

- Arguments about legal authority made by policymakers since the bankruptcy are unpersuasive. These arguments involve flawed interpretations of economic and legal concepts, and factual claims that are not accurate.
- From a detailed examination of Lehman's finances, it is clear that the firm had more than enough collateral to secure a loan to meet its liquidity needs. Such a loan could have prevented a disorderly and destructive bankruptcy, with negligible risk to the Fed.
- More specifically, Lehman probably could have survived by borrowing from the Fed's Primary Dealer Credit Facility on the terms offered to other investment banks. Fed officials prevented this outcome by restricting Lehman's access to the PDCF.

We will never know what Lehman Brothers' long-term fate would have been if the Fed had rescued it from its liquidity crisis. There are several possibilities: Lehman might have survived indefinitely as an independent firm; it might have been acquired by another institution; or it might have eventually been forced to wind down its business. Whichever of these outcomes occurred, however, would have been less disruptive to the financial system than the bankruptcy that actually happened.

If legal constraints do not explain why the Fed did not rescue Lehman, then what does? The available evidence supports the theories that political considerations were important, and that policymakers did not fully anticipate the damage from the bankruptcy. The record also shows that the decision to let Lehman fail was made primarily by Treasury Secretary Henry Paulson; Fed officials deferred to Paulson even though they had the sole authority to make such a decision under the Federal Reserve Act.

A PREVIEW OF THE ARGUMENT

The Lehman crisis and the Federal Reserve's response to it were complex, and this book examines the episode in considerable detail to determine, as precisely as possible, exactly what happened and why. Here is an overview of how the book proceeds.[4]

The Financial Crisis and Lehman's Failure

Chapter 2 presents a history of the Lehman crisis and places it within the broader financial crisis that unfolded in 2008. Other landmark events include the Fed's rescues of Bear Stearns in March and AIG in September when liquidity crises threatened those firms. As many have pointed out, a satisfactory account of Fed policy must explain why Lehman was treated differently from Bear, AIG, and other companies.

During the week that began on Monday, September 8, Lehman's liquidity was wiped out by a run. Over the weekend of September 13–14, Fed and Treasury officials tried to broker the sale of Lehman to a stronger firm, and they almost succeeded, but a deal with the British bank, Barclays, fell apart on September 14. The central issue examined in this book is what the Fed could have done after the Barclays deal failed to avert Lehman's bankruptcy on September 15.

An important detail of the story – and one that is not widely appreciated – is that not all of the Lehman enterprise failed on September 15. The entity that Barclays almost purchased on the 14th, and which famously filed for bankruptcy on the 15th, was Lehman Brothers Holdings Inc. (LBHI), a corporation with many subsidiary companies. Most of these subsidiaries immediately entered bankruptcy along with LBHI, but one did not: Lehman Brothers Inc. (LBI), Lehman's broker-dealer in New York. The Fed kept LBI in business from September 15 to September 18 by lending it tens of billions of dollars. After that, Barclays purchased part of LBI and the rest was wound down by a court-appointed trustee. These events raise another important question: Why did the Fed choose to assist LBI but not its parent, LBHI?

Section 13(3) of the Federal Reserve Act

Chapter 3 explores the law that governs lending by the Federal Reserve. Normally, the Fed lends only to depository institutions (traditional discount lending). Under Section 13(3) of the Federal Reserve

Act, however, the Fed can lend to non-depository institutions such as investment banks under "unusual and exigent circumstances." Almost everyone agrees that conditions in 2008 were unusual and exigent.

The legal controversy about Fed lending concerns the requirement under Section 13(3) that a loan be "secured to the satisfaction of the Reserve Bank" that makes the loan. Usually, security takes the form of collateral – borrower assets that the Fed can seize if the borrower defaults. Nobody has given a precise definition of "satisfactory security," but Fed officials have interpreted the concept to mean that the Fed cannot make a loan if there is a significant risk that it will lose money on the deal. In the words of the General Counsel of the Board of Governors, "You have to be pretty confident you will be repaid."

Was Lehman Solvent?

Chapter 4 analyzes LBHI's financial condition before its bankruptcy as summarized by the firm's balance sheet, and examines the controversial issue of whether Lehman was solvent. Section 13(3), as it stood in 2008, did *not* require that recipients of Fed loans be solvent by any definition. However, examining Lehman's solvency helps us to understand what assistance the firm needed to survive its liquidity crisis, and to assess its longer-term prospects.

In a financial statement for August 31, 2008, LBHI reported assets of approximately $600 billion and liabilities of $572 billion. These figures imply that the firm was solvent, with stockholder equity of $28 billion.

It is generally agreed that Lehman valued some of its assets at more than their true market values. Yet the extent of overvaluation was not as great as some commentators have suggested. About $60 billion of reported assets (primarily investments in real estate and private equity) were questionable. Other financial institutions estimated that these assets were overvalued by $15 billion to $32 billion. If we subtract that amount from Lehman's total assets, the firm's equity falls from the reported level of $28 billion to something between –$4 billion and +$13 billion. Thus, with realistic asset values, Lehman was near the border between solvency and insolvency.

These calculations are based on mark-to-market valuation of Lehman's assets, that is, on estimates of the prices at which Lehman could have sold the assets at the time of its crisis. In the distressed markets of September 2008, the prices of many assets had fallen below their fundamental values (as determined, for example, by likely repayment rates on loans). If Lehman was near the edge of solvency with mark-to-market valuation, then it was probably solvent based on its assets' fundamental values.

Fed officials have said repeatedly that Lehman was insolvent, but they have never supported this claim with an analysis of the firm's balance sheet. When pressed to back up the claim, officials have offered explanations with a number of flaws, including confusion between the concepts of insolvency and illiquidity and misinterpretations of statements by Lehman executives.

Lehman's Liquidity Crisis

After Bear Stearns nearly failed in March 2008, many commentators suggested that Lehman Brothers might also be in danger. Fears about Lehman grew throughout the summer of 2008 as the firm suffered losses on its real estate investments. Eventually Lehman experienced a run: a self-reinforcing cycle of decreases in its share price, downgrades of its bonds by rating agencies, and a flight of its customers and counterparties in various financial transactions.

The fatal part of this cycle was a liquidity crisis, which Chapter 5 examines in detail. This liquidity crisis involved a number of factors, the most important of which involved Lehman's repurchase agreements, or repos.

These repos were effectively short-term loans that Lehman took out using the firm's securities as collateral. In early 2008, Lehman's liabilities included more than $200 billion in repos, which it rolled over continuously. Lehman and other investment banks believed that repos were a stable source of funds. They were safe for lenders because the loans were secured by collateral that was worth more than the loans. In determining how much cash to provide, lenders would take off some percentage of the collateral's value, called a "haircut," to cover any costs of selling the collateral if the borrower defaulted. Investment banks believed that because lenders were protected by this over-collateralization, they would not cut off a firm's repo funding during a crisis.

A surprising aspect of the 2008 crisis was that repo funding proved *not* to be reliable. Cash lenders abruptly cut off repos with Bear Stearns in March and with Lehman in September. The reasons for these actions are not entirely clear, but whatever the reasons, the loss of repo financing was disastrous for Bear's and Lehman's liquidity.

Lehman's loss of liquidity began during July and August of 2008, and accelerated sharply during the week of September 8. On Friday, September 12, Lehman had almost no cash, and it was clear the firm would immediately default on its obligations if it opened for business on Monday, September 15.

The Fed Could Have Provided Lehman with Liquidity Support

Chapter 6 turns to the central question of this book: Could the Fed have kept Lehman in operation with a loan that was well-secured, and hence legal? This question turns on how much cash the firm needed to borrow, and how much collateral it had available. I examine this issue in three complementary ways.

A Simple Calculation On the eve of its bankruptcy, Lehman's balance sheet had two key features. First, the firm was on the borderline of solvency, which means its total assets (with reasonable valuations) and its total liabilities were approximately the same: each was about $570 billion. Second, the liabilities included $115 billion of unsecured long-term debt, meaning debt that was not due for 12 months or more. Together, these facts imply that Lehman had enough collateral for any liquidity support it might have needed.

To see this point, consider the most severe liquidity crisis imaginable: Lehman must immediately repay *all* of its short-term liabilities, defined as its liabilities less its long-term debt. Assume also that Lehman cannot liquidate any of its assets. Short-term liabilities total $455 billion ($570 billion minus $115 billion), so Lehman must borrow that much cash. It has $570 billion of assets, which are unencumbered because its only remaining liability, long-term debt, is unsecured. Therefore, Lehman's available collateral ($570 billion) exceeds the largest loan it could possibly need ($455 billion) by $115 billion, or about 25 percent.

A Likely Scenario How much would Lehman have actually needed to borrow from the Fed to stay in operation? While the answer to this question is speculative, detailed information on the liquidity drains the firm experienced allows me to make a reasonable estimate: Lehman would have needed about $84 billion of assistance to stay in operation for a period of weeks or months.

Lehman could have borrowed this $84 billion from an existing Fed facility, the Primary Dealer Credit Facility (PDCF), because the firm had at least $114 billion of available assets that were acceptable as PDCF collateral. Thus, the Fed probably could have rescued Lehman without a new Section 13(3) authorization. Instead, Fed policymakers chose to restrict Lehman's access to the PDCF.

Comparison to Liquidity Support for LBI After the bankruptcy of its parent company (LBHI), Lehman's New York broker-dealer, LBI, was permitted to borrow daily from the Fed's PDCF in amounts ranging from $20 billion to $28 billion. These loans allowed LBI to operate from September 15 to September 18, on which date Barclays acquired most of LBI. The amounts of these loans are consistent with my estimate that $84 billion could have sustained the entire Lehman enterprise for weeks or months.

Fed Pre- and Post-Bankruptcy Discussions about Liquidity Support

As Chapter 7 describes, Fed officials discussed the possibility of liquidity support for Lehman before the bankruptcy; after the bankruptcy,

Fed officials made many statements about why they withheld that support.

Discussions before September 15 From the Bear Stearns crisis in March 2008 to September 13, the staffs of the New York Fed and the Board of Governors extensively analyzed Lehman's liquidity risk and how the Fed might assist the firm if it experienced a crisis. The staffs reported to senior officials on several policy options, including loans from the PDCF to replace the cash that Lehman would lose if its counterparties refused to roll over repos.

These discussions do not explain why, in the end, the Fed chose not to lend to Lehman when its crisis actually occurred. In the available records, there is little discussion of Lehman's collateral, and no discussion at all of any legal issues related to Section 13(3).

Bernanke on September 23 Ben Bernanke first discussed the Lehman bankruptcy in Congressional testimony just eight days after it happened. On that occasion he said that "the Federal Reserve and the Treasury declined to commit public funds" to Lehman because "the troubles at Lehman had been well known for some time" and "we judged that investors and counterparties had had time to take precautionary measures." Bernanke did not mention concerns about collateral or legal barriers to assisting Lehman.

Bernanke later disavowed his initial testimony about Lehman. In 2010 he told the Financial Crisis Inquiry Commission, "I regret not being more straightforward there, because clearly it has supported the mistaken impression that in fact we could have done something [to save Lehman]." Bernanke makes a similar statement in his 2015 memoir.

Dubious Claims about Lehman's Collateral In a speech on October 7, 2008, Bernanke first claimed that Lehman had insufficient collateral for the loan it needed, thus making the loan illegal under Section 13(3). Since then he has repeated that position many times, as have other officials including Timothy Geithner (the New York Fed President in 2008) and the General Counsels of the Board of Governors and the New York Fed. However, nobody has ever presented any details about Lehman's finances to support this position.

In 2010, Bernanke testified at a public hearing of the FCIC, and several FCIC Commissioners pushed him to back up his claims about Lehman's collateral. Bernanke said that the New York Fed analyzed Lehman's finances and reported to him that "the liquidity demands on the holding company [LBHI] were much greater than the collateral that they had available to meet those demands." The FCIC sent Bernanke a follow-up letter that asked pointedly for details of the New York Fed's analysis and for "the dollar value of the shortfall of Lehman's collateral" relative to its liquidity needs. Bernanke never answered these questions.

Another witness at the 2010 FCIC hearing was Thomas Baxter, General Counsel of the New York Fed. Baxter also testified that Lehman's collateral was inadequate, but when pressed for details he deflected the question. He said that a loan to LBHI "was never seriously considered by the Federal Reserve," and that policymakers had decided before LBHI's final weekend that it must declare bankruptcy unless it was acquired by a stronger firm.

How the Fed Ensured Lehman's Bankruptcy

Fed officials did not stand by passively as Lehman failed. They took actions to force LBHI to file a bankruptcy petition, as Chapter 8 describes. On the afternoon of Sunday, September 14, after it became clear that Barclays was not going to buy LBHI, officials of the New York Fed called Lehman executives to a meeting. According to multiple accounts, General Counsel Baxter announced, "We've come to the conclusion that Lehman has to go into bankruptcy," or words to that effect. Baxter said that LBHI should file a bankruptcy petition by midnight that night.

The Fed does not have the legal authority to order a corporation to file for bankruptcy. However, officials took actions to ensure that Lehman had no good alternative. Specifically, they prevented Lehman Brothers International Europe (LBIE), the firm's London broker-dealer, from obtaining the cash it needed to meet its obligations on September 15. Because many of these obligations were guaranteed by LBHI, LBHI was also forced into default. The LBHI Board of Directors decided that bankruptcy was preferable to defaulting and then trying to operate the firm.

Fed officials denied cash to LBIE through two actions. First, they refused a request from Lehman that LBIE, as well as the New York broker-dealer LBI, be allowed to borrow from the PDCF. This refusal contrasts starkly with the Fed's treatment of other investment banks when they experienced liquidity problems. Starting on September 21, for example, the Fed granted PDCF access to the London broker-dealer subsidiaries of Goldman Sachs, Morgan Stanley, and Merrill Lynch.

Second, the Fed thwarted an effort by LBI to borrow enough to fund both itself *and* LBIE. This plan would have required LBI to gather collateral from other parts of Lehman to pledge to the PDCF. The plan was prevented by the Fed's "Friday criterion," a rule which stated that LBI could only pledge assets that were on its own balance sheet on Friday, September 12. Policymakers have never given a clear rationale for this restriction.

The Long-Term Resolution of Lehman's Crisis

An adequate loan from the Fed would have kept Lehman in business while the firm looked for long-term solutions to its problems. We will never know what the outcome would have been, but Chapter 9 outlines some possibilities.

One possibility is that the Barclays acquisition of LBHI – the plan on September 13 – would have eventually been completed. This deal failed because British regulators would not approve it without a vote by Barclays shareholders, which would have taken a month or two to organize. Liquidity support from the Fed could have kept Lehman in operation until the vote was held.

Another possibility is that Lehman would have survived as an independent firm. This outcome would have been more likely if Lehman could have removed some of its illiquid assets from its balance sheet. Before it failed, Lehman was planning to spin off its illiquid real estate assets into a real estate investment trust in early 2009. Alternatively, the Fed might have created a special purpose vehicle to buy Lehman's illiquid assets, like the Maiden Lane facilities that bought assets from Bear Stearns in March and AIG in November.

In the worst case, Lehman would eventually have had to declare bankruptcy. In this case, liquidity support from the Fed would have given Lehman the time to wind down or sell various of its businesses before declaring bankruptcy. This process could have greatly mitigated the disruption of the financial system that occurred because of the firm's sudden failure. On September 14, Lehman executives began planning a six-month wind down, but they abandoned the plan when they realized the Fed would not provide the liquidity support necessary to execute it.

The Fed's Treatment of Other Firms

Many have asked why the Fed let Lehman fail but rescued other financial institutions in 2008. The Fed's answer is that, unlike Lehman, the firms it assisted had sufficient collateral, which made it safe to lend to them. As Chapter 10 discusses, this claim is yet another Fed position that does not survive scrutiny.

The Fed's assistance to some institutions was similar to the assistance that Lehman needed and did not receive. In particular, Goldman Sachs and Morgan Stanley received large amounts of PDCF financing when their liquidity positions deteriorated after Lehman's failure. The PDCF lent to both the New York and London broker-dealers of Goldman and Morgan, and it accepted types of collateral – including speculative-grade securities and equities – that Lehman had possessed in ample quantities.

In lending to Bear Stearns in March 2008 and AIG starting in September, the Fed took on *more* risk than it would have in rescuing Lehman. Lehman probably could have survived with overnight, over-collateralized loans from the PDCF. In rescuing Bear Stearns, the Fed provided long-term financing for illiquid assets, and might have taken substantial losses had financial markets not recovered as strongly as they did in 2009. In the case of AIG, the collateral accepted by the Fed included equity in privately-held insurance companies. The value of this collateral was highly uncertain, and might well have been less than the amount the Fed lent AIG.

Who Decided to Let Lehman Fail?

There is plentiful evidence showing that lack of legal authority because Lehman had inadequate collateral was *not* the reason that the Fed refused to rescue Lehman. What then were the real reasons?

To answer this question, we must first understand who decided that Lehman should fail. Chapter 11 shows that the primary decision maker was Treasury Secretary Henry Paulson, even though he had no legal authority over the Fed's lending decisions. Paulson traveled to New York on September 12 and took charge of the negotiations about Lehman that were taking place at the New York Fed. Other officials on the scene, including New York Fed President Geithner, deferred to Paulson. Chairman Bernanke remained in Washington and received periodic reports on developments in New York.

Explaining the Decision to Let Lehman Fail

Chapter 12 asks why Secretary Paulson insisted on Lehman's bankruptcy and why Fed officials acquiesced. The available evidence supports the common theory that Paulson was influenced by the strong political opposition to financial rescues. He had been stung by criticism of the Bear Stearns rescue in March and the government takeovers of Fannie Mae and Freddie Mac just a week before the Lehman decision. He ruled out any assistance to Lehman because, in his widely-quoted words, "I can't be Mr. Bailout."

Another factor is that although Paulson and Fed officials worried about the effects of a Lehman failure, they did not fully anticipate the severe damage to the financial system that it would cause. Since the bankruptcy, Ben Bernanke has said that he knew before the event that it would be a "catastrophe" and a "calamity" for the economy, but this claim is not consistent with what he and other officials said shortly before and shortly after the bankruptcy.

SOURCES OF EVIDENCE

What distinguishes this book from others on the 2008 financial crisis is the level of detail in which it examines one specific topic, the Fed's decision not to rescue Lehman Brothers. A detailed analysis is made possible by the wealth of information on the topic that is available from a variety of public sources. Previous authors have made conflicting, unproven claims about the Fed and Lehman, but having extensively studied the available record, I can make a number of firm conclusions about what happened and why. The following are the major sources for my research. The endnotes to the book give citations for each specific piece of evidence that I present.

The Valukas Report (March 2010)

LBHI's bankruptcy petition, filed on September 15, 2008, was the first step in an extraordinarily complex bankruptcy case, which is ongoing in 2018 (*In re Lehman Brothers Holdings Inc.*, Case No. 08–13555, U.S. Bankruptcy Court, Southern District of New York). At the outset of the case, the court appointed an Examiner, Anton Valukas, and charged him with writing a report on what happened to Lehman, including its interactions with the Federal Reserve. The report does not directly address whether the Fed could have rescued Lehman, but it contains much information that bears on that question.

During his investigation, Valukas was the Chairman of Jenner and Block, an international law firm based in Chicago (where he remains in 2018). He was assisted by lawyers from his firm and elsewhere, and by the accounting firm of Duff and Phelps. Valukas's team had subpoena power, and they gained access to Lehman Brothers' records and computer systems, received documents from other financial institutions and the Fed, and interviewed more than 250 people. In March 2010, Valukas published a report of more than 2,000 pages, 8,000 footnotes, and 24 appendices.

The Valukas Report is available at jenner.com/lehman. In the online report, the footnotes include hyperlinks to most of the documents that are cited, including numerous emails, memos, and PowerPoint presentations from Lehman executives and Fed officials.

The Investigation of the Financial Crisis Inquiry Commission (FCIC) (2009–2011)

In May 2009, Congress established the FCIC to investigate the causes of the financial crisis and policymakers' responses to it. Like Valukas, the FCIC had subpoena power, and its staff gathered numerous emails and other documents related to the Lehman failure and interviewed scores of people. The Commission also held public hearings at which key actors in the Lehman crisis testified under oath. The FCIC issued its final report in January 2011.

Stanford Law School maintains a website, fcic.law.stanford.edu, with the FCIC report and the documents it cites. The FCIC website also includes transcripts of the Commission's hearings and records of staff interviews, mostly in the form of audio recordings. Additional FCIC records are held at the National Archives.

For this book, the most important FCIC documents include testimony at a 2010 hearing by two people: Ben Bernanke and Thomas Baxter, the General Counsel of the New York Fed. Commissioners questioned Bernanke and Baxter aggressively, challenged their statements about the Lehman episode, and sent follow-up questions that Bernanke and Baxter answered in writing. These exchanges produced the most detailed defenses of Fed actions that are available.

The FCIC's final report expresses some skepticism about the claim that rescuing Lehman would have been illegal. The report notes that Bernanke initially gave a different reason for inaction ("the market was prepared for the [bankruptcy]"), and it then says:[5]

> In addition, though the Federal Reserve subsequently asserted that it did not have the legal ability to save Lehman because the firm did

not have sufficient collateral to secure a loan from the Fed under Section 13(3), the authority to lend under that provision is very broad.

Reports on LBI and LBIE

When LBHI entered bankruptcy, LBIE, Lehman's broker-dealer subsidiary in London, entered a separate process of "administration," a British version of bankruptcy. LBI, the New York broker-dealer, stayed in business for several days with Fed assistance, and part of it was sold to Barclays. On September 19, however, the rest of LBI entered a Securities Investor Protection Act (SIPA) liquidation, yet another version of bankruptcy for US broker-dealers. Like the LBHI bankruptcy case, the LBIE administration and LBI liquidation are ongoing in 2018.

Both of these processes have produced reports roughly analogous to the Valukas Report on LBHI. The Joint Administrators of LBIE issued a Progress Report in 2009, and the LBI Trustee (James Giddens) has issued two reports: a Preliminary Investigation Report in 2010 and a Preliminary Realization Report in 2015. Each of these three reports contains significant details about the Lehman episode that are not available elsewhere.

Reports on AIG

Two authorities issued reports on the AIG crisis: the Special Inspector General for the Troubled Asset Relief Program (TARP), and the Congressional Oversight Panel for TARP. Each of these reports describes Federal Reserve actions to assist AIG, as well government aid through TARP. This material is helpful when comparing the Fed's policies toward AIG and Lehman.

Lehman's Financial Statements

LBHI's annual and quarterly filings with the Securities and Exchange Commission (SEC), forms 10-K and 10-Q, include extensive information about the firm's finances. The last of these reports is the

10-Q for the second quarter of 2008, which ended on May 31 under Lehman's accounting calendar. Just before its bankruptcy, the firm issued a press release with preliminary results for the third quarter, ending August 31.

It appears that Lehman reported inflated values for some of its assets. Nonetheless, we can construct a credible balance sheet for the firm by combining its statements with outside estimates of overvaluation.

Federal Reserve Records

The websites of the Board of Governors and the New York Fed contain many relevant items. A section of the Board's site called "Credit and Liquidity Programs and the Balance Sheet" describes the Fed's responses to the financial crisis in detail. Other relevant material includes speeches and Congressional testimony by Fed officials; transcripts of Federal Open Market Committee (FOMC) meetings during 2008; and the balance sheets of the Maiden Lane LLCs which bought illiquid assets from Bear Stearns and AIG.

The website of Bloomberg News contains daily data on Fed lending during the crisis, broken down by borrower. Bloomberg requested these data from the Board under the Freedom of Information Act (FOIA); the Board declined the request, but Bloomberg litigated the matter successfully and obtained the data in 2011. Reporters from Bloomberg and the *Financial Times* have analyzed these data, and I draw on their work.

Popular Books

Of the many books on the financial crisis, the most informative for my purposes is *Too Big to Fail*, by *New York Times* reporter Andrew Ross Sorkin (2009). This book includes a rich narrative of the Lehman crisis, focusing on the interactions among policymakers, Lehman executives, and others involved in the episode. Sorkin's account provides information about policymakers' deliberations and decisions that is not available elsewhere.

An important qualification is that *Too Big to Fail* is based primarily on interviews with anonymous sources. It is therefore less authoritative than the carefully documented reports of the Lehman Examiner (Valukas) and the FCIC. On the other hand, many of Sorkin's accounts are corroborated by other sources, and I do not know of any allegations of major inaccuracies.

My research also draws on David Wessel's account of the crisis, *In Fed We Trust* (2009), and on the memoirs of Henry Paulson (*On the Brink*, 2010), Timothy Geithner (*Stress Test*, 2014), and Ben Bernanke (*The Courage to Act*, 2015).

Interviews

I sought interviews with people involved in the Lehman episode, with moderate success. I talked off the record to half a dozen people with direct knowledge of events surrounding the bankruptcy or the investigations that followed. These interviews have helped me understand the Lehman episode, but the arguments in this book do not rely on specific information from the interviews. All facts and opinions that I relate come from publicly available sources.

Even with the voluminous records that are available, some aspects of the Lehman episode remain hazy. At times, I had to interpret fragmentary evidence and try to reconcile conflicting statements by different people. Nonetheless, the overall record shows clearly that a Federal Reserve rescue of Lehman would have been legal and feasible.

2 The Crisis of 2008

To understand the Fed's actions during the Lehman crisis, we need quite a bit of background not only on that specific episode but also on the broader financial crisis of 2008. This chapter reviews the major events of the crisis, focusing on facts that are undisputed. Later chapters delve into controversial details of the story.

INVESTMENT BANKING ON THE EVE OF THE CRISIS

At the beginning of 2008, Lehman Brothers was one of the so-called Big Five investment banks with headquarters in the United States. These firms, in order of assets, were Goldman Sachs ($1,120 billion), Morgan Stanley ($1,045 billion), Merrill Lynch ($1,020 billion), Lehman ($691 billion), and Bear Stearns ($395 billion). Over the course of 2008, all five faced threats to their survival.

Why Investment Banks Were at Risk

Today, there is a broad consensus about why the big investment banks experienced crises. Three aspects of their businesses combined to put them at risk.

First, in the early 2000s, the Big Five expanded their real estate investments in several directions. They originated home mortgage loans, bought mortgages from other lenders, created mortgage-backed securities, and financed commercial real estate projects. They sold parts of their real estate investments to other institutions but kept a large share of the investments on their own balance sheets. This strategy was profitable during the bubble in real estate prices from 2001 to 2006, but as the bubble deflated over 2006–2008, the investment banks started taking losses.

19

Second, the investment banks operated with high degrees of leverage: they financed their assets primarily with borrowed money rather than shareholder equity. At the five firms, equity ranged from 3.0 to 3.8 percent of assets at the end of 2007; at Lehman, it was 3.3 percent.[1] With these small equity cushions, losses on real estate threatened to push equity to zero and make the firms insolvent.

Third, much of the borrowing the investment banks used to finance their assets was short term. Indeed, a sizable fraction of the borrowed funds was *extremely* short term – overnight loans that needed to be rolled over every day. As a result, the funding that the investment banks relied on could be cut off suddenly if lenders lost confidence in them.

In retrospect, we can see how these three factors combined to cause crises at the investment banks. As the firms' losses on real estate mounted, their already thin equity cushions became even thinner, and market participants began to question whether the firms would remain solvent and viable. As confidence fell, lenders began to doubt the creditworthiness of the investment banks, and, as a result, began to cut off the banks' short-term funding. Losses of funding led to liquidity crises; the investment banks ran short of the cash they needed to operate.

Short-Term Funding through Repurchase Agreements

A crucial part of understanding the 2008 crisis is understanding the nature of the short-term borrowing done by the investment banks. The firms did some borrowing by issuing unsecured commercial paper, but they borrowed much larger amounts through repurchase agreements, or "repos." Later in this book, we will see that unexpected losses of repo funding were central to the liquidity crises experienced at the investment banks.

In a repo, one financial institution sells a security to another and agrees to buy it back for a slightly higher price in the future, often the next day. In economic terms, a repo is essentially the same as a collateralized loan: one party receives cash from the other for the period of the agreement; the lender of cash holds the borrower's security as collateral; and the increase in the security's price is like an interest payment to the lender.

In 2008, investment banks used repos to obtain hundreds of billions of dollars of cash from institutions such as mutual funds and commercial banks. They used their inventories of bonds, mortgage-backed securities, and equities as collateral.

The cash advanced in a repo is less than the value of the collateral. The purpose of this "haircut" on the collateral is to protect the cash lender from losses if the borrower defaults and the lender must seize and sell the collateral. Haircuts are larger for securities that are less liquid or have volatile prices, and are therefore more risky. According to a New York Fed analysis, typical haircuts on repo collateral in July 2008 ranged from about 1 percent for Treasury securities to 13 percent for high-yield asset-backed securities.[2]

In addition to the haircuts on collateral, repos have a second feature that enhances their safety for cash lenders: their treatment under bankruptcy law. When a corporation declares bankruptcy, an automatic stay generally prevents its creditors from demanding cash or seizing collateral immediately. Under a 2005 amendment to the bankruptcy code, however, repos are exempt from the automatic stay. If a cash borrower defaults on a repo, the lender can liquidate the collateral immediately.

Because repos are safe for cash lenders, their interest rates are low. During the summer of 2008, overnight repo rates were close to the target federal funds rate of 2 percent.[3]

Before the financial crisis, the belief that repos were safe for lenders had a corollary: repos were a stable source of funds for investment banks. When lending is unsecured, a firm's funding may be cut off suddenly if it loses the confidence of its counterparties. Indeed, unsecured funding can disappear without any good reason, just because of a self-fulfilling expectation of a crisis (as in the Diamond-Dybvig model of bank runs).[4] In theory, however, a firm should never experience a similar cutoff of repo funding because repos are secured loans. Because lenders are protected from losses by collateral, they should always be willing to roll over their repos.

Another important aspect of investment banks' funding is that they borrowed primarily in the "tri-party" repo market. A tri-party repo involves a clearing bank, an institution at which both the repo borrower and lender have cash and securities accounts, which makes executing transactions between them easier. The clearing bank also provides services such as daily repricing of collateral.

In 2008, a tri-party repo involved a series of transactions among the three parties. When a lender and borrower agreed on a repo, the clearing bank moved cash from the lender's account to the borrower's, and moved the securities serving as collateral in the opposite direction. The next morning, the clearing bank "unwound" the repo: it used its own cash to repay the lender, and returned the collateral to the borrower's account. In the afternoon, the borrower repaid the clearing bank, usually with cash from a new repo.

These arrangements meant that a repo borrower received overnight credit from its cash lender, and intraday credit – between the morning unwind and the new repo in the afternoon – from its clearing bank. As we will see, the intraday exposure of Lehman Brothers' clearing bank, JPMorgan Chase, proved to be an important problem during Lehman's crisis.[5]

THE BEAR STEARNS CRISIS AND THE FED'S RESPONSE, MARCH 2008

Bear Stearns, the smallest of the Big Five investment banks, was the first to suffer a loss of confidence and a liquidity crisis. Bear's experience was similar in many respects to the subsequent crisis at Lehman.[6]

The Crisis

Bear Stearns had especially large investments in mortgages and mortgage-backed securities, and therefore was hit hard when housing prices started to fall in 2006. An early landmark in the financial crisis was the failure in July 2007 of two hedge funds sponsored by Bear. In the fourth quarter of 2007, Bear became the first of the Big Five investment banks to report a quarterly loss. Market participants lost confidence in the firm, which led to warnings by bond rating agencies, a falling stock price, and rising prices of credit default swaps for Bear's debt. These developments further reduced confidence, and so on, in a vicious circle.

In this environment, Bear had trouble issuing unsecured commercial paper, and its commercial paper outstanding fell from $21 billion at the end of 2006 to $4 billion at the end of 2007. During this period, however, the firm was able to offset its lost funding from commercial paper with increased funding from repos, which cash lenders still considered safe. Bear's repos grew from $69 billion at the end of 2006 to $102 billion at the end of 2007.

Indeed, Bear seemed to have ample funding until a few days before its near-bankruptcy. In early March of 2008, the SEC reviewed Bear's liquidity position and found "no significant issues." Bear guarded against a crisis by holding a "liquidity pool" of cash and highly liquid securities that it could use to replace any funding it might lose. This pool ranged from $18 to $20 billion during the week of March 3, and still had $18 billion in it on Monday, March 10.[7]

Over the next several days, however, the erosion of confidence in Bear turned into a devastating run. An apparent trigger was the rating downgrades of mortgage-backed securities issued by a special purpose vehicle that Bear had sponsored. Some of Bear's counterparties refused to roll over repos, and others imposed larger haircuts. Bear also received collateral calls from counterparties to derivatives contracts. All of these developments drained cash from the firm, reducing its liquidity pool.

On Thursday, March 13, Bear's liquidity pool was down to $2 billion. The firm's executives told their board of directors that an additional $14 billion in repos were not going to roll, which would exhaust the liquidity pool and leave Bear without enough cash to pay its debts. The firm told the SEC that it would be "unable to operate normally on Friday."[8]

Explaining the Run on Repos

Bear's sudden loss of repo financing, the largest factor in its liquidity crisis, surprised both investment bankers and financial regulators. SEC Chair Christopher Cox discussed the episode in testimony before the Senate Banking Committee on April 3, 2008. Cox explained why the SEC's oversight of investment banks under the Consolidated Supervised Entities (CSE) program did not prevent the run on Bear:

> [T]he liquidity measurement has been designed to withstand the complete loss, for an entire year, of all sources of unsecured funding. But what neither the CSE regulatory approach nor any existing regulatory model has taken into account is the possibility that secured funding, even that backed by high-quality collateral such as US Treasury and agency securities, could become unavailable. The existing models for both commercial and investment banks are premised on the expectancy that secured funding, albeit perhaps on less favorable terms than normal, would be available in any market environment. For this reason, the inability of Bear Stearns to borrow against even high-quality collateral on March 13th and March 14th – an unprecedented occurrence – has prompted the Federal Reserve's action to open the discount window to investment banks.

Even after the fact, it is not clear why Bear's counterparties refused to roll over funding that seemed to be well-secured. Many explanations are vague. The FCIC report says, "Lenders were reluctant to risk the hassle of seizing collateral, even good collateral, from a bankrupt borrower." The report also quotes an executive of State Street Bank: "We don't want to go through that uncomfortable process of having to liquidate collateral."[9]

Scholars such as Darrell Duffie have suggested that, despite haircuts, there was *some* risk that a repo lender would lose money if it liquidated collateral in a distressed market. Some of the lenders were money market funds that would have had to sell collateral immediately because they were legally forbidden to own it. Also, lenders may have feared lawsuits by firms whose collateral they seized, despite their apparent protection from such litigation under bankruptcy law.[10]

Some commentators cite "headline risk" as a factor in the cutoff of repos: financial institutions feared bad publicity from dealings with troubled firms. A piece of evidence on this point comes from the later crisis at Lehman. In a September 11 memo, a member of the New York Fed Markets Group reported:[11]

> One [money market] fund did not roll about $1.5 billion in overnight positions for Treasury and agency-MBS repo. They stressed that they saw negligible risk in maintaining these positions, but found it easiest to eliminate the exposure in the face of inquiries from investors and senior management.

Counterparties did not need much incentive to cut off repos with Bear (and, later, Lehman), because they could easily invest their cash elsewhere. Duffie discusses possible risks of seizing collateral, and then says: "The repo creditors can avoid these threats, and other unforeseen difficulties, simply by reinvesting their cash in new repos with other counterparties."[12]

The Rescue of Bear Stearns, March 14–16

The Fed rescued Bear Stearns in two steps. The first was planned in a conference call among Ben Bernanke, Timothy Geithner, and Henry Paulson at 5:00 AM on Friday, March 14. The New York Fed lent $12.9 billion to JPMorgan Chase, which in turn lent the money to Bear so it could meet its obligations on Friday. The Fed used JPMorgan as an intermediary because that firm, as a commercial bank, could borrow from the Fed's discount window and Bear could not. Bear pledged $13.8 billion in securities as collateral.

The news that Bear needed Fed assistance was a new blow to confidence in the firm. All three rating agencies downgraded Bear's bonds on March 14, and the firm's stock price fell by 47 percent. It was clear that Bear could not open for business on Monday, March 17 without some kind of rescue.

This crisis was resolved over the weekend of March 15–16, when Geithner and Paulson brokered the acquisition of Bear by JPMorgan Chase. JPMorgan agreed to pay $2 per share for Bear's stock, which had traded at $159 less than a year before. (The price was later raised to $10 to ensure approval by Bear's shareholders.) As part of the deal, JPMorgan announced that it would immediately guarantee all of Bear's obligations, and that action restored confidence in Bear and stopped the run on the firm.

The Bear Stearns deal also required Bear to sell approximately $30 billion of its real estate assets that JPMorgan did not want. The Fed accommodated this requirement by creating a special purpose vehicle, Maiden Lane LLC, to purchase the assets. Maiden Lane was financed with a $29 billion loan from the New York Fed, collateralized by the $30 billion in assets, and a $1 billion subordinated loan from JPMorgan. The Board of Governors approved the New York Fed's loan, invoking its authority in "unusual and exigent circumstances" under Section 13(3).

In a 2009 interview, the FCIC asked Ben Bernanke why the Fed acted to rescue Bear Stearns. Bernanke said the main reason was fear of the consequences if Bear defaulted on its repos:[13]

> [T]he collapse of Bear Stearns might bring down the entire
> tri-party repo market, which is a two-and-a-half trillion-dollar
> market, which was the source of financing for all the investment
> banks and many other institutions as well. Because if it collapsed,
> what would happen would be that the short-term overnight
> lenders would find themselves in possession of the collateral,
> which they would then try to dump on the market. You would
> have a big crunch in asset prices. And probably what would have

happened – our fear, at least – was that the tri-party repo market would have frozen up. That would have led to huge financing problems for other investment banks and other firms; and we might have had a broader financial crisis.

The TSLF and PDCF

During the Bear Stearns crisis, the Fed invoked Section 13(3) to take two additional actions: it created the Term Securities Lending Facility (TSLF) and the Primary Dealer Credit Facility (PDCF). Both of these facilities lent to primary dealers in Treasury securities, which included the major investment banks. Their purpose was to prevent crises like Bear's from occurring at other firms.

The Fed announced the establishment of the TSLF on March 11, and it began operation on March 27 (too late to help Bear). The TSLF lent Treasury securities to primary dealers, accepting triple-A-rated mortgage-backed securities (MBSs) as collateral. These loans made it easier for investment banks to obtain repo financing because Treasury securities were more widely accepted as repo collateral than MBSs were.

The Fed created the PDCF on March 16, the same day that the JPMorgan-Bear deal was announced. This facility made overnight loans of cash. It accepted a broader range of collateral than the TSLF, including corporate bonds and MBSs with investment-grade ratings (triple-B and above). Haircuts on the collateral were a bit higher than typical haircuts in tri-party repos.[14]

The PDCF was meant to provide strong protection against runs on repos. If an investment bank could not roll a repo, it could pledge its collateral to the PDCF instead and receive the cash that its previous counterparty was no longer willing to provide. This protection against the loss of repos during a run made runs less likely in the first place, because repo lenders knew the PDCF would help borrowers avoid default. In a June 17 email, William Dudley, then head of the New York Fed Markets Group, said:[15]

PDCF remains critical to the stability of some of the IBs [investment banks]. Amounts don't matter here, it is the fact that the PDCF underpins the triparty repo system.

The PDCF had some success in boosting confidence in investment banks, including Lehman. On March 28, Citi stock analysts upgraded Lehman from "Hold" to "Buy," arguing that Lehman's stock was undervalued and that "reality will trump fear." They emphasized that "access to liquidity is a non-issue" because Lehman had "the ability to get access to over $200b in liquidity from the Fed's primary dealer credit facility." (The $200 billion figure is presumably based on Lehman's repo collateral.)[16]

There was, however, a limit on PDCF lending: the facility did not accept *all* types of collateral that were commonly used in tri-party repos. In particular, it did not accept speculative-grade securities or equities. This restriction, which became important during the Lehman crisis, was relaxed on September 14.

THE LEHMAN BROTHERS CRISIS, MARCH–SEPTEMBER 2008

At Lehman Brothers, serious signs of trouble started appearing in March 2008, during the Bear Stearns crisis. Like Bear, Lehman experienced a gradual erosion of confidence that turned into a devastating run in the firm's final week.

Lehman before the Bear Stearns Crisis

The Valukas Report gives a history of Lehman from 2006 through early 2008.[17] In 2006, the firm made a strategic decision to increase its principal investments, primarily in real estate and private equity. Lehman's total assets grew from $410 billion at the end of 2005 to $691 billion at the end of 2007, and peaked at $786 billion at the end of 2008 Q1 (February 29).

One example of Lehman's expanded investments, which became infamous, was its participation in a consortium that acquired Archstone, a real estate investment trust which owned 88,000 apartments across the United States. In May 2007, the consortium agreed to pay $22 billion for Archstone, and Lehman financed about half of that amount with loans and equity investments.

In mid-2006, the US real estate market began to weaken, as house prices fell and defaults on subprime mortgages rose. Some financial institutions became pessimistic about real estate and reduced their investments in that area, but Lehman continued to expand in real estate until early 2008. The firm's executives told its board of directors that "the current distressed environment provides substantial opportunities," and that they were pursuing "a counter-cyclical growth strategy" that would yield high returns when real estate markets recovered.[18]

In some cases, Lehman acquired real estate with the intention of reselling it quickly, but then found that it could not. For example, the firm planned to syndicate most of its investment in Archstone, but it was left with $6 billion of exposure when the Archstone deal closed in October 2007.

Despite such difficulties, Lehman did not show major signs of distress until March 2008. In its 10-K for the 2007 accounting year, which ended on November 30, the firm announced record earnings for the fourth straight year. Management attributed this result to "a record first half and a reasonably successful navigation of difficult market conditions in the second half."[19] In 2008 Q1, which ended February 29, earnings were lower but beat analysts' forecasts. Over January and February, Lehman's stock price fluctuated between $50 and $65.

Confidence in Lehman Declines

As the Bear Stearns crisis escalated, Lehman's stock price fell: on March 17, the day after the Bear rescue, Lehman's stock traded at $32 a share. On March 18, when Lehman reported its better-than-expected earnings for Q1, its stock price rebounded to $46.

After March 18, however, confidence in Lehman eroded steadily. The media and market participants speculated that crises like

Bear's could occur at other investment banks, and some singled out Lehman as especially endangered because of its heavy exposure to real estate. Lehman's stock price fell and the premiums for credit default swaps on its debt rose, indicating increased worries that Lehman might go bankrupt.

In late March and early April, the three rating agencies reduced their outlooks for Lehman. Moody's outlook changed from positive to stable and those of Fitch and Standard and Poor's (S&P) changed from stable to negative. In explaining its outlook on April 3, S&P cited the risk that declining confidence in Lehman could spark a liquidity crisis. It said, "The company's excess liquidity position is among the largest proportionately of the U.S. broker-dealers," but cautioned, "we cannot ignore the possibility that the firm could suffer severely if there is an adverse change in market perceptions, however ill-founded."[20]

At the end of Q1, Lehman had reported that its equity was $25 billion, but analysts suggested that this figure reflected unrealistic valuations of Lehman's real estate assets. In a speech he gave in May, the prominent hedge fund manager David Einhorn criticized Lehman's valuation methods, saying, "I suspect that greater transparency on these valuations would not inspire market confidence."[21] Einhorn was, at the time, shorting Lehman's stock, reflecting his belief that its price was going to fall.

Confidence in Lehman Brothers suffered a major blow on June 9, when the firm announced its quarterly earnings for Q2 (which ended on May 31) and reported its first-ever quarterly loss. This $2.8 billion loss was caused largely by write-downs of real estate assets. Three days later, Lehman replaced its President, Joseph Gregory, with Bart McDade and its CFO, Erin Callan, with Ian Lowitt.

In June and July, all three rating agencies downgraded Lehman's bonds: S&P from A+ to A; Fitch from AA- to A+; and Moody's from A1 to A2. The agencies cited Lehman's earnings report and fears that Lehman would have to write down its real estate assets by additional amounts in the future.[22] In the wake of these downgrades, Lehman's stock price fell to $17 at the end of July.

Falling confidence was exacerbated by negative press coverage. On June 11, for example, Bloomberg Business published an article titled "Lehman: Independent for How Long?" It concluded with a quote from an analyst: "Lehman is next. When you have a pack of dinosaurs, the slowest get picked off."[23]

Strains on Lehman's Liquidity

Lehman held a liquidity pool consisting primarily of cash and government securities. The firm increased this pool from $34 billion on February 29 to $45 billion on May 31. As noted earlier, S&P said in April that Lehman's liquidity compared favorably to that of the other big investment banks.

As confidence in Lehman fell, however, the firm began to experience strains on its liquidity. During 2008 Q3 (May 31 to August 31), Lehman's outstanding commercial paper fell from $8 billion to $4 billion, and some of Lehman's repo counterparties (including Dreyfus and Federated Investors) refused to roll over the funding they provided.[24] In addition, Lehman issued only $2 billion of new long-term debt, compared to $14 billion during Q2.[25]

These losses of liquidity were similar to those experienced by Bear Stearns, but Lehman also experienced a problem that Bear did not. Starting in June, JPMorgan Chase, Lehman's clearing bank for tri-party repos, became worried about its intraday exposure to Lehman under the tri-party arrangement. JPMorgan demanded billions of dollars of collateral for itself, on top of the collateral Lehman had already pledged to its repo lenders. Because JPMorgan insisted that much of the new collateral be cash or liquid securities, part of Lehman's liquidity pool became encumbered.

Despite these developments, Lehman's liquidity problems – like those of Bear Stearns – did not appear dire until the firm's last few days. Lehman's reported liquidity pool, which was $45 billion on May 31, was still $41 billion on Tuesday, September 9. This stability in Lehman's liquidity pool was made possible, in part, because the firm found some new repo lenders, and because it raised cash by issuing equity and selling illiquid assets.

However, Lehman's reported liquidity also reflected some dubious accounting. For example, its liquidity pool included some of the assets that were pledged as collateral to JPMorgan Chase. Chapter 5 analyzes this issue in detail, and finds that by one measure, Lehman's actual liquidity was only $23 billion on September 9.

Lehman Tries to Save Itself

In early 2008, some Lehman executives started to worry about the firm's exposure to real estate and its thin equity cushion. After the Bear Stearns crisis, Lehman changed its strategy drastically: from March to September, it sought to raise capital and reduce its holdings of illiquid assets, and it considered merging with a stronger firm.

The Valukas Report includes a detailed narrative of Lehman's survival strategies.[26] What follows is a review of the highlights. Some of Lehman's efforts to address its problems were successful, and others were not. Several actions were at the planning stage when Lehman declared bankruptcy in September, so we can only guess what their effects might have been.

New Capital On June 12, Lehman raised a total of $6 billion by issuing $4 billion in common stock and $2 billion in preferred stock. As a result, the firm's reported equity rose from about $26 billion at the end of Q2 to $28 billion at the end of Q3, despite Q3 net income of –$4 billion.

Sales of Illiquid Assets Lehman also sought to reduce its holdings of illiquid real estate assets, for the dual purpose of reducing risk and raising liquidity. By definition, those assets were difficult to sell; nevertheless, Lehman reduced its total holdings of mortgages and mortgage-backed securities by $14 billion from February 29 to May 31, and by another $13 billion from May 31 to August 31. (These decreases reflected markdowns in asset valuations as well as asset sales.)[27]

The Search for a Strategic Partner Between March and September, Lehman executives sought a strategic partner that would take a sizable equity stake in the firm or buy it entirely. The Valukas Report lists more than thirty prospects that Lehman approached, including investment banks around the world, private equity firms, sovereign wealth funds, and billionaire investors Warren Buffett and Carlos Slim.[28]

None of Lehman's efforts to find a partner was successful. Many commentators, including Henry Paulson and Ben Bernanke, have blamed this outcome on Lehman CEO Richard Fuld who, they say, did not appreciate the severity of his firm's problems and demanded unrealistically high prices from potential partners.

One investor with serious interest in Lehman was the Korean Development Bank (KDB). Lehman and KDB began negotiations in June, and on August 31 KDB proposed a $6 billion investment. The two parties could not agree on terms, however, and KDB ended negotiations on September 9.

Spinco A centerpiece of Lehman's survival strategy was a plan to transfer $25–$30 billion of its real estate assets to a real estate investment trust (REIT). This entity, officially named REI Global but nicknamed "Spinco," would be financed primarily by Lehman and owned initially by Lehman's shareholders, but it would be a separate publicly-traded company. The SEC approved the plan, and on September 10 Lehman announced that Spinco would be launched in the first quarter of 2009.

The Spinco plan would have benefited Lehman because of the accounting rules that govern real estate investment trusts. As an REIT, Spinco could have valued its assets on a hold-to-maturity basis rather than a mark-to-market basis, and therefore it would not have had to mark down its assets as the financial crisis reduced their market prices. Many analysts questioned whether Spinco would have saved Lehman, but we will never know. Because of the bankruptcy on September 15, Lehman did not have a chance to implement the plan.

Sale of IMD Finally, Lehman planned to sell a 55 percent stake in its Investment Management Division (IMD), which included the Neuberger Berman asset management business. Neuberger Berman was highly profitable – analysts called it Lehman Brothers' "crown jewel." Lehman announced its plans for IMD on September 10, along with the creation of REI Global, and said it expected to raise $3 billion from the transaction. But the IMD sale, like the Spinco plan, did not happen in time to save Lehman from bankruptcy. (On October 3, the Lehman bankruptcy estate sold large parts of IMD, including Neuberger, to a group of hedge funds for $2 billion.)

September 9–12

In Lehman's crisis, as in Bear Stearns's, an erosion of confidence over several months culminated in a run that wiped out Lehman's liquidity in just a few days. The key events during the run are described in chronologies from Valukas and the FCIC and are covered in more detail in later chapters.[29] Here is a summary of the fatal events.

Two blows to confidence appear to have triggered the final run on Lehman. The first was the announcement on the morning of Tuesday, September 9 that the Korean Development Bank had ended negotiations about investing in Lehman. On September 9, Lehman's stock price fell from $14 to $8; credit default swap premiums on the firm's debt rose almost 200 basis points; and S&P and Fitch placed Lehman's bond rating on a negative watch.

The second blow occurred on the morning of Wednesday, September 10, when Lehman simultaneously announced its earnings for Q3 (which ended on August 31) and its plans for REI Global and IMD. Lehman executives hoped these last two announcements would boost confidence in the firm, but the reaction was negative. Analysts expressed doubts that REI Global would be viable, and disappointment that Lehman had not raised new capital.

On the afternoon of September 10, Moody's, following S&P and Fitch, put Lehman's rating on a negative watch. Moody's threatened to downgrade Lehman by two notches if the firm did not find a strategic partner by September 15, and Fitch made the same threat on September 11. By the end of September 11, Lehman's stock price had fallen to $4 a share.

As confidence in Lehman collapsed, the firm rapidly lost liquidity. About $20 billion of repo agreements did not roll. On September 9, JPMorgan Chase demanded an additional $5 billion of collateral to clear Lehman's tri-party repos, and counterparties to derivatives contracts also demanded additional collateral to protect against a Lehman default. Overall, Lehman's liquidity fell from $23 billion on September 9 to $1.4 billion on Friday, September 12. The details of how this happened are discussed in Chapter 5.

At that point, it was clear that many other repos would not roll over on Monday, September 15, and that Lehman's liquidity would quickly hit zero. Lehman's executives knew the firm could not meet its obligations on Monday unless it was rescued by an acquirer or by a loan from the Fed.

The Role of Self-Fulfilling Expectations

Lehman's last week is a textbook example of a liquidity crisis driven by self-fulfilling expectations. Lehman's experience, like Bear Stearns's, was essentially a classic bank run, with the twist that the run was on secured, and not just unsecured, funding. The episode bore out S&P's warning in April that Lehman could experience a crisis "if there is an adverse change in market perceptions, however ill-founded."

Key aspects of Lehman's crisis included a falling stock price and rating downgrades, which reinforced each other in a vicious circle. For example, on September 9, S&P put Lehman on a negative watch based on "the precipitous decline in its share price in recent days."[30] This warning and those of Moody's and Fitch helped cause the share price to decline further over September 10–12.

Stock analysts recognized the self-fulfilling nature of Lehman's crisis. On September 11, the Buckingham Research Group downgraded Lehman from "strong buy" to "neutral," saying the firm was undervalued based on fundamentals but threatened by "rating agency risk." According to Buckingham:[31]

> [I]t does not appear that the rating agencies are willing to give LEH the time it needs to execute its strategic initiatives. And while we strongly disagree with the rating agencies' stance, perception is reality in this business and a significant downgrade would be very onerous on LEH's trading business.

Also on September 11, an analyst at Sanford Bernstein wrote to colleagues about Lehman's situation. The analyst listed questions and answers, which included the following:[32]

> 5. What does Lehman's liquidity look like? Can there be a run on the Bank?

> Lehman's liquidity profile appears fine, especially with the Fed backstopping the firm. After Tuesday's market close, every major market dealer has announced they continue to trade with the firm and we believe it is likely the Fed is encouraging other firms to continue to trade with Lehman to avoid a funding run.

> 6. How can Lehman really blow up?

> Lehman's stock price could fall to $1 or rise to $20 and the firm will be able to go about business as usual as long as firms continue to lend to it. The Fed's facilities are certainly helping to keep these lines open.

> But if a large counterparty decides to pull lines and other firms catch wind and pull their lines, then the Fed will have to decide what to do because Lehman would look to it for funding. It's a massive game theory. No large counterparty wants them to fail, so as long as people lend, it won't.

The analyst's comment about game theory refers to that discipline's concept of multiple equilibria. Lehman's lenders might continue to lend, or they might cut off lending, because either decision is rational for one lender if the others make the same decision. The analyst hopes that Lehman will survive because lenders coordinate on the better equilibrium and/or because the Fed steps in, but neither of those things happened.

LEHMAN'S FINAL WEEKEND

Lehman's fate was determined over the weekend of September 13–14, 2008. Fed and Treasury officials tried to broker an acquisition of Lehman by Bank of America (BoA) or Barclays, but these efforts failed. Lehman did not have enough cash to operate on Monday, September 15, so it filed a bankruptcy petition that day at 1:45 AM.

Two Possible Acquirers

Over the summer of 2008, Lehman explored mergers with a number of possible partners, but by September, the only firms still interested were BoA and the British bank, Barclays.

Lehman had approached BoA about a deal in July and again in August, but BoA executives were lukewarm to the idea. In early September, Treasury Secretary Paulson called BoA's CEO, Kenneth Lewis, and "asked him to take another look at acquiring Lehman, assuring him that Fuld was ready to deal."[33] BoA began a due diligence review of Lehman's finances around September 9.[34]

Lehman had also approached Barclays over the summer. Barclays CEO Robert Diamond told Fuld he was not interested in a merger because "there was too much overlap" between the two firms.[35] However, Diamond later said that a Lehman acquisition appealed to Barclays as a way to expand its business in North America. On balance, Diamond thought an acquisition might be profitable if Lehman experienced a crisis and was therefore available at a "very, very distressed price."[36]

As Lehman entered its final week, it appeared that the firm *would* be available at a distressed price. Geithner and Paulson contacted Diamond and encouraged him to consider a Lehman deal. Barclays began its due diligence on Friday, September 12.

Around the same time, BoA lost interest in Lehman Brothers. It believed that a large fraction of Lehman's assets were overvalued, and it discovered a more attractive opportunity to buy an investment bank. The CEO of Merrill Lynch, John Thain, saw the run on Lehman and feared a similar fate for his firm, so he called BoA's Lewis on September 13. The two men quickly reached a deal for BoA to acquire Merrill, and that left Barclays as the only bidder for Lehman.

The Near Deal

On Friday, September 12, Treasury Secretary Paulson traveled to New York. He spent the weekend at the New York Fed, along with NY Fed President Timothy Geithner and SEC Chairman Christopher Cox. From Friday until Sunday, Paulson and colleagues tried to broker Barclays' acquisition of Lehman Brothers.

One obstacle to the deal was that Barclays did not want to acquire some of Lehman's illiquid assets, specifically its commercial real estate and private equity. Like JPMorgan Chase when it bought Bear Stearns, Barclays demanded that someone else take the assets it did not want. While the Fed had created the Maiden Lane facility to purchase the Bear assets that JPMorgan rejected, it did *not* create such a facility to aid Lehman Brothers. Instead, policymakers sought financing of the unwanted assets from a consortium of Wall Street firms, an approach modeled on the rescue of the Long Term Capital Management hedge fund that the Fed had brokered in 1998.

To organize a consortium, policymakers invited the CEOs of twelve financial institutions to meet at the New York Fed. The group convened on Friday evening and worked through the weekend. Paulson and Geithner asked the CEOs to help devise a plan to rescue Lehman, and told them that the Fed would not contribute any money to the deal.

On Saturday, September 13, a tentative deal was reached among Lehman, Barclays, and the Wall Street consortium. The deal, as outlined in the minutes of a Lehman board meeting at 5:00 PM on the 13th, was the following:[37] Barclays would pay $3 billion and acquire all of Lehman Brothers Holdings Inc. except for a pool of illiquid assets (commercial real estate, private equity, and investments in hedge funds) valued at $40 billion. The consortium would lend $40 billion to LBHI with the illiquid assets as collateral, taking on a risk of losses if the value of the assets fell. LBHI would remain as an independent corporation, but its only assets would be the $40 billion of assets rejected by Barclays, plus the $3 billion paid by Barclays for the rest of LBHI. Its liabilities would be its $40 billion debt to the consortium.

According to the minutes of the Lehman board meeting: "The proposed structure was summarized as Barclays gets the 'good bank' and [Lehman's] stockholders get the 'bad bank.'" The bad bank was somewhat similar to the Spinco real estate investment trust that Lehman had previously planned to create: it was a vehicle that would hold Lehman's illiquid assets.

On the night of September 13, it appeared that the proposed deal would be completed the next day. On the morning of September 14, however, the deal was derailed by a problem that nobody anticipated. To approve the deal, the New York Fed required that Barclays immediately guarantee all of Lehman's obligations, just as JPMorgan Chase had guaranteed Bear Stearns's obligations. Under UK law, however, such a guarantee had to be approved by Barclays shareholders, and a shareholder vote on the matter would take 30–60 days to organize.

Geithner and SEC Chair Cox appealed to Britain's Financial Services Authority to waive the requirement of a shareholder vote, but the FSA refused. The Fed continued to insist on an immediate guarantee by Barclays, and in a final effort to save the deal, Secretary Paulson called the Chancellor of the Exchequer, Alistair Darling. They failed to resolve the impasse, and by 11:00 AM in New York on Sunday, September 14, it was clear that the Lehman-Barclays deal would not go forward.[38]

Lehman's Final Hours

On the afternoon of September 14, Lehman executives tried despe-
rately to save their firm. Fuld called the CEO of Morgan Stanley, John
Mack, and asked for some kind of help, but he was rebuffed.[39]
According to Andrew Ross Sorkin's book *Too Big to Fail*, George
Walker, a Lehman executive who was a second cousin of President
Bush, called the White House and asked to speak to the President, but
his call was not returned.[40]

A group of Lehman executives and lawyers met at the New York
Fed with officials led by the NY Fed's General Counsel, Thomas
Baxter. Baxter announced that the Fed would not assist the broad
Lehman enterprise, LBHI, and strongly advised LBHI to file for bankruptcy. Baxter said the Fed *would* assist LBI, Lehman's broker-dealer
in New York, to keep that unit in operation. (This decision is discussed in more detail in later chapters.)

LBHI's board of directors met on the evening of Sunday,
September 14. With neither a Barclays deal nor adequate Fed assistance, it was clear the firm would not have enough cash to fund its
operations on the next day. After a long discussion, the directors voted
to declare bankruptcy. Lehman's attorneys at Weil, Gotshal, and
Manges rushed to prepare a bankruptcy petition, which was submitted
to the bankruptcy court in New York at 1:45 AM on September 15.
It was 6:45 AM in London, where Lehman's European broker-dealer
LBIE was scheduled to open at 9:00.

The Fed's Damage Control

Fed officials were worried that LBHI's bankruptcy would disrupt the
financial system, and starting on September 14, policymakers took
a number of actions to try to minimize the damage.

Expansion of the PDCF and TSLF To maintain confidence in the
tri-party repo market during the Bear Stearns crisis in March 2008, the
Fed had created the Primary Dealer Credit Facility (PDCF) and the
Term Securities Lending Facility (TSLF). Officials feared that

Lehman's bankruptcy would be a new blow to confidence, which could trigger runs on the repos of other investment banks. To head off this threat, the Fed broadened the types of collateral the two lending facilities would accept.

Collateral acceptable to the PDCF was expanded "to closely match the types of collateral that can be pledged in the tri-party repo systems of the two major clearing banks."[41] This change meant that the PDCF started accepting speculative-grade securities, equities, and whole loans. For most borrowers, the Fed set haircuts on the newly-accepted types of collateral between 7 percent and 12 percent, somewhat lower than market haircuts at the time.[42]

The purpose of PDCF expansion was to completely protect investment banks from losing their repo funding. After this change, the cash lost from *any* repos that did not roll could be replaced by PDCF loans, using whatever collateral the repo lenders had stopped accepting.[43]

The TSLF, which lent Treasury securities to the major Wall Street firms, was expanded at the same time as the PDCF. Previously, the TSLF accepted only triple-A mortgage backed securities as collateral. Starting September 14, it accepted all investment-grade securities, making it easier for borrowers to strengthen their liquidity by acquiring Treasuries.

Support for LBI Lehman Brothers Inc. (LBI), Lehman's broker-dealer in New York, was a subsidiary of LBHI. On September 14, Fed officials wanted LBHI to file for bankruptcy, but they wanted LBI to stay in business for some period. According to General Counsel Baxter, Fed officials sought "to enable the broker-dealer [LBI] to wind down its trading book in an orderly manner – thereby mitigating to some degree the impact of the failure on financial markets and the economy."[44]

LBI was one part of LBHI that lacked enough cash to operate on September 15. To keep LBI open, the Fed allowed it to borrow from the PDCF for up to two weeks. LBI could pledge the same types of collateral as other borrowers, but with larger haircuts – about 17 percent for many securities.[45]

Why did the Fed assist LBI, but not the rest of LBHI? This crucial question is addressed in later chapters.

Netting Derivatives When it filed for bankruptcy, LBHI defaulted on millions of its derivatives contracts. To mitigate the effects of these defaults on other financial institutions, the New York Fed hosted a special session for trading derivatives on the afternoon of Sunday, September 14. Some firms were able to take positions that reduced their exposure to Lehman's bankruptcy.

AFTER LEHMAN'S BANKRUPTCY

The US financial crisis intensified dramatically after the Lehman bankruptcy, and so did efforts by the Fed and Treasury to contain the damage.

The Resolution of LBI

After the LBHI bankruptcy, LBI needed assistance from the PDCF, as policymakers had expected. LBI received overnight loans for three days: approximately $28 billion on September 15; $20 billion on September 16; and $20 billion on September 17.[46]

When LBHI entered bankruptcy, Barclays expressed interest in purchasing LBI from the bankruptcy estate. On September 16, Barclays and the estate agreed on a complex transaction in which Barclays acquired LBI's broker-dealer operations and some, but not all, of LBI's assets and customer accounts. This deal was approved by the LBHI bankruptcy court on September 19.

On September 18, Barclays agreed to provide liquidity to LBI as part of its takeover of LBI's operations. Barclays lent $45 billion to LBI through a tri-party repo, and LBI stopped borrowing from the PDCF.[47]

After the Barclays transaction, LBI was still a corporate entity with billions of dollars in customer accounts. On September 19, it entered liquidation under the Securities Investors Protection Act (SIPA) – a special kind of bankruptcy for regulated broker-dealers. LBI's liquidation proceeding, like LBHI's bankruptcy case, is ongoing in 2018.

The AIG Crisis and the Rescue on September 16

Like the big investment banks, American International Group (AIG), a trillion-dollar firm that owned insurance companies, bet heavily on real estate during the housing bubble. It purchased large quantities of mortgage backed securities (MBSs), and it sold credit default swaps to other holders of MBSs, insuring them against losses on the securities. As MBS prices fell over 2007 and 2008, AIG suffered losses and markets lost confidence in the firm. The effects of falling confidence were the same as those experienced by Bear Stearns and Lehman: a falling stock price, warnings from rating agencies, and a loss of liquidity.

Like Bear and Lehman, AIG lost liquidity largely because it could not roll over its short-term borrowings. In AIG's case, this funding was mostly unsecured commercial paper, not repos. Collateral calls on credit default swap contracts were another important liquidity drain.

AIG's crisis, like Lehman's, became acute in September 2008. On September 12, AIG executives met with New York Fed officials to request help. A Fed summary of the meeting predicted that AIG would run out of cash in five to ten days.[48] By Tuesday, September 16, AIG's funding had broken down completely; as the firm's CEO later put it, "nobody would lend us lunch money."[49] Once again, a huge financial institution was on the brink of bankruptcy.

As in the Lehman crisis, policymakers tried to broker a private-sector solution involving a Wall Street consortium. On September 15, President Geithner met with a group of financial institutions led by Goldman Sachs and JPMorgan Chase, and tried to arrange an AIG rescue. The financial institutions prepared a proposal for a $75 billion loan to AIG, but then, on the morning of the 16th, they decided not to pursue it. One factor that deterred the potential lenders was the panic in financial markets that followed the Lehman bankruptcy.[50]

On the evening of September 16, the Fed stepped in to rescue AIG. Citing Section 13(3) of the Federal Reserve Act, the Board of

Governors authorized the New York Fed to provide an $85 billion line of credit to AIG. According to the Board's press release:

> The purpose of this liquidity facility is to assist AIG in meeting its obligations as they come due. This loan will facilitate a process under which AIG will sell certain of its businesses in an orderly manner, with the least possible disruption to the overall economy.

The loan was collateralized by "all the assets of AIG," including the stock of AIG's insurance subsidiaries. The loan conditions were harsh: the interest rate was 850 basis points above the London Interbank Offered Rate (LIBOR), a short-term market rate, and the US government received an 80 percent equity interest in AIG.

The Fed's initial loan was not sufficient to stabilize AIG. On October 6, the Fed granted the firm an additional credit line of $38 billion. On November 10, the Fed created the Maiden Lane II facility, which bought $21 billion of MBSs from AIG, and Maiden Lane III, which financed $29 billion of complex transactions that terminated derivatives contracts between AIG and other firms. Finally, on November 10, the Treasury invested $40 billion in AIG under the Troubled Asset Relief Program.

The Money Market Crisis, September–October 2008

The Lehman failure led directly to another part of the financial crisis: the run on money market mutual funds. One large fund, the Reserve Primary Fund, held $785 million of LBHI's commercial paper, which was about 1 percent of the fund's assets. This commercial paper became almost worthless on September 15, and that caused the Reserve Primary Fund to "break the buck": it repriced shares that it had sold for $1.00 at $0.97.[51]

This event shook confidence in money market funds, which savers had come to regard as riskless. Over several days, the funds' customers withdrew about $350 billion, or 10 percent of the funds' assets, setting off a chain reaction that disrupted the economy. As the funds lost cash, they reduced their purchases of commercial paper, which corporations needed to issue to obtain working capital. Fearing that they could not raise the money they needed to operate, many corporations reduced production and laid off workers.

Policymakers eventually contained this crisis through several actions. On September 19, the Treasury temporarily guaranteed the $1 value of money market shares. On the same day, the Fed created the Asset-Backed Commercial Paper Money Market Mutual Fund Liquidity Facility, which made loans to banks that purchased commercial paper from money market funds. Finally, on October 7, the Fed boosted the demand for commercial paper by creating the Commercial Paper Funding Facility, which purchased commercial paper directly from issuers.

Goldman Sachs and Morgan Stanley

After Lehman failed and Merrill Lynch was acquired by BoA, only two of the Big Five investment banks were left: Goldman Sachs and Morgan Stanley. These firms had also suffered losses on real estate, and market participants started to question their viability. John Mack, Morgan Stanley's CEO, told the FCIC:[52]

> As soon as we come in on Monday [September 15], we're in the eye of the storm with Merrill gone and Lehman gone ... Now we're the next in line.

Yet again, a loss of confidence produced a loss of repo financing and other liquidity drains, which threatened the survival of Goldman and Morgan. According to Ben Bernanke:[53]

> [W]hen that huge funding crisis hit all the investment banks, even Goldman Sachs, we thought there was a real chance that they would go under.

Goldman Sachs and Morgan Stanley were able to offset their liquidity drains by borrowing from the PDCF and TSLF. Much of this borrowing was collateralized with equities and speculative-grade securities, as allowed by the September 14 expansion of the PDCF. Goldman's total borrowing from Fed facilities peaked at $69 billion on December 31; Morgan Stanley's peaked at $107 billion on September 29.[54] Morgan Stanley borrowed far more than 100 percent of its liquidity pool, which was $55 billion in mid-September.[55] This fact suggests that Morgan Stanley would have run out of cash if not for Fed assistance.

Goldman and Morgan Stanley also took steps to restore confidence in their firms. Both applied to become bank holding companies (BHCs), and the Fed approved their requests on September 21. BHC status implied greater oversight by the Fed, which made the companies appear safer to their customers and lenders.

In addition, the two firms raised new capital. Goldman received $5 billion from Warren Buffett's Berkshire Hathaway Inc. on September 23, and Morgan Stanley received $9 billion from Mitsubishi UFJ on September 29. Both firms also received capital from the government's Troubled Asset Relief Program.

The Troubled Asset Relief Program, October 2008

In late September, Congress voted to establish the Troubled Asset Relief Program (TARP), and President Bush signed the legislation on October 3. TARP allocated $700 billion to the Treasury department to aid troubled financial institutions. Over the next several months, the Treasury used this money to purchase equity stakes in most of the large US financial institutions, including Goldman Sachs, Morgan Stanley, and AIG.

As the financial system stabilized over 2009–2011, the Treasury sold most of the equity it had bought under TARP, and the Fed closed most of its lending facilities. The Fed closed the PDCF and TSLF in February 2010.

The Great Recession of 2008–2009

The financial crisis caused a credit crunch throughout the US economy. Banks cut lending sharply, loan securitization came to a halt, risk premia on corporate debt spiked upward, and firms had trouble issuing commercial paper. The crisis also produced a 50 percent fall in the stock market, an acceleration of the decline in house prices, a rising number of foreclosures on homes, and record lows in consumer confidence. All of these factors reduced spending, employment, and production throughout the economy.

The Great Recession pushed the US unemployment rate to 10 percent in 2009, and it spilled over into recessions around the globe. The damage has persisted until today. In 2018, US output is still expected to be 5 or 10 percent lower than it would have been if the economy had followed the path it was on before 2008.[56]

This chapter has given an overview of events in 2008: the growing stresses in the financial system in the spring and summer; the Lehman bankruptcy on September 15; and the dire financial and economic crisis that followed the bankruptcy. We have seen that the Federal Reserve lent money to a number of financial institutions to save them from failure, but refused to rescue Lehman. To understand the financial crisis, we must understand why the Fed let Lehman Brothers fail.

The remainder of this book addresses this question by analyzing the voluminous record on Lehman's crisis, especially the evidence gathered by Bankruptcy Examiner Valukas and by the Financial Crisis Inquiry Commission. The evidence shows clearly that Fed officials' explanation for not rescuing Lehman – a lack of legal authority due to inadequate collateral – is not correct. The real reasons for the Fed's decision apparently include political opposition to a rescue and a failure to fully anticipate the damage that Lehman's bankruptcy would cause.

3 The Legal Criteria for Fed Assistance

The central question of this book is whether a Federal Reserve rescue of Lehman Brothers would have been legal. Before examining the facts of the case, I review the relevant law.

SECTION 13(3) OF THE FEDERAL RESERVE ACT

Section 10B of the Federal Reserve Act authorizes the Fed to lend to depository institutions through the "discount window." Ordinarily, the Fed may *not* lend to non-depository institutions such as investment banks and insurance companies. However, Section 13(3) of the Federal Reserve Act allows loans to these institutions (and even non-financial firms and individuals) under special circumstances.

Section 13(3) was added to the Federal Reserve Act in 1932, and it has been amended three times: in 1935; in 1991, as part of the FDIC Improvement Act; and in 2010, as part of the Dodd-Frank Wall Street Reform Act. What matters for our purposes is Section 13(3) as it stood in 2008, before the 2010 amendments.

Under 13(3), a Federal Reserve Bank can make a loan to a non-depository institution if it is authorized to do so by five members of the Fed's Board of Governors. In 2008, the Board could authorize a loan if three requirements were met:

- The Board must find that "unusual and exigent circumstances" exist.
- The Reserve Bank must "obtain evidence that [the borrower] is unable to secure adequate credit accommodations from other banking institutions."
- The loan must be "indorsed or otherwise secured to the satisfaction of the Reserve Bank."

Between 1932 and 1936, the Board of Governors invoked Section 13(3) to authorize a total of $1.5 million in loans by various

Reserve Banks. Then Section 13(3) was dormant for more than seventy years. In March 2008, the Board invoked it to authorize the New York Fed's loan to Maiden Lane LLC, which bought illiquid assets from Bear Stearns, and to establish the Term Securities Lending Facility (TSLF) and the Primary Dealer Credit Facility (PDCF). In the Fall of 2008, the Fed used Section 13(3) to create several more lending facilities and to support AIG.[1]

In 2008, few questioned that the financial crisis had created unusual and exigent circumstances, the first requirement for lending under Section 13(3). The second requirement, that borrowers be unable to secure other credit, was also generally satisfied by the firms that the Fed assisted. The Fed lent to firms that had lost their normal sources of funds, such as investment banks that could not roll repos and corporations that could not issue commercial paper. Lehman Brothers was definitely unable to secure adequate credit to fund its operations, which is why it declared bankruptcy.

The tricky part of Section 13(3) is the requirement that a borrower must provide satisfactory security for a loan. Fed officials have asserted that this condition was met for all the lending they approved in 2008, but that it could not have been met for a loan to rescue Lehman. I will carefully examine the concept of satisfactory security in what follows.

Before tackling the definition of satisfactory security, we should take note of two other significant features of Section 13(3) as it stood in 2008. First, 13(3) did *not* require that a borrower be solvent in any sense of the word. Second, the Federal Reserve System had sole authority over its lending decisions: to make loans, a Reserve Bank such as the New York Fed needed only the approval of the Board of Governors.

Both of these features of 13(3) were changed by the Dodd-Frank Act of 2010. The law now prohibits loans to "borrowers that are insolvent" or to "a failing financial company," and it requires that loans be approved by the Secretary of the Treasury in addition to the Fed's Board of Governors. Dodd-Frank also restricts the Fed's authority under 13(3) in another major way: the Fed can create lending programs for a broad category of financial firms, but it may not make special deals with a single firm. Under current law, the Primary Dealer Credit Facility established in 2008 would still be legal, because nineteen financial institutions could borrow from it. But current law would have prevented the Fed's loan to Maiden Lane LLC which enabled the Bear Stearns rescue and the loans to AIG which rescued that firm.

Under the 2008 version of Section 13(3), the requirements for Fed lending were similar to those that Walter Bagehot advocated for the Bank of England in his classic book *Lombard Street* in 1873.[2] Bagehot argued that a central bank should serve as the "lender of last resort" to banks that lose their normal sources of funds in a panic. Like Section 13(3), Bagehot's book stresses the security of loans, saying that a central bank should require "good banking securities" as collateral and that "no advances need be made by which the Bank will ultimately lose." Bagehot does not mention the concept of solvency, although commentators sometimes misquote him and say that he advocates loans only to solvent institutions.[3]

WHAT IS "SATISFACTORY SECURITY"?

The Section 13(3) requirement that a loan be "secured to the satisfaction of the Reserve Bank" is vague. The legislative history of Section 13(3) does not clarify the term, and it has not been interpreted by the courts.[4] However, two sources shed light on the Fed's definition of satisfactory security in 2008: a memo written by the Board's Legal Division, and statements by Ben Bernanke about lending decisions. Apparently, the Fed interpreted satisfactory security to mean simply that a loan was likely to be repaid.

The Legal Division's Memo on the Commercial Paper Funding Facility

Each time the Board of Governors authorized lending under Section 13(3) in 2008, its Legal Division, led by General Counsel

Scott Alvarez, wrote a memo about the decision. One of these memos – the one on the Commercial Paper Funding Facility (CPFF), which was established in October 2008 – was released by the FCIC when it issued its report.[5] This memo is the only publicly available document in which the Legal Division formally interprets Section 13(3).[6]

The CPFF memo includes a general discussion of security for 13(3) loans, and describes several types of security. One type that Section 13(3) mentions explicitly is "indorsement," a guarantee of repayment by a party other than the borrower. Collateral is a second type of security, and a third type is an insurance fee (which was the security for loans from the CPFF).

In discussing these types of security, the Legal Division emphasizes that "the scope of the Reserve Bank's discretion in deciding what will be 'satisfactory' to it in connection with section 13(3) lending is extremely broad." In keeping with this theme, the memo focuses more on what is *not* required for satisfactory security than what *is* required. For example, the memo points out that 13(3) does not limit the types of assets that can serve as collateral. In this respect, lending under 13(3) differs from some kinds of Fed lending, which require specific types of collateral.

In many credit markets, the value of the collateral that secures a loan must exceed the amount of the loan (i.e., lenders impose haircuts). For a 13(3) loan, however, the Legal Division says the value of collateral can be *less* than the loan:

> The [Federal Reserve] Act could have provided that section 13(3) credit must be secured solely by collateral whose fair market value at the time credit is extended is at least equal to the amount of credit extended. . . . Congress imposed no such limitations under section 13(3). Therefore, the Reserve Bank has the discretion to accept as collateral securing [a loan] collateral of any value, including collateral that at the time of the extension of credit may have a current market value that is less than the amount of credit extended . . .

At only one point does the memo hint at an affirmative requirement concerning collateral:

> [T]he language of section 13(3) imposes no requirements on the amount or type of security obtained by a Reserve Bank in connection with [a loan] other than that the credit be secured "to the satisfaction of the Reserve Bank." This requirement has traditionally been met by collateral that secures the repayment of the credit.

The last sentence borders on the tautological, but we might interpret "secures the repayment" as meaning that the Fed will not lose money on a loan.

This interpretation is consistent with a comment by General Counsel Alvarez in his 2010 FCIC interview. Asked about the CPFF memo, Alvarez summarized its definition of satisfactory security as, "You have to be pretty confident you will be repaid."[7]

Statements by Ben Bernanke

In explaining why the Fed did not assist Lehman Brothers, Ben Bernanke has often referred to 13(3)'s requirement of satisfactory security. Bernanke's working definition of this term appears similar to Alvarez's.

One example is Bernanke's speech to the National Association for Business Economics on October 7, 2008. On that occasion, Bernanke said a Lehman rescue would have been unlawful because it "would have involved the assumption by taxpayers of billions of dollars of expected losses." He added:

> [T]he Federal Reserve's loans must be sufficiently secured to provide reasonable assurance that the loan will be fully repaid. Such collateral was not available in [Lehman's] case.

Bernanke contrasted this situation with the case of AIG, in which "the Federal Reserve was able to provide emergency credit that was judged to be adequately secured by the assets of the company."

Similarly, in an October 15 speech at the Economic Club of New York, Bernanke said:

> A public-sector solution for Lehman proved infeasible, as the firm could not post sufficient collateral to provide reasonable assurance that a loan from the Federal Reserve would be repaid . . .

And again he said that the Fed's loan to AIG was "adequately secured."

Bernanke made a similar statement to the Bankruptcy Examiner in December 2009. His exact words are not recorded, but the Valukas Report summarizes them:[8]

> Bernanke did not believe that the Fed had the legal authority to bail out Lehman in September 2008. He noted that a Federal Reserve Bank such as the FRBNY could make a loan only if it was satisfactorily secured, that is, that the bank could reasonably expect a 100 percent return.

Bernanke said this condition was not satisfied because Lehman lacked adequate collateral.

Bernanke's requirement of a "reasonable assurance" of repayment is somewhat imprecise, but it is similar to Scott Alvarez's view that the Fed must be "pretty confident" of repayment. We should keep these definitions of satisfactory security in mind when we examine the collateral that Lehman Brothers had available for a loan.

4 Lehman's Balance Sheet and Solvency

This chapter begins to examine the financial condition of Lehman Brothers in detail. It gives an overview of Lehman's business, and then analyzes its balance sheet, the evidence on its overvaluation of assets, the firm's solvency, and the destruction of value caused by Lehman's bankruptcy.

In 2008 solvency was not a requirement for Fed assistance under Section 13(3). Yet Lehman's solvency is relevant in determining the type of liquidity support the firm needed, and in examining the possibilities for a long-term resolution of its problems. Solvency is also important because Fed officials have claimed that Lehman's insolvency was a factor in their decision not to rescue the firm.

AN OVERVIEW OF LEHMAN BROTHERS HOLDINGS INC.

The activities of Lehman Brothers Holdings Inc. (LBHI), like those of many financial firms, were organized along two dimensions: business line and legal entity.

Lehman's Businesses

LBHI was organized into three business segments, each of which operated around the world. The firm described these business segments in its filings with the Securities and Exchange Commission (forms 10-Q and 10-K):

- The Investment Banking segment provided services such as underwriting securities and advising corporations and governments.
- The Investment Management segment managed assets for institutions and wealthy individuals, and invested Lehman's money in private equity and hedge funds.

- The third business segment, Capital Markets, operated in markets for fixed-income securities, equities, and derivatives. It served as an intermediary, buying or borrowing securities from clients and selling or lending them to other clients; it was a prime broker for hedge funds; and it took proprietary positions. The Capital Markets segment also included divisions that originated residential mortgages and invested in commercial real estate.

Lehman's Corporate Structure

Lehman had a complex corporate structure that did not align with its business segments. This structure was based partly on geography, and it was influenced by taxation and capital requirements in various countries.

Lehman Brothers Holdings Inc. was at the top of the corporate structure. LBHI directly owned assets including real estate and securities, and it had sixteen subsidiaries. These subsidiaries included broker-dealers in New York, London, and Tokyo: Lehman Brothers Inc. (LBI), Lehman Brothers International Europe (LBIE), and Lehman Brothers Japan Inc. Other important subsidiaries included the investment management firm Neuberger Berman, and Lehman Brothers Bankhaus, a German commercial and investment bank.

The subsidiaries of LBHI had subsidiaries of their own. For example, LBI owned Lehman Derivative Products Inc. and Lehman Commercial Paper Inc. Altogether, the Lehman enterprise included thirty-six corporate entities in 2007.[1]

LBHI and several of its subsidiaries issued long-term debt and commercial paper. Lehman's repo financing (which became a key factor in the firm's crisis) occurred mainly at LBI and LBIE, the New York and London broker-dealers. LBHI managed liquidity throughout its enterprise: it collected excess cash from subsidiaries and sent it to subsidiaries with shortages.[2]

LBHI's quarterly and annual financial statements (Forms 10-Q and 10-K) reported a consolidated balance sheet for the firm and its subsidiaries. The annual statements also reported unconsolidated balance sheets for LBHI, LBI, and "other subsidiaries." In this accounting, LBHI held equity in its subsidiaries, and LBHI and the subsidiaries had debts to each other. All equity in subsidiaries and intra-Lehman debts netted to zero on the consolidated balance sheet.

Before LBHI's bankruptcy, its corporate structure was not salient to its senior managers, who ran the firm as a single business. Corporate structure suddenly became important when LBHI entered bankruptcy, however, because many Lehman subsidiaries entered separate bankruptcy proceedings of various types (including LBI's Securities Investor Protection Act (SIPA) proceeding and LBIE's administration proceeding in the United Kingdom). This break-up along corporate entity lines disrupted Lehman's businesses, and it produced extensive litigation between different parts of the firm over their debts to one another.

LBHI'S BALANCE SHEET

Exhibits 4.1 and 4.2 are the asset and liability sides of LBHI's consolidated balance sheet for May 31, 2008, the end of 2008 Quarter 2 in the firm's accounting calendar. This balance sheet is reproduced from LBHI's 10-Q for the quarter, the last 10-Q Lehman filed before the September 2008 bankruptcy. Exhibit 4.3 is a preliminary financial statement for August 31, 2008, the end of Quarter 3, which LBHI released on September 10 just prior to the bankruptcy.[3]

LBHI's balance sheets were based on complex accounting conventions, which are described in lengthy notes in its 10-Q. The next sections review the largest items on the balance sheets, starting with the numbers from the 2008 Q2 balance sheet.

Assets on May 31

Exhibit 4.1 lists LBHI's assets on May 31 and compares them to its assets on November 30, 2007. The firm's total assets on May 31 were $639 billion, down from $691 billion, a decrease due in part to sales of real estate assets.[4] The bulk of Lehman's assets – $606 billion out of $639 billion – belonged to three broad categories:

LEHMAN BROTHERS HOLDINGS INC.
Consolidated Statement of Financial Condition
(Unaudited)

In millions	At	
	May 31, 2008	Nov 30, 2007
Assets		
Cash and cash equivalents	$6,513	$7,286
Cash and securities segregated and on deposit for regulatory and other purposes	13,031	12,743
Financial instruments and other inventory positions owned (includes $43,031 in 2008 and $63,499 in 2007 pledged as collateral)	269,409	313,129
Collateralized agreements:		
Securities purchased under agreements to resell	169,684	162,635
Securities borrowed	124,842	138,599
Receivables:		
Brokers, dealers and clearing organizations	16,701	11,005
Customers	20,784	29,622
Others	4,236	2,650
Property, equipment and leasehold improvements (net of accumulated depreciation and amortization of $2,697 in 2008 and $2,438 in 2007)	4,278	3,861
Other assets	5,853	5,406
Identifiable intangible assets and goodwill (net of accumulated amortization of $361 in 2008 and $340 in 2007)	4,101	4,127
Total assets	$639,432	$691,063

See Notes to Consolidated Financial Statements.

EXHIBIT 4.1   Lehman Brothers Holdings Inc., Assets on May 31, 2008.
Source: LBHI Form 10-Q for 2008 Q2, p. 5.

- *Financial instruments and other inventory positions owned* ($269 billion) This category includes securities, derivatives contracts with positive market values, private equity, commercial real estate, and whole mortgage loans.[5]
- *Collateralized agreements* ($295 billion) This category has two sub-categories: "securities purchased under agreements to resell," also known as reverse repos, and "securities borrowed." These two types of assets are

LEHMAN BROTHERS HOLDINGS INC.
Consolidated Statement of Financial Condition (Continued)
(Unaudited)

In millions, except share data	At May 31, 2008	Nov 30, 2007
Liabilities and Stockholders' Equity		
Short-term borrowings and current portion of long-term borrowings		
(including $9,354 in 2008 and $9,035 in 2007 at fair value)	$35,302	$28,066
Financial instruments and other inventory positions sold but not yet purchased	141,507	149,617
Collateralized financings:		
Securities sold under agreements to repurchase	127,846	181,732
Securities loaned	55,420	53,307
Other secured borrowings		
(including $13,617 in 2008 and $9,149 in 2007 at fair value)	24,656	22,992
Payables:		
Brokers, dealers and clearing organizations	3,835	3,101
Customers	57,251	61,206
Accrued liabilities and other payables	9,802	16,039
Deposit liabilities at banks		
(including $10,252 in 2008 and $15,986 in 2007 at fair value)	29,355	29,363
Long-term borrowings		
(including $27,278 in 2008 and $27,204 in 2007 at fair value)	128,182	123,150
Total liabilities	613,156	668,573
Commitments and contingencies		
Stockholders' Equity		
Preferred stock	6,993	1,095
Common stock, $0.10 par value:		
Shares authorized: 1,200,000,000 in 2008 and 2007;		
Shares issued: 612,948,910 in 2008 and 612,882,506 in 2007;		
Shares outstanding: 552,704,921 in 2008 and 531,887,419 in 2007	61	61
Additional paid-in capital	11,268	9,733
Accumulated other comprehensive loss, net of tax	(359)	(310)
Retained earnings	16,901	19,698
Other stockholders' equity, net	(3,666)	(2,263)
Common stock in treasury, at cost		
(60,243,989 shares in 2008 and 80,995,087 shares in 2007)	(4,922)	(5,524)
Total common stockholders' equity	19,283	21,395
Total stockholders' equity	26,276	22,490
Total liabilities and stockholders' equity	$639,432	$691,063

See Notes to Consolidated Financial Statements.

EXHIBIT 4.2 Lehman Brothers Holdings Inc., Liabilities and Equity
on May 31, 2008.
Source: LBHI Form 10-Q for 2008 Q2, p. 6.

similar in economic terms: both reflect transactions in which Lehman
temporarily lends cash to customers in exchange for securities. The cash
due back to Lehman is counted in the firm's assets. (The securities that
Lehman must send back to its customers do not appear on either side of
Lehman's balance sheet.)

LEHMAN BROTHERS HOLDINGS INC.
SELECTED STATISTICAL INFORMATION
(Preliminary and Unaudited)
(Dollars in millions, except share data)

	At or for the Quarter Ended				
	Aug 31, 2008	May 31, 2008	Feb 29, 2008	Nov 30, 2007	Aug 31, 2007
Income Statement					
Net Revenues	$(2,903)	$(668)	$3,507	$4,390	$4,308
Non-Interest Expenses:					
Compensation and Benefits	1,950	2,325	1,841	2,164	2,124
Non-personnel Expenses	971	1,094	1,003	996	979
Income before provision for income taxes	(5,824)	(4,087)	663	1,230	1,205
Net Income	(3,927)	(2,774)	489	886	887
Net Income Applicable to Common Stock	(4,090)	(2,873)	465	870	870
Earnings per Common Share:					
Basic	$(5.92)	$(5.14)	$0.84	$1.60	$1.61
Diluted	$(5.92)	$(5.14)	$0.81	$1.54	$1.54
Financial Ratios (%)					
Return on Average Common Stockholders' Equity					
(annualized)	NM	NM	8.6%	16.6%	17.1%
Return on Average Tangible Common Stockholders'					
Equity (annualized)	NM	NM	10.6%	20.6%	21.1%
Pre-tax Margin	NM	NM	18.9%	28.0%	28.0%
Compensation and Benefits/Net Revenues	NM	NM	52.5%	49.3%	49.3%
Effective Tax Rate	32.6%	32.1%	26.3%	27.9%	26.4%
Financial Condition					
Total Assets	$600,000	$639,432	$786,035	$691,063	$659,216
Net Assets	310,915	327,774	396,673	372,959	357,102
Common Stockholders' Equity	19,450	19,283	21,839	21,395	20,638
Total Stockholders' Equity	28,443	26,276	24,832	22,490	21,733
Total Stockholders' Equity Plus Junior Subordinated					
Notes	33,362	31,280	29,808	27,230	26,647
Tangible Equity Capital	29,277	27,179	25,696	23,103	22,164
Total Long-Term Capital	143,043	154,458	153,117	145,640	142,064
Book Value per Common Share	27.29	34.21	39.45	39.44	38.29
Leverage Ratio	21.1x	24.3x	31.7x	30.7x	30.3x
Net Leverage Ratio	10.6x	12.1x	15.4x	16.1x	16.1x
Other Data (#s)					
Employees	25,935	26,189	28,088	28,556	28,783
Assets Under Management (in billions)	$273	$277	$277	$282	$275
Common Stock Outstanding (in millions)	689.0	552.7	551.4	531.9	529.4
Weighted Average Shares (in millions):					
Basic	691.2	559.3	551.5	542.6	540.4
Diluted	691.2	559.3	572.8	563.7	565.8

EXHIBIT 4.3 Lehman Brothers Holdings Inc., Financial Statement for August 31, 2008.

Source: LBHI press release, September 10, 2008.

- **Receivables** ($42 billion) This category includes cash due to Lehman as a result of various transactions. It also includes assets that belong to Lehman, but are posted as collateral for derivatives contracts.

Liabilities and Equity on May 31

Exhibit 4.2 summarizes LBHI's liabilities and equity. Total liabilities on May 31 were $613 billion. The bulk of these liabilities ($539 billion) belonged to four categories:

- *Financial instruments and other inventory positions sold but not yet purchased* ($142 billion) This category covers Lehman's short positions, including derivatives contracts with negative market values.
- *Collateralized financings* ($208 billion) This category is the opposite of collateralized agreements on the asset side of the balance sheet. It reflects transactions such as repos and securities loans, in which Lehman temporarily borrows cash in exchange for securities. The cash owed by Lehman is a liability of the firm. (The securities due back to Lehman are included in the "financial instruments" category on the asset side.)
- *Payables* ($61 billion) This category includes cash due from Lehman in various transactions, collateral posted to Lehman by counterparties in derivatives contracts, and customer balances in prime brokerage accounts.
- *Long-Term Borrowings* ($128 billion) This category comprises unsecured debt that is not due for a year or more. Of the total, $110 billion is senior unsecured debt and $18 billion is subordinated debt.[6]

Notice that commercial paper was not a major part of Lehman's liabilities. The balance sheet includes $35 billion of "short-term borrowings and current portion of long-term borrowings." Of this total, only $8 billion is commercial paper; most of the rest is long-term debt coming due within a year.[7]

With $639 billion in assets and $613 billion in liabilities, Lehman reported stockholder equity of $26 billion on May 31.

Developments in 2008 Quarter 3

Exhibit 4.3 is a preliminary financial statement that was part of a press release from Lehman on September 10, five days before its bankruptcy. In this statement, the firm pre-announced its earnings for 2008 Q3, which ended August 31, and it reported some balance-sheet items. Lehman never filed a 10-Q for 2008 Q3.

Lehman's total assets fell from $639 billion on May 31 to $600 billion on August 31, as the firm continued to sell illiquid assets. The firm's investments in real estate fell by $19 billion.[8]

The decline in total assets included net revaluations of –$5.6 billion, which primarily reflected declines in the prices of real estate assets. Net income including revaluations was –$3.9 billion – Lehman's second straight quarterly loss. The effect of this loss on stockholder equity was more than offset, however, by $6 billion of new stock that Lehman had issued in June. As a result, equity rose by $2.1 billion, from $26.3 billion on May 31 to $28.4 billion on August 31.[9]

ASSET VALUATION AND LEHMAN'S SOLVENCY

Economists usually define a solvent institution as one with assets greater than liabilities, or equivalently, with positive equity. The definition of solvency is the same in bankruptcy law.[10] As just seen, according to Lehman's financial statements, the firm was solvent before its bankruptcy.

Despite the numbers reported in Lehman's financial statements, many analysts have questioned the firm's solvency. They contend that Lehman inflated the values of its assets, and that more realistic valuations would have implied that equity was negative. Discussions of the Lehman episode often take it as given that the firm was insolvent. For example, a New York Fed study in 2013 said the Primary Dealer Credit Facility (PDCF) "could not prevent the trouble experienced by Lehman ... due to solvency problems."[11]

The next section examines the issue of Lehman's solvency by looking closely at the value of Lehman's assets. With realistic mark-to-market valuations, it is hard to say whether Lehman was solvent: it appears that its true equity was near zero. With valuations based instead on fundamentals – on assets' expected cash flows – Lehman was probably solvent.

A Review of Lehman's Asset Valuations

The first step in assessing Lehman's solvency is to review the methods it used to value its assets. Specifically, how extensively did the firm use subjective methods that might have produced unreasonably high values? The information to answer this question appears in Lehman's 10-Q for 2008 Q2 (ending May 31).

As shown in Exhibit 4.1, most of Lehman's assets fall under one of three categories: *Collateralized agreements; Receivables;* and *Financial instruments and other inventory positions owned.* Assets in the first two categories are primarily cash owed to Lehman, which does not require subjective valuation. To my knowledge, nobody has questioned the valuations of the assets in these two categories.

Discussions of overvaluation have focused on the Lehman assets in the *Financial instruments and other inventory positions owned* category: real estate assets, corporate debt and equity, government securities, and derivatives. At the end of 2008 Q2, Lehman valued these assets at a total of $269.4 billion.

Of this $269.4 billion in assets, a total of $248.7 billion was reported at "fair value," as defined by the Financial Standards Accounting Board (FSAB).[12] In 2008, the FSAB's definition of fair value was "the price at which an asset could be exchanged in a current transaction between knowledgeable, willing parties."[13] This concept of fair value is also known as "mark to market" value. (The remaining $20.7 billion of the total was valued in a more complicated way, discussed later.)

Following FSAB guidelines, Lehman used three types of "inputs" to determine the fair value of its assets.[14] Level 1 inputs are asset prices in active markets, such as stock prices on an exchange. Level 2 inputs are "alternative pricing sources with reasonable levels of price transparency," such as price quotes from dealers or market prices for similar but not identical assets. Level 3 inputs are the most subjective, and are used to value an asset only when Level 1 and 2 inputs are unavailable. Level 3 inputs "reflect the Company's assumptions that it believes market participants would use in pricing the assets," and may be derived from proprietary data and asset-pricing models.

This analysis of Lehman's asset valuations assumes that valuations based on Level 1 or 2 inputs are reasonable, an assumption that appears consistent with the assessments of Lehman's valuations by other financial institutions (discussed next). Lehman's valuations based on subjective Level 3 inputs, on the other hand, might be inflated.

LEHMAN BROTHERS HOLDINGS INC.
Notes to Consolidated Financial Statements
(Unaudited)

In millions	Assets at Fair Value as of May 31, 2008			
	Level 1	Level 2	Level 3	Total
Mortgage and asset-backed securities	$347	$51,517	$20,597	$72,461
Government and agencies	11,002	15,986	—	26,988
Corporate debt and other	77	44,332	5,590	49,999
Corporate equities	26,785	10,606	10,158	47,549
Commercial paper and other money market instruments	4,757	—	—	4,757
Derivative assets	2,597	39,395	4,999	46,991
	$45,565	$161,836	$41,344	$248,745

EXHIBIT 4.4 Lehman Brothers Holdings Inc., Assets at Fair Value on May 31, 2008, by Level of Inputs Used for Valuation. *Source*: LBHI Form 10-Q for 2008 Q2, p. 29.

Exhibit 4.4 is a table from Lehman's 10-Q for 2008 Q2.[15] It shows the breakdown of Lehman's assets at fair value ($248.7 billion) by the type of asset and by the level of inputs used to value them. According to the table, a total of $41.3 billion of assets were valued with Level 3 inputs. These assets were mostly mortgages and asset-backed securities ($20.6 billion) and private equity ($10.2 billion).

A complication: Out of Lehman's $269.4 billion in the *Financial instruments and other inventory positions owned* category of assets, $20.7 billion is not included in Exhibit 4.4. These assets are "real estate held for sale," which were reported at "the lower of carrying amount or fair value less cost to sell."[16] The 10-Q does not give details about the valuation of these assets, but presumably it involved judgments by Lehman about real estate values that are open to question.

To summarize, Lehman's balance sheet included two types of questionable assets: those valued with Level 3 inputs, which were $41.3 billion at the end of 2008 Q2, and real estate held for sale, which were $20.7 billion. Adding these two amounts yields a total of $62.0 billion of assets that Lehman may have overvalued. The true fair value of these assets was presumably positive, but less than Lehman reported. Therefore, at the end of 2008 Q2, the total overvaluation of Lehman assets was somewhere between zero (the level if all valuations were accurate) and $62 billion (the level if the questionable assets were worthless).

We have less detail about Lehman's assets at the end of 2008 Q3 (August 31). It appears, however, that the quantity of questionable assets fell during Q3, because Lehman sold some of the assets and wrote down the values of others. Thus, the questionable assets were probably less than $62 billion at the end of Q3.

Analyses of Lehman's Valuations by Other Financial Institutions

The most credible assessments of Lehman's valuations come from other financial institutions that examined Lehman's balance sheet before its bankruptcy. Two of these firms, Bank of America (BoA) and Barclays, examined Lehman as they considered whether to acquire the firm. Another assessment comes from the consortium organized by the Fed to help rescue Lehman on its final weekend. Three members of this group – Citi, Goldman Sachs, and Credit Suisse – were tasked with reviewing Lehman's valuations by New York Fed President Geithner.

An Overview of the Analyses BoA, Barclays, and the consortium reached similar conclusions on some major points. They all found that about $50–$70 billion of Lehman's reported assets had questionable valuations, and that these assets were primarily real estate assets and private equity. These findings confirm my analysis of Lehman's financial statements for 2008 Q2 and Q3.

The different assessments also produced similar estimates of the size of Lehman's overvaluation of the questionable assets. Taken together, the evidence suggests that the assets' reported values exceeded their true mark-to-market values by a total of $15 billion to $32 billion.

On the preliminary balance sheet for the end of 2008 Q3 (Exhibit 4.3), Lehman reported equity of $28 billion. If the firm overvalued its assets by $15–$32 billion, then its actual equity was between –$4 billion and +$13 billion.

The BoA, Barclays, and consortium analyses of overvaluation were done hurriedly, so it is not certain they were accurate. We will never know for sure whether Lehman's equity based on ideal fair-value accounting was positive or negative. But either way, it appears that equity was small relative to Lehman's $600 billion in assets. With equity close to zero, Lehman was near the border between solvency and insolvency.

Lehman's liabilities included $18 billion in subordinated debt (when last reported, for Q2). If the firm's equity was between –$4 billion and $13 billion, then the sum of equity and subordinated debt was between $14 billion and $31 billion. It seems likely, therefore, that this sum was positive. In other words, the firm's assets exceeded its liabilities excluding subordinated debt by a positive amount between $14 billion and $31 billion. This calculation suggests that a resolution of Lehman was possible in which losses, if any, were absorbed by holders of subordinated debt, and all other creditors were repaid fully.

The Details of the Analyses The following details of the analyses by Barclays, Citi/Goldman/Credit Suisse, and BoA support my conclusions about Lehman's solvency.

- *Barclays* A memo on Lehman's asset valuations was circulated within Barclays on September 13. The Bankruptcy Examiner made this memo public, and Exhibit 4.5 shows the first page.[17] In the memo, "Long Island" or "LI" is a code name for Lehman Brothers; Barclays is called "Baltimore."

  The memo summarizes the asset write-downs needed to "bring L.I. marks in line with Baltimore's valuation policies." In other words, the memo states the amounts by which Barclays thought Lehman overvalued its assets. A previous Barclays analysis had found total overvaluations of $7.5 billion, but the September 13 memo raises that figure to $23–$27 billion. The Barclays analysts, like others, found that most of the assets with inflated values were real estate and private equity.[18]

- *The Consortium* The analysis by Citi, Goldman, and Credit Suisse is summarized in several places. One is an email circulated among New York Fed staff in the early hours of September 14,[19] which reports that the consortium had estimated that Lehman's real estate assets (which it reported were worth $58 billion) were overvalued by $29–$32 billion. According to this email, the consortium had not yet examined Lehman's private equity or derivatives positions.

Long Island key exposures – key due diligence findings

Key exposures

- In the previous report to the Board, we estimated a total of $7.5 billion in further write-downs to Long Island assets based on a high level analysis of the risks of the valuation of key assets

  - The largest components of this estimate were a further 15% write-down of L.I.'s commercial mortgage portfolio and Real Estate held for sale ($5 billion) and a 5–10% write-down of their RMBS assets ($2 billion)

- Based upon due diligence undertaken in the last 24 hours, this estimate of the further immediate write-downs to L.I.'s book has increased significantly to $23 billion – $27 billion, the largest components being:

  - $16 billion write-down to the $32 billion exposure to Commercial Real Estate and Real Estate held for sale
  - $3–5 billion trading write-downs, primarily relating to RMBS
  - $4–6 billion relating to Private Equity and alternative investment portfolio
  - Analysis on Leveraged & Corporate Lending and Muni portfolios are still in progress and excluded from current write-down estimate

- These revisions are based upon:

  - Bringing L.I. marks in line with Baltimore's valuation policies
  - Review of risk reports and reserving policies
  - For the most material segments (e.g., CMBS) this estimate is based on an asset-by-asset basis, while elsewhere, where markets are highly illiquid, these are conservative top-down estimates

BCI-EX-00081255

EXHIBIT 4.5 Barclays Bank, Analysis of Asset Overvaluation by Lehman Brothers, September 13, 2008.
Source: Report of the LBHI Bankruptcy Examiner, footnote 7788.

Other sources give somewhat smaller figures for the consortium's estimate of overvaluation. In his memoir, Treasury Secretary Paulson says that the consortium identified a total of $52 billion of "bad real estate and private equity investments" that were overvalued by $22–$25 billion.[20] Merrill Lynch CEO John Thain told the FCIC that the consortium identified total overvaluation between $15 and $25 billion.[21]

- **Bank of America** Like Barclays, BoA reviewed Lehman's asset valuations as it considered acquiring the firm. No contemporaneous account of BoA's analysis is available, but a number of people, including Fed officials, Treasury Secretary Paulson, and BoA chief executive Kenneth Lewis, summarized BoA's findings in FCIC interviews and elsewhere. All these reports are similar.

The most detailed summary appears in Secretary Paulson's memoir. Paulson describes a report by BoA's "deal team" at a meeting on September 13:[22]

> [A]fter poring over Lehman's books, Bank of America now believed that to get a deal done it would need to unload between $65 and $70 billion worth of bad Lehman assets. BoA had identified, in addition to $33 billion of soured commercial mortgages and real estate, another $17 billion of residential mortgage-backed securities on Lehman's books that it considered to be problematic. In addition, its due-diligence team had raised questions about other Lehman assets, including high-yield loans and asset-backed securities for loans on cars and mobile homes, as well as some private-equity holdings. The likely losses on all of those bad assets, they estimated, would wipe out Lehman's equity of $28.4 billion.

The conclusion about wiping out equity suggests that Lehman's total over-valuation was on the order of $28.4 billion.

Solvency Based on Fundamentals

Based on the fair-value or mark-to-market prices of Lehman's assets, Lehman was near the border between solvency and insolvency. What happens to the solvency question if we instead base our assessment on the assets' fundamental values, that is, on the present values of their expected cash flows? This version of solvency is relevant to Chapter 9's discussion of Lehman's long run prospects if it had survived its liquidity crisis.

Economists generally agree that the mark-to-market values of many assets, especially real estate assets, were lower than their fundamental values in the stressed markets of September 2008. Therefore, if Lehman overvalued its assets by $15–$32 billion relative to their true mark-to-market values, the assets were overvalued by less than that amount relative to their fundamental values, or might even have been *undervalued* relative to fundamentals. If Lehman's true equity was near zero based on mark-to-market asset values, it was probably positive based on the higher fundamental values.

Some evidence on this point comes from a September 10 conference call in which Lehman CFO Ian Lowitt discussed Lehman's Q3 earnings with analysts from other firms.[23] Lowitt argued that Lehman's valuations of mortgage assets were "exceptionally conservative" relative to fundamentals, because the valuations were low enough to imply healthy returns under pessimistic assumptions about the performance of mortgages. Specifically:

> At current prices, our US residential portfolio generates a 12% yield or approximately LIBOR plus 800 if approximately 50% of the loans default and average recovery rates are only 40%.
>
> This base case assumes national home prices drop 32% peak to trough, vs. 18% to date, with California down 50% versus 27% to date. For a 0% yield and only principal repayment, over 80% of the borrowers would need to default with an average 35% recovery rate . . . .
>
> In our nonprime portfolio, the assets would generate a yield of LIBOR plus 1100 with 59% defaults, LIBOR plus 100 with 76% defaults, and a 0% yield at 85% defaults, each with a 20% to 30% recovery rate assumption.

The default rates in Lowitt's calculations exceeded analysts' forecasts at the time. The calculations suggest, therefore, that Lehman's mortgage assets were undervalued relative to reasonable projections of cash flows.

We could view Lowitt's calculations skeptically given his strong incentive to talk up his firm, but the calculations gain credibility from their specificity and I do not know of anyone who has questioned them.

Evidence from the Valukas Report

The Valukas Report carefully reviews many, but not all, of Lehman's asset valuations.[24] For most asset classes, the Report "finds insufficient evidence to support a finding that Lehman's valuations were unreasonable during the second and third quarters of 2008."[25] The Report reaches this conclusion for Lehman's residential and commercial mortgages, mortgage-backed securities, collateralized debt obligations, and derivatives.

However, in two cases the Report finds "sufficient evidence to conclude that certain assets were not reasonably valued." The first case concerns Lehman's Principal Transactions Group (PTG), which held stakes in real estate projects that it valued at $7.8 billion at the end of 2008 Q3. The Valukas Report criticizes PTG's valuation methods but does not estimate the amount of overvaluation.[26] The second case concerns Lehman's investment in the Archstone real estate investment trust, which the firm valued at $4.2 billion. The Report estimates that the Archstone position was overvalued by $140–$400 million.[27]

The overvaluations reported by Valukas are modest compared to Lehman's reported equity of $28 billion. The Report emphasizes, however, that its review of Lehman's assets is not comprehensive, and does not yield conclusions about total overvaluation or Lehman's solvency.

In lieu of a comprehensive valuation analysis, the Valukas Report analyzes Lehman's solvency in a different way: it presents a "market-based solvency analysis" by the accounting firm of Duff and Phelps.[28] Duff and Phelps developed a method for assessing solvency based on the market prices of Lehman's equity and debt. They found that Lehman was insolvent starting on September 8 or earlier, and that its "solvency equity" was approximately –$35 billion when it declared bankruptcy.

However, the Duff and Phelps analysis is flawed. Based on some complex reasoning, Duff and Phelps argue that a firm is solvent if the market value of its equity exceeds the difference between the book and market values of its liabilities:

Solvent if
> market value of equity > (book value of liabilities) – (market value of liabilities).

Yet this condition may not hold for a firm that is solvent by the usual definition that assets exceed liabilities. In particular, the condition may fail in the situation that Lehman faced after September 8: markets saw that Lehman's liquidity crisis was likely to force the firm into bankruptcy, and the bankruptcy was expected to destroy value.

To see this point, note that the prospect of bankruptcy drives the market value of equity close to zero, because bankruptcy will wipe out equity holders. In addition, even if Lehman is initially solvent, the value destruction during bankruptcy might cause substantial losses to creditors, and the risk of this occurring pushes the market value of liabilities substantially below their book value. In this situation, the gap between book and market values on the right side of the Duff-Phelps condition may exceed the near-zero equity on the left, so the condition does not hold. The Duff-Phelps calculation implies that Lehman is insolvent, even if it is actually solvent.[29]

FED OFFICIALS' CLAIMS ABOUT LEHMAN'S SOLVENCY

Fed officials have repeatedly asserted that Lehman was insolvent before its bankruptcy on September 15, 2008. In his 2015 memoir, Ben Bernanke says:[30]

> [I]t became evident that Lehman was deeply insolvent, even allowing for the likelihood that fire sales and illiquid markets had pushed the values of its assets to artificially low levels. [Lehman CEO] Fuld would later claim Lehman wasn't broke, but the capital figures he cited were based on the firm's inflated asset valuations and greatly overstated the true capital.

Fed officials have never backed up their insolvency claim with any details from Lehman's balance sheet like those presented and analyzed earlier in this chapter. To my knowledge, the only instances in which officials presented any reasons for believing that Lehman was insolvent were in their exchanges with the Financial Crisis Inquiry Commission (FCIC). The FCIC pressed two people on the solvency issue: Ben Bernanke and Thomas Baxter, the General Counsel of the New York Fed. Bernanke and Baxter responded with a total of four arguments, each of which purports to show Lehman was insolvent and each of which is flawed.[31]

Argument #1: Lehman Could Not Meet Its Obligations

Baxter advanced one argument in testimony before the FCIC on September 1, 2010. His argument involves a confusion between the basic concepts of insolvency and illiquidity.

Earlier in the hearing, Lehman CEO Richard Fuld had asserted that Lehman was solvent, citing its $28 billion in reported equity and claiming that overvaluations were modest. FCIC Commissioner Peter Wallison refers to Fuld's testimony in questioning Baxter: "Mr. Fuld has said [Lehman] was solvent; and I haven't heard anyone actually contradict that yet." Wallison argues that if Lehman *was* solvent, the Fed should have offered liquidity support when the firm experienced a run.[32]

Baxter disagrees with Wallison, and a confusing debate ensues.[33] The debate between the two men concludes with the following exchange:

WITNESS BAXTER: We saw no end to the run.

COMMISSIONER WALLISON: If they're solvent, then there is always an end to the run.

WITNESS BAXTER: Commissioner Wallison, one definition of "insolvent" is failure to pay your debts as they come due. And that was the situation that Lehman was experiencing at the end of Lehman week. And it couldn't pay its debts as they came due. No one would extend credit to it.

Economists usually use the term "illiquidity," not "insolvency," to describe the situation that Baxter describes. He is correct that one definition of insolvency is the one he cites. Bankruptcy attorneys sometimes distinguish between "cash-flow insolvency," an inability to pay debts as they come due, and "balance-sheet insolvency," in which liabilities exceed assets.[34] Nonetheless, Baxter's reply to Wallison is unsatisfactory for two related reasons.

First, CEO Fuld's testimony concerned Lehman's solvency in the balance-sheet sense, and Wallison clearly has the same concept in mind when he questions Baxter. Baxter's remarks about cash flows are not responsive to Wallison's question.

Second, illiquidity or cash-flow insolvency was not a valid reason for the Fed to deny assistance to Lehman. Firms that the Fed did assist, such as Bear Stearns and AIG, were also unable to obtain credit or pay their current debts. Indeed, under Section 13(3), the Fed can *only* lend to firms that are "unable to secure adequate credit accommodations from other banking institutions." Baxter's position is nonsensical: he cites Lehman's satisfaction of one requirement for a loan as a reason for the Fed *not* to lend.

Argument #2: Lehman Knew It Was Insolvent

Both Baxter and Ben Bernanke say that Lehman's attorneys and board of directors knew the firm was insolvent. They make this claim in written responses to follow-up questions after their testimony before the FCIC.[35] Both Baxter and Bernanke cite the minutes of the LBHI board of directors meeting on September 14, 2008 – the meeting at which the directors voted for bankruptcy.

Baxter wrote to the FCIC on October 15, 2010. His letter states that "the LBHI board minutes are extremely helpful in establishing. . . important points that were raised during the September 1 hearing." One of these points has the heading "<u>Lehman was insolvent</u>" [underlined in the original]. The text below the heading is:

> With regard to the question whether Lehman Brothers was in sound financial condition on September 14, 2008, and had plenty of good collateral, the minutes reflect that attorneys from Weil, Gotshal & Manges, LLP, LBHI's bankruptcy counsel, advised the Lehman board that "it was likely the Corporation would ultimately have to file for protection under Chapter 11" (p. 4), and the Lehman board recognized that bankruptcy was an "ultimate inevitability" (p. 5).

Bernanke wrote to the FCIC on November 4, 2010, and echoes Baxter:

> By Sunday of Lehman Weekend, Lehman's board of directors recognized that Lehman was either already insolvent or would imminently be insolvent.

In a footnote to this sentence, Bernanke cites the minutes of the board meeting. I presume that he is referring to the statements quoted by Baxter.

In the statements that Baxter quotes, Lehman's attorneys and board recognize that the firm faces bankruptcy. This does not imply, however, that they think the firm is balance-sheet insolvent, and nothing in the minutes suggests such a belief. Instead, it is clear that meeting participants expect bankruptcy because Lehman has run out of cash, that is, because of illiquidity. (Chapter 5 discusses this board meeting in detail.)

When Baxter testified before the FCIC, he was part of a panel that also included attorney Harvey Miller of Weil Gotshal. Miller was explicit about why bankruptcy was inevitable. He testified that Lehman filed a bankruptcy petition "after consideration of the inevitability of bankruptcy *because of the lack of liquidity*" (emphasis added).[36]

Again, one can say that illiquidity is a type of insolvency, but that type cannot be used to justify the Fed's treatment of Lehman.

Argument #3: Valukas Said Lehman Was Insolvent

In Bernanke's letter to the FCIC, he says:

> After extensive analysis, the Lehman Bankruptcy Examiner, Mr. Anton Valukas, determined that there is sufficient evidence to show that Lehman Brothers Holdings Inc. ("LBHI") was insolvent as of September 8, 2008, and perhaps was insolvent as early as September 2, 2008.

Bernanke cites p. 1573 of the Valukas Report, which summarizes the solvency analysis of Duff and Phelps. As discussed earlier, Duff and Phelps's "market-based" method is not a credible way to assess solvency.

Argument #4: Lehman's Estate Was Insolvent in 2010

Finally, Bernanke's letter to the FCIC discusses a report from Alvarez and Marsal, the corporate restructuring firm that managed the LBHI bankruptcy estate. This report describes the estate's financial condition in 2010. Bernanke mentions the report immediately after his comments about the Lehman board meeting and the Valukas solvency analysis, so it appears he is trying to bolster his argument that Lehman was insolvent. Bernanke writes:

> [T]he recent report of the managers of the Estate of LBHI strongly suggests that a decision by the Federal Reserve to fund Lehman in

September 2008 would have resulted in substantial losses to the Federal Reserve and taxpayers. On September 22, 2010, Alvarez and Marsal, representing the LBHI Estate, estimated that the value of assets currently available to LBHI – which would have been the debtor in a hypothetical loan from the Federal Reserve – was approximately $57.5 billion as of June 30, 2010. Importantly, these assets are currently all that is available to fund what the Estate estimates to be approximately $365 billion in likely allowed claims still pending against the Estate – that is, claims representing roughly 6 times the value of the assets available.

Here, Bernanke points out that the bankruptcy estate's assets were much less than its liabilities in 2010. The estate *was* insolvent at that point, but this fact does not determine LBHI's solvency before its bankruptcy. Economists believe that bankruptcies destroy value, so a firm that is insolvent after bankruptcy may have been solvent before. Lehman's bankruptcy destroyed lots of value, as I discuss next.[37]

LEHMAN IN BANKRUPTCY

Lehman was solvent, or at least close to solvent, when it filed for bankruptcy on September 15. Its assets were approximately equal to its liabilities, which suggests it should have been able to pay its creditors. At worst, any losses should have been absorbed by the holders of subordinated debt.

Yet Lehman's creditors suffered large losses. In March 2014, the LBHI estate had $304 billion of allowed claims and only $86 billion available to distribute among the claimants.[38] These figures imply that more than $200 billion of value disappeared during the bankruptcy.

What accounts for this loss? Many discussions of the bankruptcy emphasize the lack of planning. On September 14, after New York Fed officials instructed Lehman to declare bankruptcy, the firm's attorneys rushed to prepare a bankruptcy petition in a few hours. The lead attorney, Harvey Miller, later said that the petition was "the most bare-bones chapter 11 petition ever filed,"[39] even though LBHI's bankruptcy was the largest ever in US history. A 2014 study from the New York Fed concludes, "Lehman's poor pre-bankruptcy planning may have substantially reduced the value of Lehman's estate."[40]

Clearly the bankruptcy was chaotic. Bryan Marsal, who mana-ged the LBHI bankruptcy estate, described the situation in a 2013 interview.[41] Marsal, the head of the corporate restructuring firm Alvarez and Marsal, was first contacted by Lehman's board at 10:30 PM on Sunday, September 14. He recounts:

> I showed up at 8:30 the next morning, and people with boxes were coming out of the building. I said, "Oh, my God." Four days later, all the people, the operating businesses, the building and all the infrastructure of the business were sold to Barclays [when it purchased most of LBI]. So we had $650 billion worth of assets and no people on the fourth day.

Flows of money among LBHI and its subsidiaries stopped on the 15th as the different units entered separate insolvency proceedings. In addition, Lehman's global accounting system shut down. Marsal says:

> [O]ne of the dangers of a global entity is that these walls go up and you really don't have access to your basic financial information. We didn't know for 90 days who we owed money to or what assets were ours, what loans were ours, as we tried to reconstruct.

Marsal says, "the kind of losses that were experienced by the Lehman creditors were pretty much unnecessary," and stemmed from the disorder of the bankruptcy.

Value destruction is one of the murkiest aspects of the Lehman bankruptcy. Nobody has clearly identified the channels through which the chaos described by Marsal caused losses to the LBHI estate, and more research is needed on this topic. The available records suggest that three factors played a significant role in the value destruction, although it is not clear how much of the $200 billion loss they explain.

- **Termination of Derivatives Contracts** Lehman's bankruptcy gave its derivatives counterparties the right to terminate contracts and seize collateral. When that happened, the counterparties were allowed to value contracts in ways that were unfavorable to Lehman and favorable to the counterparties. The details are complex, but one aspect is that asset values were based on the less favorable of bid and ask prices.

  Lehman's derivatives had a total notional value of $35 trillion, so modest changes in valuation produced large losses. Bryan Marsal's restructuring firm estimated that these losses were between $50 billion and $75 billion.[42]

- **Fire Sales of Subsidiaries** Shortly after the bankruptcy, the LBHI estate sold a number of its subsidiaries and the assets they held at fire-sale prices.

  Here, the most important item is the sale of most of LBI to Barclays. The bankruptcy court approved the sale on September 19, only four days after the LBHI filing, saying "time is of the essence" in preserving the viability of LBI's broker-dealer business.[43] The LBHI estate suffered losses on this sale for two distinct reasons. First, the panic between September 15 and 19 reduced the value of LBI's assets by $30 billion, and those losses were reflected in the terms of the sale.[44] Second, even after these markdowns, the assets received by Barclays exceeded the liabilities it took on by $8–$13 billion, according to the LBI Trustee.[45]

  On October 3, the LBHI estate sold parts of its Investment Management Division, including the Neuberger Berman asset management business, to a group of hedge funds for $2 billion. Critics argued that the sale price was reduced by a flawed bidding process. Other sales that were arranged hurriedly included LBHI's interests in R3 Capital Management and in Eagle Energy Partners.[46]

- **Disruption of Investment Projects** At the time of its bankruptcy, Lehman had hundreds of ongoing investment projects, largely in real estate development. In many cases, the firm was part of a syndicate of investors. The bankruptcy caused many projects to lose financing and fail. Lehman lost its stakes in the projects, and other parties made claims on the Lehman estate for losses they suffered from Lehman's defaults. Harvey Miller, Lehman's bankruptcy attorney, emphasized these costs in his FCIC testimony.[47] Nobody has quantified this part of Lehman's losses, but it may have been substantial.

As part of their explanation for Lehman's failure, Fed officials have asserted that the firm was insolvent before its bankruptcy, or "deeply insolvent" (Bernanke's memoir). In fact, the best available evidence suggests that Lehman was on the border between solvency and insolvency based on realistic mark-to-market accounting, and it was probably solvent based on its assets' fundamental values. Nonetheless, other financial institutions lost confidence in Lehman, triggering a liquidity crisis that drove the firm into bankruptcy. The next chapter tells that story.

5   Lehman's Liquidity Crisis

This chapter looks closely at Lehman's liquidity crisis. I describe the firm's strategy for liquidity management, the basic ways in which this strategy failed, and the details of the liquidity drains that pushed Lehman into bankruptcy. Understanding this story helps us see how the Fed might have rescued Lehman.

LEHMAN'S STRATEGY FOR LIQUIDITY MANAGEMENT

Lehman's liquidity management was based on a strategy it developed after the financial crisis of 1998, when Russia defaulted on its debt and the hedge fund Long Term Capital Management nearly failed. These events shook confidence in financial institutions, leading many, including Lehman, to lose liquidity. To guard against future crises, Lehman adopted a "funding framework" that it believed would ensure it always had enough cash to operate.

The firm described this framework in its 10-Ks and 10-Qs for various years, and in presentations to rating agencies and regulators.[1] The following sections describe the key elements of the framework.

Sources of Funds

The basic goals of the funding framework were for Lehman to raise funds to finance all of its assets, and to always maintain that funding, even in "stressed liquidity environments." To that end, the firm divided its assets into liquid and illiquid categories, and it funded these assets in different ways. Lehman defined liquid assets as those "for which the Company believes a reliable secured funding market exists across all market environments."[2] This meant that Lehman could always raise cash to finance these assets by pledging them as collateral in repos; it did not necessarily mean the assets were easy to sell outright. By Lehman's account, its liquid assets included various equities, bonds, and mortgage-backed securities, including some with speculative-grade ratings.

Illiquid assets included those not commonly accepted as repo collateral, such as private equity, investments in real estate development projects, and corporate loans. The illiquid category also included collateral posted by Lehman in derivatives contracts. Lehman financed illiquid assets with stable sources of funds that it called "cash capital": equity, long-term debt, and core deposits at Lehman's bank subsidiaries. The firm also used cash capital to finance the haircuts on liquid assets pledged in repos.

Commercial paper was a modest source of funds ($8 billion at the end of 2008 Q2). Lehman used commercial paper "to mitigate short-term liquidity outflows such as unforeseen operational friction."[3]

The Liquidity Pool

Another part of Lehman's funding framework was a "liquidity pool" held by LBHI to protect itself against any losses of cash. The terminology here is confusing because the types of assets included in the pool were narrower than those considered liquid in determining sources of funding. The liquidity pool was "primarily invested in cash instruments, government and agency securities, and overnight [reverse] repurchase agreements collateralized by government and agency securities."[4] These assets could be turned into cash quickly. Assets included in the liquidity pool were *not* pledged as repo collateral or otherwise encumbered.

LBHI's liquidity pool was $44.6 billion at the end of 2008 Q2 (May 31), up from $34.9 billion at the end of 2007. As Lehman claimed, the pool consisted *primarily* of highly liquid assets such as cash and government securities. However, the pool also included about $4 billion of collateralized loan obligations, which presumably were less liquid.[5]

LBHI's liquidity pool was "primarily intended to cover expected cash outflows for twelve months in a stressed liquidity environment."

Its 10-Q for 2008 Q2 listed types of outflows that it thought might occur, of which the most significant were:[6]

- repayment of commercial paper and long-term debt due within a year, if Lehman could not roll over these debts;
- take-ups of commitments by Lehman to extend credit to clients;
- collateral calls in derivatives contracts that would be triggered by rating downgrades of LBHI's bonds; and
- "reduced borrowing availability" in the repo market or increased haircuts on repo collateral.

Notice that the last point hedges on the claim elsewhere in the 10-Q that Lehman's repo financing was reliable in all market environments.

Lehman's broker-dealer subsidiaries in New York (Lehman Brothers Inc., LBI) and London (Lehman Brothers International Europe, LBIE) had their own liquidity pools of $0.3 billion and $7.0 billion respectively at the end of 2008 Q2.[7] Regulations forbade LBHI from accessing these pools, but liquidity could flow in the other direction, from LBHI to a subsidiary. In that case, LBHI recorded a receivable on its unconsolidated balance sheet and the subsidiary recorded a payable.

Reliable Repo Funding

At the end of 2008 Q2, Lehman had $188 billion of collateral pledged in repo agreements.[8] This amount greatly exceeded its liquidity pool of $44.6 billion, which meant the pool could absorb some loss of repo funding but not too much. Thus, another goal of Lehman's funding framework was to ensure that its repo funding was stable.

Many of Bear Stearns's counterparties refused to roll over repos with Bear during its crisis in March, and that episode shook Wall Street's faith in the reliability of repo funding. In its 10-Q for 2008 Q2 and in statements to investors and regulators, Lehman took pains to argue that it was different from Bear and could maintain adequate funding in a crisis.[9] The firm made several points about its repos:

- *Relationships with Counterparties* Lehman claimed its repo funding was secure because it had "broad and long-established relationships" with counterparties, and the counterparties understood the assets they were accepting as collateral. In addition, Lehman's management would respond to any crisis with phone calls "to address rumors and reassure key stakeholders."

- *Quality of Collateral* Of Lehman's $188 billion in repo collateral, $83 billion was Treasury and agency securities, which could always be monetized easily. Of the remaining $105 billion, $65 billion was investment-grade securities and publicly traded equities for which, Lehman insisted in its 10-Q for 2008 Q2, "there exists a very active, reliable and liquid secured funding market." That left only $40 billion of lower-quality collateral that counterparties might reject.

- *Bank Subsidiaries* Of the lower-quality assets, $8 billion were pledged in repos with LBHI's banking subsidiaries. These units would always roll over repos with their parent, and they could even provide additional funding to it.

- *Overfunding* Lehman "overfunded" its non-Treasury/agency repos, which meant that it could lose some of its repo financing without needing to draw on its liquidity pool. Total overfunding was $27 billion at the end of 2008 Q2. The accounting here is subtle, with two types of overfunding:[10]

  First, Lehman had $11 billion of "excess collateral" for its repos. That meant that $11 billion of the non-Treasury/agency collateral that it pledged to its repo counterparties was borrowed from other institutions, which received cash from Lehman. If some of Lehman's repo agreements did not roll, it could offset the loss of liquidity by returning borrowed collateral and taking back its cash.

  Second, Lehman had $16 billion of "ticket" overfunding. That meant repo counterparties agreed to accept $16 billion more in non-Treasury/ agency collateral than Lehman actually had. Lehman delivered $16 billion of liquid Treasury and agency securities to the counterparties in place of the agreed-on less liquid collateral, but it could switch to delivering the less liquid collateral if it wanted to. Lehman would make such a switch if some of its other repos did not roll, leaving non-Treasury/ agency collateral that it needed to finance. In this case, Lehman presumed, the Treasuries and agencies that it stopped delivering could be financed through new repos.

Assessments of Lehman's Liquidity by Lehman and Others

In May and June 2008, Lehman told regulators and rating agencies that it was "building a liquidity fortress."[11] It supported this claim with stress tests which showed that the firm generally survived hypothetical liquidity crises.[12] One of Lehman's key assumptions in these stress tests was that most of its repos with investment-grade securities or equities as collateral (not just its Treasury and agency repos) would continue to roll over.

After the Bear Stearns crisis, the Fed performed its own stress tests on the remaining investment banks. These tests generally found that Lehman would *not* survive a liquidity crisis. Yet the Fed's conclusions were not alarmist. In May, Fed analysts characterized Lehman's liquidity as "poor but improving." In June, they said, "Lehman recognizes its vulnerabilities and is trying to reduce illiquid assets and extend maturities where possible … Lehman should improve its liquidity position by $15 billion."[13]

For a time, rating agencies were optimistic about Lehman's liquidity. On March 17, the day after the Bear Stearns rescue, Moody's reported, "Lehman's liquidity management and position remain robust and are underpinned by a funding framework that is scaled to the firm's expectations for, and vetting of, reliable secured funding." On April 1, Fitch said, "Liquidity remains strong with Lehman's lower reliance on short-term funding relative to its peers."[14]

S&P's view was more cautious. On April 3, it said:[15]

[Lehman's] excess liquidity position is among the largest proportionately of the U.S. broker-dealers … Nonetheless we cannot ignore the possibility that the firm could suffer severely if there is an adverse change in market perceptions, however ill-founded.

In retrospect, Lehman's claims about a liquidity fortress seem like wishful thinking. The Valukas Report criticizes the firm's liquidity management, saying Lehman should have known that its repo funding was unreliable and that its liquidity pool was inadequate.[16]

Lehman started experiencing liquidity problems after May 31, the end of its Q2. This section chronicles developments between May 31 and September 9, when bad news about earnings and the Korean Development Bank triggered the fatal run on the firm. Over this period, LBHI reported a fairly stable liquidity pool, with losses of funding offset by sales of real estate assets. Yet this stability masked problems that would ultimately contribute to Lehman's crisis and failure.

The information on Lehman's liquidity comes primarily from memos from the firm's treasury department, which are available through links in the Valukas Report footnotes. One key memo is "Funding Lehman Brothers," written on September 10 as the firm struggled to survive.[17] Another is "Liquidity of Lehman Brothers," a post-mortem review of the crisis written on October 7.[18]

Factors Affecting LBHI's Liquidity Pool

The September 10 memo summarizes Lehman's liquidity management during Q3 (which had ended August 31):

> Despite a challenging market environment, Lehman Brothers was able to maintain the status quo broadly in terms of liquidity – primarily as a result of deleveraging its balance sheet (which was done for risk reasons).

Lehman provided details of this deleveraging in its press release about its Q3 earnings. During the quarter, the firm shed $23.3 billion of illiquid assets, including $18.9 billion of real estate and $4.4 billion of "high yield acquisition finance."[19]

The "challenging market environment" that Lehman acknowledged included decreases in several types of its funding. These funding losses are listed in the September 10 and October 7 memos:

- **Long-term debt** Lehman issued only $2 billion of long-term debt in Q3, down from $14 billion in Q2. The stock of long-term debt fell from $128 billion to $115 billion.

- *Commercial paper* Commercial paper outstanding fell from $8 billion at the end of Q2 to $4 billion at the end of Q3.
- *Repos* Lehman's repo agreements fell by about $10 billion. The firm had to pay back the $10 billion of cash it had received from the lost repos, which cut into its liquidity pool. (Lehman maintained a constant level of overfunding of its repos, choosing not to absorb its losses through reduced overfunding.)[20]

Overall, Lehman's claim that it "maintained the status quo" was consistent with LBHI's reported liquidity pool, which fell only slightly from $45 billion at the end of Q2 to $42 billion at the end of Q3 and $41 billion on September 9.

Factors Not Accounted for in LBHI's Liquidity Pool

The stability of LBHI's liquidity pool masked several problems:

- *Questionable Assets in the Liquidity Pool* As noted earlier, LBHI's liquidity pool included some non-Treasury/agency securities that were not very liquid. These assets grew from $4 billion at the end of Q2 to $7 billion, probably before September 9. Lehman was unable to monetize these securities during its crisis.
- *Clearing-Bank Collateral* Starting in June, JPMorgan Chase, Lehman's clearing bank for tri-party repos, demanded collateral – either cash or liquid securities – to cover its intraday exposure to Lehman. Other banks that cleared transactions for Lehman demanded "comfort deposits" of cash. These other banks included Citi, which cleared Lehman's currency trades, and HSBC, which cleared its trades of securities denominated in British pounds. These demands by clearing banks totaled $11.5 billion on September 9. Lehman included assets held by clearing banks in its liquidity pool, but that practice is criticized in the Valukas Report[21] and in Lehman's October 7 post-mortem. The collateral held by JPMorgan was released every night, but it was not available to meet Lehman's obligations during the day. Theoretically, Lehman had the right to withdraw comfort deposits from Citi and HSBC, but those banks might have stopped clearing Lehman's transactions as a result.
- *Broker-Dealer Liquidity Pools* As confidence in Lehman fell, the separate liquidity pools at LBI and LBIE were depleted: From May 31 to September 9,

LBIE's pool fell from $7.0 billion to $0.8 billion, and LBI's fell from $0.3 billion to zero. The reasons are not completely clear, but one factor was a loss of cash in LBIE's prime broker business. After September 9, the broker-dealers had essentially no liquidity of their own, so they drew on LBHI's liquidity pool.

Arguably we can measure Lehman's true liquidity by adding the broker-dealers' liquidity pools to LBHI's pool, and subtracting clearing bank collateral and illiquid assets included in the pool. By this measure, liquidity was approximately $48 billion at the end of Q2 ($52 billion in liquidity pools minus $4 billion of illiquid assets). Liquidity fell to $23 billion on September 9 ($42 billion minus $7 billion of illiquid assets and $12 billion held by clearing banks).

Lehman and the PDCF

The Fed created the Primary Dealer Credit Facility (PDCF) in March 2008 to help investment banks cope with losses of liquidity. Lehman borrowed $2 billion from the PDCF on April 16, but did not access the PDCF as its liquidity fell over the summer. It did not borrow again until LBI accessed the facility after LBHI's bankruptcy.

It is not completely clear why Lehman did not borrow more before September 14. A likely factor is that the PDCF did not accept speculative-grade securities or equities as collateral. A substantial fraction of Lehman's repos used those types of collateral, and it was those repos that were the most difficult to roll when markets lost confidence in the firm. PDCF access, therefore, was not enough to protect Lehman from a severe run. At the same time, Lehman probably feared that borrowing from the PDCF would signal that the firm was in trouble, making a run more likely.

This situation changed dramatically on September 14. On that date, the Fed changed the rules to allow the PDCF to accept all tri-party repo collateral, and Lehman desperately sought PDCF support. Lehman probably would have borrowed enough from the PDCF on September 14 to avert its bankruptcy the next day, if not for a decision by Fed policymakers to restrict the firm's access to the facility. Chapter 8 examines this Fed decision in detail.

Between April and September, Lehman borrowed Treasury securities from the Term Securities Lending Facility (TSLF) in amounts ranging from $10 billion to $20 billion, using agency securities and triple-A mortgage-backed securities as collateral. Access to the TSLF did not help Lehman during its crisis because of the narrow range of collateral the facility accepted.

THE RUN ON LEHMAN, SEPTEMBER 10–12

Lehman had the same experience as Bear Stearns: an erosion of liquidity over several months and then a sudden, fatal run. Lehman's run occurred from Wednesday, September 10 to Friday, September 12. The firm's post-mortem from October 7 describes the run in detail.

It seems that the run was triggered by two pieces of bad news: the failure of negotiations with the Korean Development Bank on September 9, and Lehman's disappointing announcement about its earnings and strategic plan on September 10. These blows to confidence were reinforced by warnings about Lehman's condition from rating agencies.[22]

Over September 10–12, about $20 billion of Lehman's repo financing was cut off (including $5 billion of repos with Fidelity Investments). Lehman absorbed $18 billion of this loss by reducing its overfunding of repos, so its liquidity pool lost only $2 billion. This outcome meant, however, that little overfunding remained to absorb any further repo losses.

Over the same three-day period, collateral pledged to clearing banks rose by about $4 billion, as JPMorgan Chase reacted to Lehman's crisis by demanding more collateral for clearing its tri-party repos.

A number of other factors reduced Lehman's liquidity in its final days. The October 7 memo summarizes these factors in a chart, shown here as Exhibit 5.1. Some of the factors affected LBHI directly and

Liquidity Situation Post Q3 Earnings Announcement

◆ Post earnings announcement on September 9, Holdings' liquidity decreased by $16 billion from $41 billion to $25 billion –$16 billion of which was required by clearing banks at the start of the day and approximately $7 billion of which was in liquid securities that became near impossible to monetize immediately in this extremely stressed market environment – primarily because of a loss of repo capacity.

◆ As a result, the result of "free cash" available intra day was less than $2 billion. With LBIE facing a projected cash shortage of $4.5 billion on September 15, Lehman had no choice but to place LBIE into administration because of potential director liability. This resulted in a cross-default of and triggered the filing on September 15.

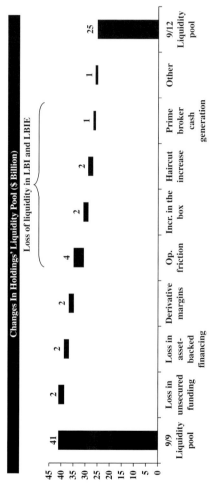

Changes In Holdings' Liquidity Pool ($ Billion)

Loss of liquidity in LBI and LBIE

| | | |
| 9/9 Liquidity pool | Loss in unsecured funding | Loss in asset-backed financing | Derivative margins | Op. friction | Incr. in the box | Haircut increase | Prime broker cash generation | Other | 9/12 Liquidity pool |

41   2   2   2   4   2   2   1   1   25

LEHMAN BROTHERS

EXHIBIT 5.1 Estate of Lehman Brothers Holdings Inc., Analysis of Lehman's Liquidity Crisis, October 7, 2008.
Source: Report of the LBHI Bankruptcy Examiner, footnote 6341.

some affected its broker-dealers, which LBHI had to fund because their liquidity pools were gone.

The chart in Exhibit 5.1 shows the following drains from LBHI's liquidity pool:

- **Loss in unsecured funding, $2 billion:** commercial paper that did not roll over.
- **Loss in asset-backed financing, $2 billion:** the failure of deals to issue asset-backed commercial paper.
- **Derivative margins, $2 billion:** demands for additional collateral by counterparties in derivatives contracts.
- **Operational friction, $4 billion:** withdrawals from prime broker accounts at LBIE; a temporary loss due to delays in transferring assets which Lehman expected to disappear in a few days.
- **Increase in the box, $2 billion:** The $2 billion loss of cash from repos was reflected in an increase in "boxed" assets, meaning assets that were not pledged as repo collateral.
- **Haircut increase, $2 billion:** modest increases in haircuts demanded by lenders that continued to roll over Lehman's repos.
- **Loss of prime broker cash, $1 billion:** a permanent loss of cash from shrinkage in LBIE's prime broker business.

These specific liquidity losses, plus another $1 billion drain of "Other," totaled $16 billion. They reduced LBHI's reported liquidity pool from about $41 billion on September 9 to $25 billion on September 12. As the October 7 memo acknowledges, the remaining pool included $16 billion of clearing bank collateral and $7 billion of "liquid securities that became near impossible to monetize immediately" (an oxymoron). Subtracting these amounts from $25 billion left true liquidity (which the memo calls "free cash") of less than $2 billion. With less rounding of figures, the actual amount was $1.4 billion.

LEHMAN'S PREDICAMENT ON SEPTEMBER 13–14

Over the weekend of September 13–14, it became clear that if Lehman opened for business on September 15, it would quickly run out of cash and default on various payments due to its counterparties. With this grim outlook, LBHI's board of directors approved a bankruptcy petition on the night of Sunday, September 14.

Liquidity Calculations for Monday, September 15

Several analyses concluded that Lehman's liquidity needs on September 15 would greatly exceed its $1.4 billion of available cash:

- A Lehman memo, apparently from Saturday, September 13, made detailed liquidity projections for the following week.[23] The memo predicted that $7.6 billion of repo agreements would not roll over on the 15th. It also predicted additional cash drains of $5.0 billion, but assumed that Lehman could replace $4.5 billion of these losses by drawing on credit lines.
- Lehman Brothers hired Lazard, another investment bank, to advise it during its crisis, and Lazard prepared a memo on Lehman's liquidity on September 14.[24] This Lazard memo was more pessimistic than Lehman's: it estimated that $16 billion of repos would not roll on the 15th; that, because of rating downgrades, derivatives counterparties would demand an additional $2 billion of collateral; and that banks would cut off the credit lines that Lehman planned to access. The memo concluded, using "Green" as a code name for Lehman: "absent a sale transaction or extraordinary government intervention, Green believes it will not be able to open for business on Monday."
- Lehman's October 7 post-mortem memo highlights the untenable liquidity position of LBIE, the London broker-dealer. LBIE projected a cash shortage of $4.5 billion at the beginning of September 15.

Looming Catastrophes

Even if Lehman had opened for business and had somehow managed to meet its immediate obligations, it faced two imminent disasters:

- **Rating downgrades** On September 10 and 11, Moody's and Fitch threatened to downgrade Lehman by two notches if it did not find a strategic partner by

September 15.[25] Presumably these downgrades would have accelerated the run on Lehman if it had tried to stay in business.

- **Clearing banks** On September 11, JPMorgan Chase, worried about its exposure to Lehman, threatened to stop clearing Lehman's tri-party repos. If that happened, Lehman would lose access to any financing through the tri-party market. According to the Lazard memo:

> JPMorgan CEO indicated to Green CEO Thursday evening September 11, that Green needed to announce a sale transaction by market open Monday September 15 or JPM would immediately discontinue doing business with Green and effectively "put Green out of business."

Also on September 11, Citi threatened to stop clearing Lehman's currency trades.

The Final Board of Directors Meeting

On Sunday, September 14, the LBHI board of directors convened at 5:00 PM. The meeting adjourned at 6:10 and reconvened at 7:55; it is not clear when it ended. The meeting is summarized in the board's minutes, and accounts also appear in Sorkin's *Too Big to Fail* and in the FCIC testimony of Harvey Miller, Lehman's lead bankruptcy attorney.[26]

Lehman executives described the firm's predicament to the board. The Barclays deal had failed, the firm was out of cash, and the Fed would not lend it enough to operate the next day. LBIE faced a special problem because, under British law, its directors faced *criminal* liability if they tried to operate the firm without sufficient cash. LBIE was planning to file for administration, the British version of bankruptcy, and would default on payments due Monday. Because LBHI guaranteed those payments, it, too, would be in default.

At one point the meeting was interrupted by a phone call from SEC Chair Christopher Cox and New York Fed General Counsel Thomas Baxter, who urged the board to "make a quick decision" about bankruptcy. Chapter 8 describes the details of this call.

After the phone call, LBHI's board debated what to do. One director suggested "calling the government's bluff" and attempting to open for business on Monday.[27] In the end, however, the board concluded that opening on Monday would produce chaos, and that Lehman's stakeholders would fare better under bankruptcy. The attorneys from Weil Gotshal rushed to prepare a bankruptcy petition and filed it with the bankruptcy court at 1:45 AM on Monday September 15.

6   Lehman's Collateral and the Feasibility of Liquidity Support

Beginning with this chapter, we turn from describing what happened to Lehman Brothers to discussing how things might have been different. We will see that assistance from the Fed could have prevented Lehman's disorderly bankruptcy and mitigated the broader financial crisis.

An alternative resolution of Lehman's crisis would have involved two steps:

- First, the Fed would have provided liquidity assistance to keep LBHI in operation for a period of weeks or months, and Lehman would have posted collateral that protected the Fed and taxpayers from losses, as required by Section 13(3) of the Federal Reserve Act. The feasibility of these actions is discussed in this chapter.
- Second, policymakers and Lehman executives would have worked on a long-term resolution of the firm's crisis. A range of outcomes would have been possible, but whichever one of them occurred, it would likely have been less disruptive to the financial system than was Lehman's bankruptcy on September 15. Chapter 9 examines what Lehman's long-term fate might have been.

The feasibility of the first step, Fed liquidity support, depends on how much Lehman would have needed to borrow from the Fed to survive, and on whether Lehman had enough collateral to secure such a loan. Three complementary approaches illuminate these issues:

- The simplest approach uses two facts about Lehman's balance sheet. First, the firm's assets were approximately equal to its liabilities (that is, its equity was close to zero). Second, its liabilities included $115 billion in long-term unsecured debt, which it did not need to repay for a year or more. Together, these facts imply that Lehman's assets greatly exceeded all liabilities that might come due over the next year, which, in turn, implies that Lehman had ample collateral to borrow any cash it might have needed.

- A more ambitious approach involves using available information on Lehman's liquidity crisis to estimate the amount of Fed assistance that Lehman needed. The bottom line is that Lehman probably could have stayed in business if it had received about $84 billion from the Fed. The firm could have borrowed that amount from the Fed's Primary Dealer Credit Facility (PDCF), because it had at least $114 billion of assets that it could have pledged to the PDCF as collateral under the rules established on September 14.
- Finally, looking at the liquidity support that the Fed actually provided to Lehman's New York broker-dealer, LBI, after the bankruptcy of its parent, LBHI, gives us an idea about how much Lehman needed to borrow. Support to LBI peaked at $28 billion, a fact that is consistent with the estimate that $84 billion of assistance would have rescued all of LBHI.

THE IMPLICATIONS OF LEHMAN'S LONG-TERM DEBT

This section shows that Lehman's cushion of long-term debt meant the firm had ample collateral to borrow any cash it needed to survive in the weeks and months after September 15.

A Condition for Adequate Collateral

In a liquidity crisis or run, a financial institution faces extraordinary demands to pay off its liabilities with cash. For example, it must repay short-term credit that it cannot roll over; it must meet demands for withdrawals from customer accounts; and counterparties may force it to close out various contracts that have negative values. During a run, a firm may not have enough cash to meet such obligations.

Can a central bank rescue a financial institution from such a crisis without taking on significant risk for itself? The answer turns on whether the firm has enough collateral to secure a loan that meets its need for cash. Economists often argue that a firm has sufficient collateral if it is solvent, that is, if its assets exceed its liabilities. A solvent firm, by definition, would have enough collateral to borrow the cash it needs to pay off any or all of its liabilities.

There is, however, a less stringent condition which guarantees that a firm has adequate collateral: a firm will have enough collateral for any loan it needs if its assets exceed its liabilities *excluding its long-term unsecured debt*. In a run on a financial institution, many of the institution's liabilities entitle other parties to demand cash immediately or almost immediately, but holders of long-term debt cannot demand cash before the debt matures. Therefore, the sum of all liabilities except long-term debt is the largest amount of cash that the firm might need to pay out during the short-term phenomenon of a run. The total of these liabilities is, then, an upper bound on the loan the firm might need from the central bank, and on the assets needed to fully collateralize the loan.

This condition for adequate collateral is:

assets > liabilities – long-term debt.

We can rewrite this condition as:

(assets – liabilities) + long-term debt > 0,

or, using the definition of equity (assets – liabilities),

equity + long-term debt > 0.

A firm has adequate collateral for any liquidity assistance it might need if the sum of its equity and long-term debt is positive.

I have not seen this condition for adequate collateral presented elsewhere. However, policymakers at the Federal Reserve and elsewhere have suggested that long-term debt reduces the risk of disorderly failures of financial institutions.[1] This idea is one rationale for the Net Stable Funding Ratio Rule proposed by the Basel Committee on Banking Supervision and by the Fed, which would require financial institutions to hold minimum levels of stable funding including long-term debt.[2]

Applying the Condition to Lehman

In its last financial statement, for August 31, 2008, Lehman reported $28 billion of equity and $115 billion of long-term unsecured debt (defined as debt not due for a year or more).[3] Based on these figures, the sum of Lehman's equity and long-term debt was $143 billion, so the firm easily met the condition that this sum exceed zero. Therefore, according to its financial statement, Lehman had more than enough collateral to secure any liquidity support it might have needed.

Chapter 4 showed that Lehman probably overvalued its assets by $15–$32 billion relative to market prices. However, if we subtract the upper bound of $32 billion from the firm's reported assets, and therefore from its equity, the sum of equity and long-term debt falls only from $143 billion to $111 billion. Even if we suppose that Lehman's approximately $70 billion of questionable assets were completely worthless, its equity plus long-term debt is still $73 billion – far above zero. It is difficult to escape the conclusion that Lehman had more than enough collateral for liquidity support.

Because long-term debt as measured here is not due within a year, well-secured liquidity support for Lehman could have lasted for a year or more. Given that amount of time, policymakers and Lehman executives probably would have been able to find a more orderly resolution of the firm's crisis than the September 15 bankruptcy. In fact, shortly before the bankruptcy, New York Fed staff considered liquidity support for two months to a year. (The memo that presents this idea is discussed in detail in Chapter 7.)[4]

An Upper Bound on the Assistance Lehman Might Have Needed

In addition to determining the adequacy of Lehman's collateral, we can ask the related question of how large a loan Lehman might have needed to survive a run. An upper bound on this amount is given by Lehman's total liabilities excluding long-term debt, which is how much cash the firm would have needed if all those liabilities had come due at once. In this worst-case run scenario, Lehman cannot roll over any short-term funding; loses all deposits in its bank subsidiaries; has to eliminate all its payables; must close out all derivatives positions with negative values; and must cover all its short positions. Once again, a run does *not* force Lehman to pay off its long-term debt.

In its August 31 financial statement, Lehman reported total liabilities of $572 billion, of which $115 billion were long-term debt. Therefore, the cash that Lehman needed to borrow could not have exceeded $457 billion ($572 billion – $115 billion).

In the same financial statement, Lehman reported assets of $600 billion. Assuming $32 billion of overvaluation, its true assets were $568 billion. Again, we see that, even taking overvaluation into account, Lehman's assets exceeded the largest loan it could have needed by at least $111 billion ($568 billion – $457 billion). This surplus is 24 percent of the maximum loan, which implies that any necessary loan could have been overcollateralized by 24 percent or more.[5]

A REALISTIC SCENARIO FOR FED ASSISTANCE

The previous section considered a hypothetical worst case in which Lehman has to immediately pay off all its liabilities except its long-term debt. This section presents a more realistic scenario and estimates how much Fed assistance Lehman actually would have needed if it had stayed in business after September 15. This exercise requires some guesses about the liquidity drains that Lehman would have experienced, but they are educated guesses because there is considerable information about the firm's situation.

In this scenario, Lehman would have needed about $84 billion of liquidity assistance from the Fed to stay in business over the four weeks from September 15 to October 13. This total reflects $85 billion of cash losses offset by $1 billion of cash that Lehman had on hand on September 15. The $85 billion of cash losses include $66 billion from repos that would not have rolled and $19 billion from other liquidity drains.

This section also discusses the type of assistance that Lehman could have received from the Fed. It appears the Fed could have kept Lehman in operation with overnight lending through the PDCF – the type of support it actually provided to LBI after the LBHI bankruptcy. The PDCF could have provided liquidity to the entire Lehman enterprise because at least $114 billion of the firm's available assets were acceptable as PDCF collateral. This finding means the Fed could have rescued Lehman without a new authorization under Section 13(3).

The scenario considered here is more realistic than the worst-case scenario presented in the previous section, in which all short-term liabilities come due at once. Yet it is still a worst case, in a sense. The analysis assumes that the run on Lehman would have accelerated on September 15, a likely outcome if the firm had opened for business without Fed support. A commitment of support by the Fed, however, might have boosted confidence in Lehman and ended the run. In that case, Lehman might have survived without actually needing to borrow much from the Fed.

Assumptions about Lehman's Liquidity Needs

This section presents the basic assumptions I use in estimating how much liquidity support LBHI would have needed if it had stayed in operation on Monday, September 15 and beyond.

- **Assumption 1** Lehman's counterparties continue to roll over repos in which Lehman's collateral is Treasury or agency securities. This assumption is realistic because counterparties rolled over most of LBI's Treasury and agency repos even after the LBHI bankruptcy.[6]
- **Assumption 2** Counterparties do *not* roll over any of Lehman's repos with collateral other than Treasuries and agencies. Lehman's advisors at Lazard predicted that few of Lehman's non-Treasury/agency repos would roll on September 15 or later,[7] and that prediction proved true for LBI after the bankruptcy (as discussed below).
- **Assumption 3** JPMorgan Chase continues to clear Lehman's tri-party repos. This assumption is realistic because Fed officials persuaded JPMorgan to continue clearing for LBI after September 15 because the PDCF was supporting it. I assume officials could have made a similar case for all of Lehman if the PDCF were supporting all of it.[8]
- **Assumption 4** In addition to its lost repos, Lehman experiences several other liquidity drains, including collateral calls and losses of cash at its

prime brokerages. I identify these liquidity drains based on Lehman's pre-bankruptcy experience, predictions by Lehman and Lazard on September 13–14, and the Fed's stress tests from May and June.[9]

- **Assumption 5** Lehman does *not* experience liquidity drains that are theoretically possible but that, during the actual crisis, nobody expected to happen. For example, Lehman's bank subsidiaries do not lose any of their deposits.

- **Assumption 6** Lehman cannot replace any of its lost cash with new private credit or by selling assets – a conservative assumption. On September 13–14, Lehman predicted that if it stayed in business, it could draw on lines of credit during the following week, but Lazard believed those lines would be cancelled.

Quantifying Lehman's Liquidity Needs

Starting from the assumptions in the last section, in this section I estimate how much Fed assistance Lehman would have needed to stay in operation during the four weeks from September 15 to October 13. This analysis draws on predictions with four-week horizons made by Lehman and the Fed.

Various factors would have drained about $85 billion of cash from Lehman. Because the firm had $1 billion of cash on September 14,[10] it would have needed to borrow $84 billion from the Fed. To put that figure in perspective, note that the Fed committed a total of $123 billion to AIG on September 16 and October 6 and that its lending to Morgan Stanley through the PDCF and the Term Securities Lending Facility (TSLF) peaked at $107 billion on September 29.

The following are estimates of the various liquidity drains that Lehman would have experienced if it had stayed in business from September 15 through October 13.

- **Lost Repos ($66 billion)** In their September 13–14 analyses of Lehman's liquidity, Lehman and Lazard reported the collateral in Lehman's non-Treasury/agency repos, which I have assumed would not roll over. Total collateral in these repos was $80 billion according to Lehman and $77 billion according to Lazard. To be conservative, I use the $80 billion number in my calculations. At least 10 percent of the repos had maturities beyond four weeks, so I assume that repos secured by $72 billion of collateral (90 percent of $80 billion) would have matured and failed to roll within four weeks.

Because of haircuts on the collateral, the cash that Lehman received from those repos before the bankruptcy was less than $72 billion. According to a JPMorgan Chase memo on September 11, the average haircut for LBI's non-Treasury/agency repos was about 8 percent.[11] Assuming the same haircut for repos at other units of Lehman (primarily LBIE), Lehman's loss of cash from repos would have been about $66 billion (92 percent of $72 billion).

- *Unsecured Funding ($6 billion)* I assume Lehman could not have rolled its $2 billion of commercial paper outstanding.[12] I also assume that $4 billion of long-term debt would have come due within the four-week horizon and could not have been replaced. The $4 billion figure is a guess based on the fact that $8.5 billion or less was coming due within three months.[13] Including both commercial paper and maturing long-term debt, Lehman would have lost a total of $6 billion in unsecured funding in the four-week period.

- *Collateral Calls ($5 billion)* On September 13–14, Lazard predicted that rating downgrades on September 15 were going to trigger $2 billion in collateral calls on Lehman's derivatives contracts. In a September 11 email to Ben Bernanke, a New York Fed analyst predicted that downgrades would trigger collateral calls of $2.9 billion (for a one-notch downgrade) or $4.4 billion (for a two-notch downgrade).[14] The Fed's earlier simulations of Lehman liquidity crises had predicted collateral calls of $3 billion (May stress test) or $9 billion (June stress test). Assuming $5 billion of collateral calls seems reasonable given the range of estimates.

- *Commitments ($8 billion)* The New York Fed stress test in June included $8 billion of "on-boarding and other commitments." The Lehman and Lazard analyses do not mention this item, and I am not certain what it is. It may reflect the need to fund special purpose vehicles during a crisis. To again be conservative, I am including the Fed's $8 billion figure among Lehman's liquidity losses.

- *Operational Friction ($0)* As discussed in Chapter 5, in the days before the LBHI bankruptcy, LBIE temporarily lost $4 billion of cash due to withdrawals from its prime brokerage. It expected to regain that cash during the week of September 15, but additional withdrawals could have produced new friction. In the absence of a better idea, I have assumed the net change in operational friction is zero.[15]

Lehman's Available PDCF Collateral

This section examines the assets that Lehman had available to collateralize a loan from the Fed. I focus on assets that were acceptable collateral for the PDCF, and find that Lehman had more than enough of these assets to borrow the $84 billion of cash it needed. This finding implies that the firm could have survived if it had had unfettered access to the PDCF. (Chapter 8 describes the fatal limits that the Fed imposed on Lehman's PDCF borrowing.)

I first describe the types of collateral accepted by the PDCF, and then calculate how much of this collateral Lehman owned.

Collateral Accepted by the PDCF From when it was established in March 2008 until September 13, the PDCF accepted only high-quality securities as collateral: Treasury and agency securities and investment-grade MBSs and bonds. On September 14, however, the Fed expanded the PDCF as part of its efforts to mitigate the effects of the impending Lehman bankruptcy. Acceptable collateral was expanded "to closely match the types of collateral that can be pledged in tri-party repos," which included speculative-grade securities, equities, and whole loans (loans that were not split up and securitized).[16]

PDCF borrowers took advantage of this collateral expansion. Bloomberg News analyzed the collateral pledged on September 29, when PDCF lending peaked.[17] Borrowers pledged a total of $164 billion of collateral, no more than $46 billion of which would have been acceptable to the PDCF before September 14. Of the remaining $118 billion of newly-acceptable collateral, there were $18 billion of speculative-grade securities ($1 billion of which had a D rating), $28 billion of securities with "rating unavailable," and $72 billion of equities.

From September 15 to September 18, the PDCF lent $20–$28 billion to the broker-dealer LBI to keep it operating after the LBHI bankruptcy. The collateral pledged by LBI included significant quantities of risky and/or illiquid assets. Of the assets pledged on September 15, 72 percent were investment-grade securities and 28 percent were speculative-grade, unrated, or equities.[18]

Even some of the LBI collateral with investment-grade ratings was actually illiquid and of dubious value. This collateral included $5 billion of asset-backed commercial paper called RACERS, which had the top commercial-paper rating of A1, and collateralized mortgage obligations called SASCO, rated A2 by Moodys. Attorneys for JPMorgan Chase discussed these securities in a lawsuit related to Lehman's bankruptcy:[19]

> On Tuesday night, September 16, many of the riskiest securities that were eligible for the triparty repo had been financed by the Fed [i.e., LBI pledged them to the PDCF]. Those securities included RACERS, as well as securities called SASCO, which, like RACERS, were backed largely by Lehman's own credit, were priced on the basis of Lehman's own marks, and had never traded. Numerous other illiquid securities were also financed by the Fed on Tuesday night. Those securities – RACERS in particular – were known by LBHI to be illiquid structured securities that were not appropriate collateral for the triparty repo or to secure JPMorgan's clearing advances.

The JPMorgan attorneys quoted emails among Lehman employees who denigrated the RACERS securities, calling them "very toxic collateral" and "goat poo." When a counterparty refused to accept RACERS in a pre-bankruptcy transaction, a Lehman employee told a colleague that "another one doesn't want your toxic racer crap."

It appears, therefore, that the PDCF was liberal in the types of Lehman assets it accepted as collateral for loans to LBI. That fact makes it easier to identify additional assets that Lehman might have pledged to borrow more cash and avert LBHI's bankruptcy.

Fed officials have said little about the collateral pledged by LBI to the PDCF. I have found only a brief comment in Timothy Geithner's memoir in which he says that loans to LBI were "secured by its higher-quality assets."[20] This remark conflicts with the view inside Lehman that its collateral included goat poo.

Available Collateral: Overview Did Lehman have enough PDCF-eligible collateral under the post-September 14 rules to borrow the cash it needed? This question can be answered by carefully examining the assets on Lehman's balance sheet. But even without such an analysis, we can see that the firm probably had adequate collateral, because of the nature of its liquidity losses.

In particular, most of Lehman's cash needs starting on September 15 were due to repo agreements that were not going to roll. According to my estimates, lost repos account for $66 billion out of a projected cash shortfall of $84 billion. With the PDCF in place, the loss of repo financing should have been an easy problem to solve: the collateral that Lehman's counterparties no longer accepted could have been pledged to the PDCF instead. Indeed, backstopping repos was the purpose for which the PDCF was created and then expanded on September 14.[21]

I have estimated that Lehman needed $19 billion of cash to replace liquidity drains other than lost repos, such as collateral calls and losses of unsecured funding. To borrow this $19 billion, the firm needed assets that were eligible as PDCF collateral and had not previously been pledged in repos, so they could be used as collateral for new borrowing. Lehman had substantial quantities of such assets.

Many of these assets were whole loans, including both home mortgages and corporate loans. Whole loans were sometimes used as collateral in tri-party repos, and the Fed included them when it expanded PDCF collateral on September 14. Lehman's assets included tens of billions of dollars of whole loans, only a small fraction of which ($1.1 billion on May 31) had previously been pledged in repos.[22]

Lehman could have pledged whole loans to the PDCF, or it could have created securities backed by the loans and pledged the securities. Lehman had taken the latter approach when it borrowed from the PDCF in April. It packaged sixty-six corporate loans to create the

Freedom Collateralized Loan Obligation (CLO), with a senior tranche of $2.2 billion and an equity tranche of $0.6 billion. The senior tranche received a single A rating and Lehman pledged it to the PDCF.[23]

In addition to whole loans, Lehman held significant quantities of corporate bonds, equity, and mortgage-backed securities that were eligible as collateral for the PDCF and were not being used as repo collateral on September 14. These securities included $12 billion of collateral freed up when previous repos did not roll ($10 billion from Q3 and $2 billion from September).[24] They also included securities that were apparently never used in repos: securities in the "boxes" of LBI and LBIE, and debt and equity held by LBI's subsidiary Lehman Commercial Paper Inc. (LCPI).[25]

Available Collateral: Details Here I count up the Lehman assets that the firm could have pledged to the PDCF after the collateral expansion on September 14. Figures are for August 31 (the end of 2008 Q3) and come mainly from two sources: the preliminary financial statement that Lehman released on September 10, and a "balance sheet footnote" that apparently was intended for LBHI's never-completed 10-Q for 2008 Q3.[26] My calculations exclude Treasury and agency securities, which I have assumed Lehman would continue to pledge in repos with private institutions.

Lehman's total holdings of PDCF-eligible collateral were at least $122 billion, and they comprised the following items:

- *Equities ($26.0 billion)* The balance sheet footnote lists $43.2 billion of equities, but that includes private-equity stakes that the PDCF might not have accepted. The figure of $26.0 billion is the quantity of equities valued with Level 1 inputs, which means they were traded on public exchanges.
- *Corporate Debt ($41.7 billion)* This category includes corporate bonds and corporate loans, all of which were PDCF-eligible. Again, the loans could have been pledged directly to the PDCF, or Lehman could have securitized them and then pledged the securities.
- *Mortgages and Asset-Backed Securities ($45.8 billion)* This category includes whole mortgages and securities backed by mortgages and other types of loans. All of these assets were PDCF-eligible. The figure of

$45.8 billion comes from the balance sheet that Lehman released on September 10.[27]

- *Money Market Instruments ($4.6 billion)*
- *Municipal Bonds ($3.5 billion)* Munis were one kind of non-Treasury/agency repo collateral. The available balance sheets do not report Lehman's holdings of munis (they are included in the broader class of government bonds). We know, however, that Lehman owned at least $3.5 billion of munis on September 10, when it pledged that quantity in repos.[28]

Although Lehman owned $122 billion of assets that were eligible for PDCF financing, we must make one adjustment to determine how much collateral the firm could have pledged to the facility. Recall my earlier estimate that, on September 13–14, $8 billion of Lehman's repo collateral (10 percent of the total) was securing repos with maturities exceeding four weeks. These assets would have continued to secure the same repos over the four-week horizon in my liquidity calculations, and therefore Lehman could not have pledged them to the PDCF. (In contrast, the assets securing repos with shorter maturities would have become unencumbered when the repos failed to roll.)

The amount of collateral that Lehman could have pledged to the PDCF is the total of its eligible assets ($122 billion) minus the collateral for repos exceeding four weeks ($8 billion). This final amount is $114 billion.

Haircuts and Risk for the Fed

I have estimated that Lehman needed $84 billion of liquidity support to avoid bankruptcy, and that it had $114 billion of collateral it could have pledged to the PDCF. Assistance from the PDCF could have kept Lehman in operation, even with substantial haircuts on its collateral.

In particular, Lehman could have absorbed the large haircut actually imposed by the PDCF when it lent to LBI after the LBHI bankruptcy. This haircut was 16.7 percent for all collateral except Treasuries and agencies.[29] With that haircut, Lehman's $114 billion of collateral could have yielded $95 billion in cash, more than the $84 billion the firm needed.

The Fed's 16.7 percent haircut provided more than adequate protection against losses from assisting Lehman. There are several reasons to think that loans with this haircut were highly conservative:

- The Fed's haircut was considerably higher than the repo haircuts imposed by private institutions. A memo from JPMorgan Chase lists haircuts for Lehman's repos on September 11, and all were less than 16.7 percent. Haircuts for various asset classes included 5 percent for corporate bonds, 8 percent for equities, and 9 percent to 16 percent for mortgage-backed securities.[30]
- The normal PDCF haircuts after September 14 – those imposed on all borrowers except LBI – were also well below 16.7 percent: 6.5 percent for corporate bonds and equities, and 6.5 percent to 9.1 percent for MBSs.[31]
- New York Fed General Counsel Thomas Baxter said the large haircuts on LBI's collateral "were taken to account for LBI's diminished creditworthiness resulting from the loss of its parent's support" – in other words, from the LBHI bankruptcy.[32] That rationale would not have applied if PDCF support had prevented the bankruptcy.
- The New York Fed's William Dudley stressed the high haircuts on LBI's collateral when he reported to the Federal Open Market Committee (FOMC) on September 16. He said, "We think that's about roughly three times the market level that investors had been charging previously, so I think that gives us a fair degree of protection."[33]

COMPARISON TO ACTUAL ASSISTANCE TO LBI

So far I have estimated Lehman's liquidity needs in a counterfactual scenario in which the firm receives enough support from the Fed to avoid bankruptcy. As a check on this analysis, I now examine a relevant part of actual history: the Fed's liquidity assistance to the Lehman subsidiary LBI. This assistance, which lasted from September 15 to September 18, kept LBI in operation until most of it was acquired by Barclays. Is LBI's experience consistent with my estimate of the assistance needed by LBHI, the whole Lehman enterprise?

In particular, I check a key feature of my counterfactual sce-nario: Lehman needs Fed assistance mostly to replace lost repos, because other liquidity losses are modest. Here I ask whether lost repos accounted for most of the Fed assistance that LBI actually needed.

I focus on LBI's experience on September 15, because we have precise information about its repos on that day. On September 15, LBI borrowed $28 billion in cash from the PDCF. It also received $2 billion in new repo financing from Barclays, which wanted to support LBI as it negotiated an acquisition.[34] Liquidity support from the PDCF and Barclays totaled $30 billion.[35]

Of this funding, approximately $6.4 billion from the PDCF was collateralized by some of LBI's Treasury and agency securities.[36] In my earlier analysis of hypothetical assistance to LBHI, I assumed that Treasuries and agencies were repoed to private institutions, and there-fore could be ignored in calculating both liquidity needs and available collateral. To do comparable calculations for LBI, I focus on liquidity support collateralized by LBI assets other than Treasuries and agen-cies. The amount of this support was $23.6 billion ($30 billion from the PDCF and Barclays minus $6.4 billion).

Of this $23.6 billion, how much did LBI need to replace repos that failed to roll? A September 12 memo from JPMorgan Chase lists the LBI repos that were due to mature on September 15, the amounts of various collateral types pledged in these repos, and the haircuts on the collateral.[37] Using these figures, we can compute the cash that LBI had received from its counterparties in the maturing repos, cash it was due to return to the counterparties on September 15. The total cash due in non-Treasury/agency repos was $18.7 billion.

I assume that few or none of LBI's non-Treasury/agency repos rolled on September 15. Lazard predicted this outcome on September 14, and it appears to have occurred based on a JPMorgan Chase memo that summarizes LBI's repos at the end of September 15.[38] The memo reports that LBI's non-Treasury/agency repos with counterparties besides the Fed and Barclays were "mainly term repos," that is, repos that LBI did not need to roll on September 15.

Under the assumption that LBI could not roll any of the repos maturing on September 15, it lost the $18.7 billion of cash due back to counterparties. This loss accounts for most of the $23.6 billion that LBI needed to borrow from the PDCF and Barclays on September 15.

Notice that LBI's $18.7 billion loss of cash from repos is much less than the $66 billion loss of repo cash in the counterfactual scenario examined earlier. There are two reasons for this difference. First, the $66 billion figure includes losses in all parts of Lehman, not just LBI. More than half of the firm's repos were located at subsidiaries (primarily LBIE) other than LBI.[39] Second, the loss calculated for LBI is its loss just on September 15, whereas the earlier scenario includes losses from September 15 through October 13. Some of LBI's repos were term repos that did not mature on September 15 but would mature by October 13.

If $18.7 billion of the liquidity support needed by LBI went to replace lost repos, then the other $4.9 billion out of $23.6 billion presumably was needed to cover other liquidity drains. It is not clear how these other LBI losses compare to losses that LBHI would have suffered if it had remained in business. Some of LBI's losses would not have occurred if all of Lehman had still been operating. One example of a loss that would not have occurred is cash due to LBI from LBIE, which was cut off when LBIE entered administration (bankruptcy in the United Kingdom).[40] Another example is cash lost as customers fled LBI's prime brokerage: LBI probably would have lost fewer customers if its parent had not filed for bankruptcy. On the other hand, if LBHI had remained in business, it might have suffered some liquidity losses that did not occur for LBI. One such loss is collateral calls on derivatives contracts, because Lehman's derivatives were held mostly by LBHI, not its subsidiaries.[41]

Because of these factors, we cannot directly extrapolate from LBI's actual experience to LBHI's hypothetical liquidity needs if it had stayed in business. Yet LBI's experience is consistent with my broad conclusion that LBHI would have needed Fed assistance mainly to replace non-Treasury/agency repo funding. In particular, my estimates imply that lost repos account for 79 percent of the liquidity losses that LBI replaced with borrowing from the PDCF and Barclays ($18.7 billion out of $23.6 billion). In my hypothetical scenario for LBHI, lost repos again account for 79 percent of the firm's borrowing needs ($66 billion out of $84 billion). Again, all losses of repos would have been easy to offset with loans from the PDCF, which Lehman could have secured with the collateral previously accepted by its private repo counterparties.

This chapter has examined Lehman's liquidity needs from several angles, and the conclusions are always the same: LBHI could have avoided its bankruptcy filing if it had received a sufficient loan from the Fed, and the firm had plenty of collateral to secure such a loan. Because a loan to rescue Lehman would have been well-secured, it would have been legal under Section 13(3) of the Federal Reserve Act. The frequent and strong statements to the contrary by Fed officials, which the next chapter reviews, are not correct.

7 Fed Discussions of Collateral and Liquidity Support

Chapter 6 examined the evidence on Lehman's liquidity needs and available collateral on the eve of its bankruptcy. The goal was to determine whether a Fed rescue of the firm would have been legal and feasible. This chapter looks at the questions of liquidity, collateral, and the feasibility of a rescue from a different point of view: a critical review of statements on these topics made by Fed officials, both before and after the bankruptcy.

Documents gathered by the Bankruptcy Examiner Anton Valukas and the Financial Crisis Inquiry Commission (FCIC) show that Fed officials extensively analyzed possible liquidity support for LBHI. This analysis began during the summer of 2008 and continued until at least September 13. Officials focused on the idea that loans from the Primary Dealer Credit Facility (PDCF) could replace Lehman's lost repo funding – the main type of assistance that the firm ended up needing to survive. In their pre-bankruptcy discussions, officials rarely questioned the legality of lending to Lehman or the adequacy of the firm's collateral.

Ben Bernanke made his first public comments on Lehman's September 15 bankruptcy in Congressional testimony on September 23. On that occasion, Bernanke said the Fed "declined to commit public funds" to prevent the bankruptcy because "we judged that investors and counterparties had had time to take precautionary measures" to mitigate the effects of the bankruptcy. He did not say anything about legal constraints or Lehman's collateral.

The first time that Bernanke said the Fed could not legally rescue Lehman, and cited inadequate collateral as the reason, was in a speech to the National Association for Business Economics on October 7. Since then Bernanke has repeated those points many times, and other Fed officials have echoed him.

Yet Fed officials have never supported their claims about legality and collateral with any evidence about Lehman's financial condition. In public hearings and written interrogatories, the FCIC repeatedly pressed both Bernanke and New York Fed General Counsel Thomas Baxter for quantitative details about Lehman's liquidity needs and collateral, but to no avail. Bernanke failed to respond to some of the FCIC's questions, and both he and Baxter replied to other questions with answers that do not make sense.

DISCUSSIONS BEFORE SEPTEMBER 15

After the Bear Stearns crisis in March 2008, Fed officials and staff extensively discussed what they might do if Lehman experienced a run. Some people suggested that PDCF lending could keep Lehman in operation. It is not clear from the record why policymakers ultimately did not take this course.

New York Fed Stress Tests

The New York Fed staff performed stress tests in May and June 2008 in which they simulated liquidity crises at Lehman. These analyses do not explicitly discuss whether the Fed could rescue Lehman from a crisis, but the test results shed light on this question.

In contrast to results of stress tests performed by Lehman, the firm failed the Fed's tests: the cash outflows in the Fed's stress scenarios exceeded Lehman's liquid assets. The Fed's tests assumed, however, that Lehman would receive no liquidity assistance from the Fed. A closer look at the Fed's scenarios reveals that the firm could have covered its cash shortfall with Fed loans that were well-collateralized.

The basic reason for this conclusion is that the largest liquidity drain in the tests – as in the actual crisis in September – was Lehman's loss of repo financing. If Lehman can borrow from the Fed, this problem mostly solves itself: when counterparties refuse to roll repos, that action frees up collateral that Lehman can then pledge to the Fed in return for loans to replace the cash it has lost.

Specifically, let us consider the stress test called the "Bear scenario," the most dire of the scenarios that the Fed examined. New York Fed analysts reported the results of this test to colleagues in a May 12 memo, and the Lehman Bankruptcy Examiner obtained the memo and included it among the documents linked to the Examiner's Report.[1] (The original memo examined the Bear scenario not only for Lehman, but also for Goldman Sachs, Morgan Stanley, and Merrill Lynch, but the test results for those other firms were redacted when the Fed sent the memo to the Lehman Examiner.)

The Bear stress test assumed "a run on the bank in all business areas." In the test, Lehman loses $88 billion of repo financing; suffers $33 billion of other cash drains including lost commercial paper, collateral calls, and operational friction; and is able to offset $17 billion of these losses by selling assets, drawing on credit lines with banks, and other means. The net loss of liquidity is $104 billion ($88 billion + $33 billion − $17 billion). The firm starts the scenario with liquidity of $37 billion, which falls short of its net loss by $67 billion. Thus, Lehman runs out of cash and cannot operate.

Notice, however, that the $88 billion of lost repo financing exceeds the $67 billion shortfall of cash. The collateral that was previously pledged in the repos – assets worth more than $88 billion – would be more than sufficient for borrowing $67 billion from the Fed, even if the Fed imposed large haircuts.

The New York Fed performed its final stress test on June 26.[2] For reasons that are not clear, this test assumed less severe liquidity drains than the Bear scenario, so the total cash shortfall is only $18 billion. Once again, the loss of repos – $35 billion in this case – exceeds the cash shortfall, suggesting that Lehman could survive this stress scenario with Fed assistance.

These stress tests appear to be the most careful analyses of Lehman's liquidity that the Fed ever performed. I have found no evidence that Fed officials reviewed the tests during Lehman's crisis in September; but if they did not, they could have. Heading into the crisis, the Fed's best analysis implied that it could rescue Lehman with well-collateralized liquidity support.

Discussions in July

During July 2008, staff at the New York Fed and the Board of Governors discussed possible liquidity support for Lehman in a number of memos and email exchanges. These discussions are documented in the FCIC Lehman Chronology.[3]

The discussions began with a July 11 memo to President Timothy Geithner from New York Fed staff, including Lucinda Brickler and Til Schuermann. The memo discusses how the Fed might react if a major broker-dealer lost its tri-party repo financing, and analyzes Lehman Brothers as an example.

The memo points out that a firm could lose tri-party repo financing either because counterparties refuse to roll its repos or because the firm's clearing bank refuses to provide intraday credit. The Fed could step in to replace either the counterparties or the clearing bank. The memo describes the rationale for such an intervention:

> Should a dealer lose the confidence of its investors or clearing bank, their efforts to pull away from providing credit could be disastrous for the firm and also cast widespread doubt about the instrument [tri-party repos] as a nearly risk-free, liquid overnight investment. In the event a firm faced this situation, the Federal Reserve could step in and provide overnight financing as it does now through the PDCF, and by replacing the credit provided by the clearing bank during the day . . .. By allowing a dealer to provide a strong face to the market, this approach is intended to support market confidence in the dealer and, by continuing the smooth functioning of the market, in the tri-party repo instrument itself.

The memo also says that the PDCF might need to accept all types of tri-party collateral, anticipating the expansion of the facility that occurred on September 14.

Schuermann sent the memo to Geithner and sixteen others at the New York Fed. An accompanying email said, "I will bring printed copies now," suggesting there was a meeting to discuss the memo. Brickler forwarded the memo to Patrick Parkinson, Deputy Director of the Board of Governors' Division of Research and Statistics, saying, "We are talking through collateral, margin, legal agreement, operating issues, etc., today to put together a plan in the event it becomes necessary to consider this."

Over the next two days, July 12–13, there is a lively email exchange among New York Fed and Board staff, including Brickler, Schuerman, Parkinson, and several others. Generally the emails are not sent to top policymakers; instead, the staff discusses "what we should tell Tim [Geithner]." They debate a wide range of policy options in the event of a run on Lehman.

The Board's Patrick Parkinson takes a leading role in these exchanges. He expresses confidence that the PDCF could replace any loss of repo funding by Lehman and keep the firm afloat. At one point he writes:

> [T]he point of our PDCF lending would be to head off a massive run. Perhaps in a world where "headline risk" is an important concern a run would still occur. But if so we would end up lending at the end of the day an amount that still would be no higher (and could be far smaller) than what others seem to want to commit to lend at the beginning of the day.

On July 20, Parkinson reported on Lehman's problems to top Board officials including Ben Bernanke.[4] For reasons that are not clear, Parkinson is less optimistic on that occasion than he is on July 13. Even if the PDCF replaced all of Lehman's repo financing, he suggests, "our action would not ensure LB's [Lehman Brothers'] survival" because the firm could face other liquidity drains. Parkinson concludes, "That's not to imply that [a rescue] would not be worth the gamble, but it would be a gamble."

The Last Week

After July, the discussions about Lehman's liquidity died down, as far as one can tell from the public record. The topic re-emerged as an urgent one on September 10, when it became clear that Lehman was facing an acute crisis. The FCIC Lehman Chronology documents extensive analyses performed by Fed staff from September 10 through September 13.

The discussions about Lehman were complex, and some are difficult to interpret because they refer to non-public documents. Yet two broad points emerge from the evidence. First, numerous staff at the New York Fed and the Board of Governors developed plans for liquidity support for Lehman, partly at the request of President Geithner. Second, there is no sign that anyone was concerned about the adequacy of Lehman's collateral or the legality of assisting the firm.

The following are highlights of the discussions:

Geithner's Options On Wednesday, September 10, President Geithner led a conference call with staff from the New York Fed and the Board. The discussion is summarized in an email from Mark Van Der Weide of the Board's Legal Division:[5]

> At 4:15pm FRBNY/Board call, same three options were laid out once again by Tim. Working groups were directed to spend the next few hours fleshing out how a Fed-assisted BofA acquisition transaction might look, how a private consortium of preferred equity investors transaction might look, and how a Fed take out of tri-party repo lenders would look.

The last of the three options sounds like the plans for liquidity support discussed in July. Van Der Weide also says, "Tim seemed to think that Lehman would survive into the weekend, but may need some PDCF help tomorrow [September 11] or Friday [September 12]."

The "Gameplan" On September 10 and 11, a memo referred to as a "liquidity consortium gameplan" was circulated among

New York Fed and Board staff and Board Vice Chair Donald Kohn.[6]
It is not clear who wrote the memo. It presented a plan for the meeting
of Wall Street CEOs that began at the Fed on September 12.
The meeting's purpose was to "explore possibilities of joint funding
mechanisms that avert Lehman's bankruptcy."

For our purposes, two parts of the Gameplan memo are significant. One is headed "FRBNY financial commitment." This section
discusses liquidity support for Lehman:

> Term of any liquidity support should be long enough to guard
> against a fire sale, but on a short enough fuse to encourage
> buyers of Lehman assets to come forward. Two months to a year
> in duration?

Here, the memo envisages the policy intervention that I analyze
throughout this book: liquidity support to give Lehman time to find
the best possible resolution of its crisis.

The other relevant part of the memo is a section titled "Legal,"
which is part of a larger section titled "Open Issues." The Legal section lists a number of questions, including what approvals for a deal
would be needed from Lehman shareholders and US and foreign regulators. It also asks, "Can we obtain necessary FOMC [Federal Open
Market Committee] approval for whatever funding facility is fash-
ioned to facilitate a consortium?"[7]

The most interesting aspect of the Legal section is what it does
not discuss: It does not mention any concerns about the legality of
liquidity support or the adequacy of Lehman's collateral.

Kohn Email On the afternoon of Friday, September 12, Vice
Chair Kohn sent a brief email to Bernanke and Governor Kevin
Warsh, in which he reported on discussions he had had with Fed Bank
Presidents.[8] Kohn says:

> I was quizzed closely by Fisher [President of the Dallas Fed] on the
> appetite for Fed/Gov't involvement beyond liquidity provision.
> I told him strong predilection against by both Treas. and Fed . . .

The important point here is the implicit one that policymakers were considering liquidity provision. "Involvement beyond liquidity provision" may refer to a capital injection or the establishment of a Maiden Lane facility to purchase Lehman assets.

Final Staff Debates Some of the staff who had followed Lehman since the summer – Parkinson and Van Der Weide of the Board and Brickler of the New York Fed – exchanged a flurry of emails on September 12 and 13.[9] This discussion is hard to follow because it centers on a non-public memo by Brickler called the "tri-party cheat sheet." Yet we can infer some of the thinking about support for Lehman.

Brickler attached the cheat sheet to a September 12 email, saying, "Attached are some thoughts on tri-party repo for the weekend." She added:

> I've also attempted to briefly describe a few things we may need to consider in the event that JPMC refuses to unwind Lehman's positions on Monday – assuming they're still in business, but haven't been rescued – and the policy makers believe an intervention is necessary to protect the market from the fallout of a sudden default.

As in July, Brickler is worried that JPMorgan Chase will stop clearing Lehman's repos.

Van Der Weide replies on September 13 and comments on several policy options that apparently were listed in Brickler's memo. One comment is:

> Option 1: need to discuss whether this fits within existing PDCF authorization or would need to be new 13(3)/10B loan (like the Bear March 14 loan).

From this comment, it appears that Option 1 is overnight lending against repo collateral, which would be similar to PDCF lending and to the Bear loan on Thursday, March 14 (but not the subsequent loan to Maiden Lane to purchase Bear assets).[10]

Van Der Weide's Report to Alvarez Late on September 13, there is a cryptic email exchange between Van Der Weide and Board General Counsel Scott Alvarez.[11] At 7:39 PM, Van Der Weide mentions "the tri-party solution structure we spoke with you about just now," and says, "FRBNY legal and policy thinks our proposal is workable and the best option we have right now." Evidently, New York Fed staff had some plan to help Lehman maintain its repo financing.

Van Der Weide sent this email about thirty hours before LBHI filed for bankruptcy. Nothing in the real-time record explains why policymakers did not follow through on plans to assist LBHI.

BERNANKE'S TESTIMONY ON SEPTEMBER 23

As discussed throughout this book, Ben Bernanke and other Fed officials have insisted repeatedly that they could not legally rescue Lehman because the firm lacked adequate collateral for a loan. However, that is not what Bernanke said the first time he commented on the bankruptcy.

On September 23, 2008, just eight days after the bankruptcy, Bernanke testified about the AIG and Lehman crises before the Senate Banking Committee.[12] In his written testimony, Bernanke says the Fed rescued AIG on September 16 because "a disorderly failure of AIG would have severely threatened global financial stability." He then discusses Lehman:

> In the case of Lehman Brothers, a major investment bank, the Federal Reserve and the Treasury declined to commit public funds to support the institution. The failure of Lehman posed risks. But the troubles at Lehman had been well known for some time, and investors clearly recognized – as evidenced, for example, by the high cost of insuring Lehman's debt in the market for credit default swaps – that the failure of the firm was a significant possibility. Thus, we judged that investors and counterparties had had time to take precautionary measures.

In saying the Fed "declined" to assist Lehman, Bernanke suggests that it could have done so if it had wanted to. He does not cite legal barriers, saying instead that the expected effects of Lehman's failure were not sufficiently dire to warrant a rescue because "the troubles at Lehman had been well known for some time."

During Bernanke's testimony before the FCIC in 2010, its Chairman, Phil Angelides, reminds him of his 2008 testimony, and summarizes Bernanke's 2008 position as, "Lehman was not rescued essentially because the market, the participants, had had time to prepare in the wake of market developments." Angelides adds, "it seems to me the decision to allow Lehman to fail was a conscious policy decision."[13]

Bernanke responds:[14]

> Let me just say one word about the testimony you referred to, which has gotten – which has supported this myth that we did have a way of saving Lehman. This is my own fault, in a sense, but the reason we didn't make the statement in that testimony, which was only a few days after the failure of Lehman, that we were unable to save it was because it was a judgment at the moment, with the system in tremendous stress and with other financial institutions under threat of run, or panic, that making that statement might have, might have even reduced confidence further and led to further pressure. That being said, I regret not being more straightforward there, because clearly it has supported the mistaken impression that in fact we could have done something. We could not have done anything.

Later in his testimony, Bernanke says, "I was very, very confident that Lehman's demise was going to be a catastrophe."[15]

In this testimony, Bernanke disavows his initial account of why the Fed let Lehman fail. He says he was not "more straightforward" because he feared the market's reaction if he revealed what he says was the true reason for the Fed's decision: that a rescue would have been illegal.

The Final Report of the FCIC notes the difference between Bernanke's testimony in 2008 and in 2010: "As Bernanke acknowledged to the FCIC, his explanation for not providing assistance to Lehman was not the explanation he offered days after the bankruptcy."[16]

Bernanke discusses his initial testimony about Lehman in his 2015 memoir. His account there is similar to his 2010 statement to the FCIC, with the added detail that he planned his initial Senate Banking Committee testimony of September 23 in collaboration with Treasury Secretary Paulson. Bernanke says:[17]

> In congressional testimony immediately after Lehman's collapse, Paulson and I were deliberately quite vague when discussing whether we could have saved Lehman. We spoke about the true, but ultimately irrelevant, fact that financial firms had more time to prepare for Lehman's collapse than for a Bear Stearns failure. But we had agreed in advance to be vague because we were intensely concerned that acknowledging our inability to save Lehman would hurt market confidence and increase pressure on other vulnerable firms. Today I wonder whether we should have been more forthcoming . . ..

Bernanke says he is not sure whether, on balance, his "caginess" in his September 23 testimony was a good idea.[18]

FED CLAIMS ABOUT LEGAL AUTHORITY, OCTOBER 2008–PRESENT

Bernanke first cited legal barriers to rescuing Lehman and the firm's inadequate collateral in a speech to the National Association for Business Economics on October 7, 2008 – fourteen days after his testimony to the Senate Banking Committee and twenty-two days after the Lehman bankruptcy. Since then, Bernanke and other Fed officials have consistently repeated the claims made in that speech.

In the October 7 speech, Bernanke explained why Lehman was not rescued as follows:

With respect to public-sector solutions, we determined that either facilitating a sale of Lehman or maintaining the company as a free-standing entity would have required a very sizable injection of public funds – much larger than in the case of Bear Stearns – and would have involved the assumption by taxpayers of billions of dollars of expected losses. Even if assuming these costs could be justified on public policy grounds, neither the Treasury nor the Federal Reserve had the authority to commit public money in that way; in particular, the Federal Reserve's loans must be sufficiently secured to provide reasonable assurance that the loan will be fully repaid. Such collateral was not available in this case.

Bernanke made similar claims about collateral and legal authority in speeches on October 15 and December 1, 2008 and in an interview on CBS's *Sixty Minutes* broadcast on March 12, 2009. At the Fed's Jackson Hole conference on August 21, 2009, he said:

[T]he company's available collateral fell well short of the amount needed to secure a Federal Reserve loan of sufficient size to meet its funding needs. As the Federal Reserve cannot make an unsecured loan, and as the government as a whole lacked appropriate resolution authority or the ability to inject capital, the firm's failure was, unfortunately, unavoidable.

The staff of the FCIC interviewed Bernanke in November 2009 and later released a transcript. On this occasion Bernanke repeats his claims about legal authority in particularly strong language, saying: "I will maintain to my deathbed that we made every effort to save Lehman, but we were just unable to do so because of a lack of legal authority."[19] He also says:[20]

I've said the following under oath and I'll say it again under oath if necessary: we wanted to save Lehman. We made every possible effort to save Lehman ... We could not. We did not have the legal authority to save it.

Members of Bankruptcy Examiner Valukas's team interviewed Bernanke in December 2009. No transcript is available, but the Examiner's Report summarizes what Bernanke said:[21]

> Bernanke did not believe that the Fed had the legal authority to bail out Lehman in September 2008. He noted that a Federal Reserve Bank such as the FRBNY could make a loan only if it was satisfactorily secured, that is, that the bank could reasonably expect a 100 percent return. Bernanke said a "fundamental impediment" existed for Lehman: By mid-September, Lehman lacked not just "standard" collateral, but "any" collateral. Lehman's tangible assets and securities fell "considerably short of the obligations that would come due."

Bernanke has maintained this position in subsequent discussions of the Lehman crisis. In his 2012 lectures at George Washington University, he says that legal constraints left the Fed "helpless" to save Lehman.[22] In his 2015 memoir, he says:[23]

> Unlike AIG, which had sufficient collateral to back a large loan from the Fed, Lehman had neither a plausible plan to stabilize itself nor sufficient collateral to back a loan of the size needed to prevent its collapse.

At another point in his memoir, Bernanke recounts a September 14 conversation with Timothy Geithner, when Geithner called him to report the failure of the Barclays deal. Bernanke says, "I asked Tim whether it would work for us to lend to Lehman on the broadest possible collateral to try to keep the firm afloat," and he summarizes Geithner's answer:[24]

> "No," Tim said. "We would only be lending into an unstoppable run." He elaborated that, without a buyer to guarantee Lehman's liabilities and to establish the firm's viability, no Fed loan could save it. Even if we lent against Lehman's most marginal assets, its private-sector creditors and counterparties would simply take the

opportunity to pull their funds as quickly as possible . . . . We would be left holding Lehman's bad assets, having selectively bailed out the creditors who could exit the most quickly, and the firm would fail anyway. "Our whole strategy was based on finding a buyer," Tim said. It was a question of practicality as much as legality. Without a buyer, and with no authority to inject fresh capital or guarantee Lehman's assets, we had no means of saving the firm.

Here again, Bernanke maintains that the Fed could not have saved Lehman with a well-secured loan, and that it lacked authority for more effective assistance. (In my reading of this passage, Bernanke's distinction between practicality and legality is not important for the substance of his position.)

Geithner makes similar claims about Lehman in his own 2014 memoir:[25]

[W]e didn't believe we could legally lend them the scale of resources they would need to continue to operate, because we didn't believe they had anything close to the ability to repay us.

Later, Geithner says:[26]

We had shown that we could push the boundaries of our authority to take on some modest risk, but the Fed's emergency authorities limited how much risk we could take; we were the central bank of the United States, and we weren't going to defy our own governing law to lend into a run. We could [only] make loans to solvent institutions against solid collateral.

THE FCIC CHALLENGES FED OFFICIALS

On most occasions when Fed officials have discussed Lehman, their accounts of the episode have not been challenged strongly. These cases include most of the interviews of officials by the staff of the FCIC, which are available on the FCIC website. These sessions had a friendly tone, with the interviewers seeming to accept officials' claims uncritically.

Fed officials were treated differently at the public hearings of the FCIC, where they were questioned by members of the Commission rather than its staff. On September 1–2, 2010, Chairman Bernanke, New York Fed General Counsel Baxter, and Board General Counsel Alvarez testified under oath at a hearing titled "Too Big to Fail." On that occasion, several Commissioners cross-examined the officials aggressively, questioning their claims about Lehman's collateral and the Fed's authority to lend. The FCIC pushed Bernanke and Baxter further with follow-up questions sent in writing on October 1, 2010.

In response to questions posed at the hearing and in writing, Fed officials provided the most detailed information about their treatment of Lehman that is available anywhere. A careful review of this record shows that officials (most notably, Ben Bernanke) were nonresponsive to some of the FCIC's questions. On other issues, the claims of different officials conflict with each other or with facts established elsewhere in the record.

Bernanke's FCIC Testimony

On September 2, 2010, Bernanke testified before the FCIC about various aspects of the financial crisis. The transcript of his testimony is 121 pages. Commissioners questioned Bernanke about the Lehman episode at several points.

Early in the hearing, FCIC Chairman Angelides asks Bernanke to explain why the Fed did not assist Lehman – "the things you were trying to weigh, the decision-making factors."[27] He questions the legal-authority explanation, in part because Bernanke did not mention it in his first statement about the bankruptcy on September 23, 2008. Angelides reviews the discussions among Fed staff about possible support for Lehman and concludes, "I don't see any documents or discussion along the way about legal bars or government analysis of a shortage of collateral."

In reply, Bernanke says in part:[28]

Now on Sunday night of that weekend, what was told to me was that – and I have every reason to believe – was that there was a run proceeding on Lehman, that is people were essentially demanding liquidity from Lehman; that Lehman did not have enough collateral to allow the Fed to lend it enough to meet that run; therefore, if we lent the money to Lehman, all that would happen would be that the run would succeed, because it wouldn't be able to meet the demands, the firm would fail, and not only would we be unsuccessful but we would have saddled the taxpayer with tens of billions of dollars of losses . . .. The unanimous opinion that I was told, and I heard from both the lawyers and from the leadership at the Federal Reserve Bank of New York, was that Lehman did not have sufficient collateral to borrow enough to save itself. And therefore any attempt to lend to Lehman within the law would be futile and would only result in loss of cash.

Later, Angelides asks Bernanke why the Fed lent money to LBI but not to LBHI.[29] Bernanke replies that LBI "had sufficient collateral to support the loan," whereas "the calculations were that the liquidity demands on the holding company [LBHI] were much greater than the collateral that they had available to meet those demands." Angelides asks Bernanke about the source of his information:

CHAIRMAN ANGELIDES: Was that based on an analysis? Or was that based on the private consortium's analysis?

WITNESS BERNANKE: That was based on analysis at the Federal Reserve Bank of New York, primarily, which had been going on through the weekend. And of course prior to that, we had done a lot of analysis based on our presence at Lehman during the summer.

Later in the hearing, Commissioner Peter Wallison pursues a similar line of questioning with Bernanke.[30] He asks whether the Board of Governors could have authorized a loan to LBHI, leading to the following exchange:

WITNESS BERNANKE: We are able to do so under the law so far as we have sufficient collateral. And we were prepared to do that. And I was in Washington ready to call the Board together to do that, if that was going to be helpful. However, what I was informed by those working on Lehman's finances was that it was far too little collateral available to come to our window to get enough cash to meet what would be the immediate liquidity runs on the company …. So it was our view that we could not lend enough to save the company under the restriction that we could only lend against collateral.

COMMISSIONER WALLISON: And you are saying, then, that even if the collateral was illiquid, you could have lent against it, but you concluded – or someone in the New York Fed concluded – that there wasn't enough of such even illiquid assets for you to make this loan?

WITNESS BERNANKE: That's correct.

COMMISSIONER WALLISON: Did you do a study of the collateral that was available? Does the New York Fed have a study of the collateral that was available so we could –

WITNESS BERNANKE: Well I would refer you to them. Remember, we were working with the SEC to do these liquidity stress tests that we did over the summer. And then over the weekend, there was 24-hour analysis going on that included not only the staff of the New York Fed, but also assistance from the private sector companies that were gathered there. I don't have any – to my knowledge, I don't have a study to hand you. But it was the judgment made by the leadership of the New York Fed and the people who were charged with reviewing the books of Lehman that they were far short of what was needed to get the cash to meet the run. And that was the judgment that was given to me. So that was my understanding.

Still later in the hearing, Bernanke has similar exchanges with Commissioner Douglas Holtz-Eakin and with Vice Chairman Bill Thomas.[31] Thomas pushes for details about the collateral shortfall, asking whether "it wasn't sufficient collateral by an inch, by a mile?" In reply, Bernanke relates what he heard from the policymakers gathered at the New York Fed (President Geithner, Secretary Paulson, and SEC Chairman Christopher Cox):

> [W]hat I heard from them was just the sense of defeat. You know, that it's just way too big a hole. And my own view is it's very likely that the company was insolvent, even, not just illiquid.

What should we make of this testimony? Bernanke says repeatedly that his judgment about Lehman's collateral was based on analysis at the New York Fed during the firm's final weekend. He says that "people who were charged with reviewing the books of Lehman" worked around the clock on "calculations" of the firm's liquidity needs and collateral. But Bernanke does not provide any details of this analysis, or even evidence that it occurred. There is no way to prove that such an analysis did *not* occur, but there are several reasons to question Bernanke's account.

First, as Angelides points out, there is an extensive record of Fed emails and memos from the final weekend, and nobody discusses the adequacy of Lehman's collateral. Such discussions are also absent from detailed accounts of the weekend in Sorkin's *Too Big to Fail* and in the memoirs of Henry Paulson and Timothy Geithner (although Geithner states that Lehman's collateral was inadequate).

Second, Bernanke says "the private sector companies" helped analyze the adequacy of Lehman's collateral, and that does not appear to be true. By all accounts, the firms gathered at the New York Fed were divided into three groups with different tasks, which Geithner describes as:[32]

> one to analyze Lehman's toxic assets to help facilitate a potential merger, one to investigate an LTCM [Long Term Capital Management]-style consortium that could take over the firm and gradually wind down its positions, and one to explore ways to prepare for a bankruptcy and limit the attendant damage.

None of these tasks involved analysis of Lehman's liquidity needs or the collateral available to secure a Fed loan.

Finally, Bernanke cites the New York Fed stress tests from the summer of 2008. These tests do address Lehman's liquidity needs, but they do not support the claim of inadequate collateral. As discussed earlier, the tests found that a run would have left Lehman with unencumbered repo collateral that exceeded its borrowing needs.

The FCIC's Follow-up Questions to Bernanke

On October 1, 2010, a month after Bernanke's testimony, the FCIC sent him a follow-up letter with six questions. The first two questions concern Wells Fargo's acquisition of Wachovia, and the last requests a list of readings on the financial crisis. The other three questions concern Lehman:

3. Please provide any information about Lehman's financial condition or its collateral in the weeks leading up to the company's bankruptcy.
4. During your testimony, you stated that the Federal Reserve Bank of New York conducted a collateral analysis of Lehman Brothers, upon which you relied to make your decision not to use the Federal Reserve's Section 13(3) authority. Please provide the collateral analysis, the name of the person who communicated the collateral analysis to you, and the time and location when you were informed of the collateral analysis. Please inform the Commission of the name or names of persons who conducted the collateral analysis for the Federal Reserve Bank of New York.
   In addition, please provide a list of persons with whom you or your staff consulted with regards to this matter in the White House or the Treasury and any related memoranda, documents, emails, etc.
5. Please report the dollar value of the shortfall of Lehman's collateral relative to the collateral necessary to issue a bridge loan or other secured assistance to Lehman on September 14, 2008.

With these follow-up questions, the Commission is trying hard to pin Bernanke down on the details of the Fed's collateral analysis.

On November 4, 2010, Bernanke replied to the Commission in a fifteen-page letter saying:

This letter responds to the supplemental questions you sent me on October 1, 2010 and provides additional information regarding the issues you raised in your letter inviting me to testify before the Commission. To most effectively and efficiently respond to the questions posed in your two letters, my responses are organized by topic.

The topics in the letter are "Supervision," "Monetary Policy," "Emergency Assistance" (which discusses Wachovia and 13(3) lending in general), "Lehman Brothers Bankruptcy," and "Reading List." The Lehman Brothers section is the part that is relevant here.[33]

In his letter, Bernanke reiterates, "The contention that the Federal Reserve believed it had viable options to rescue Lehman, but chose not to use them, is simply untrue." He reviews policymakers' unsuccessful efforts to arrange a Barclays acquisition, and then writes:

Without a merger partner, the Federal Reserve saw no viable options for avoiding a Lehman bankruptcy. Lehman was in immediate need of substantial capital and liquidity to fund its operations as counterparties pulled funding away or sought better lending terms and more collateral. Although we did not have precise information about their credit needs at the time, the balance sheet of Lehman readily illustrated that the credit relied on by Lehman to remain in operation was in the hundreds of billions of dollars and the lack of confidence that led counterparties to pull away from Lehman suggested that Lehman would need a credit backstop of all its obligations in order to prevent a debilitating run by its counterparties. Moreover, the value of a substantial portion of assets held by Lehman, especially its investments in RMBS [residential mortgage-backed securities], loans, and real estate, was falling significantly. Derivative positions were subject to continuing collateral calls that required amounts of Lehman funding that could not easily be quantified in advance. And clearing parties were demanding collateral as a condition for serving as an intermediary in transactions with Lehman. We saw no evidence that Lehman had sufficient collateral to support these types and amounts of taxpayer support from the Federal Reserve . . . .

This information was conveyed to me by phone that weekend by FRBNY officials. As you know, Lehman's primary dealer [LBI] did have sufficient collateral to support a limited loan through the PDCF and other existing FRBNY liquidity facilities, and that credit was provided.

After this passage, Bernanke's letter turns to the issue of Lehman's solvency. He suggests Lehman was insolvent based on dubious arguments involving the minutes of the September 14, 2008 meeting of Lehman's board of directors, the Valukas Report, and a 2010 report from the managers of the Lehman estate.[34]

In his letter to the FCIC, Bernanke does not respond to the Commission's follow-up questions. Question 4 asks for many details about the New York Fed's collateral analysis and how Bernanke learned about it ("the name of the person who communicated the collateral analysis to you," and so on), but Bernanke's relevant response is a single sentence: "This information was conveyed to me by phone that week-end by FRBNY officials." In response to Question 5, about "the dollar value of the shortfall" between Lehman's liquidity needs and collateral, Bernanke says vaguely that Lehman needed "hundreds of billions of dollars," and says nothing quantitative about its available collateral.

Bernanke lists some of the specific liquidity drains that Lehman faced, including collateral calls by derivatives counterparties and clearing banks, but does not quantify these factors. His assertion that collateral calls for derivatives "could not easily be quantified in advance" is at odds with a New York Fed memo he received on September 11, which estimated that Lehman faced $2.9 billion to $4.4 billion of collateral calls.[35]

Baxter's FCIC Testimony

On September 1, 2010, the day before Chairman Bernanke's FCIC testimony, New York Fed General Counsel Baxter testified in a session devoted to Lehman Brothers. He was part of a panel that included Richard Fuld, the CEO of Lehman at the time of the bankruptcy; Lehman's lead bankruptcy attorney, Harvey Miller; and Barry Zubrow, the Chief Risk Officer of JPMorgan Chase.

In written testimony for the hearing, Baxter states the same position on Lehman as Bernanke. He writes:[36]

> Lehman had no ability to pledge the amount of collateral required to satisfactorily secure a Fed guarantee, one large enough to credibly withstand a run by Lehman's creditors and counterparties.

Baxter, like Bernanke, was pushed by several Commissioners to back up his claim. He responded with two different points, one regarding Lehman's liquidity needs and another regarding the firm's long-term prospects.

LBHI's Liquidity Needs Commissioner Holtz-Eakin asks Baxter why the Fed provided liquidity assistance to keep LBI in operation, but not all of LBHI. Baxter replies:[37]

> So what you're talking about with additional funding to rescue the Lehman parent is it comes on top of the $60 billion that was already committed to the broker-dealer [LBI]. So, you know, if you take what was offered in one of the statements that there was another $40 billion needed, we're up to $100 billion now. Now where's the collateral coming? How are you doing that? Those things are all completely obscure.

This testimony is noteworthy because, to my knowledge, it is the only place where a Fed official gives a numerical estimate of Lehman's liquidity needs. As Baxter clarifies elsewhere, the $60 billion in support for LBI is an estimate that aggregates the $28 billion in PDCF lending on September 15, 2008 and loans of cash and securities through the Term Securities Lending Facility (TSLF) and the Fed's open-market operations (OMO).[38] The TSLF and OMO lending were roughly the same before and after the LBHI bankruptcy.[39]

The key point in Baxter's testimony is the suggestion that LBHI needed $40 billion of additional funding to survive. Baxter does not cite the source of this figure, but says it "was offered in one of the statements [the written testimony for the hearing]." It appears that Baxter is referring to the written testimony of Lehman attorney Harvey Miller, which says, "It has been estimated by some commentators that a government-sponsored wind-down [of LBHI], with limited guarantees, might have cost $40 to $50 billion."[40] Miller's figure, however, is an estimate of the ultimate cost of resolving LBHI, not an estimate of the firm's short-term liquidity needs.[41]

In any case, because LBI borrowed $28 billion from the PDCF, Baxter's $40 billion figure implies that LBHI could have survived with total PDCF support of $68 billion (along with unchanged support from the TSLF and OMOs). This estimate of LBHI's borrowing needs is on the *low* side compared to the estimate of $84 billion arrived at in Chapter 6.

Baxter says the source of collateral for additional borrowing is "completely obscure," but this statement is not true. As we have seen, an analysis of Lehman's financial records shows that the firm clearly had enough collateral. The firm had at least $114 billion of assets that it could have pledged to the PDCF under the September 14 rules, and it had many additional assets that could have served as collateral under a new 13(3) resolution.

"A Bridge to Nowhere" At several points in Baxter's testimony, Commissioners press him about the Lehman decision and he does *not* say anything about Lehman's collateral or the Fed's legal authority. Instead, Baxter says that policymakers decided before the weekend of September 13–14 that Lehman should declare bankruptcy if it was not acquired by another firm. They did not consider liquidity support for Lehman because that would not have improved the outcome of the firm's crisis: it would have been "a bridge to nowhere."

Baxter first takes this position under questioning by Chairman Angelides. Angelides makes a point that he later makes to Ben Bernanke: memos and emails suggest that policymakers discussed liquidity support for Lehman extensively, and were not concerned about the firm's collateral or their legal authority. Angelides reviews the evidence and says, "I never see anyone say during the months, we can't even consider financial assistance because the condition of Lehman won't allow it."[42] He asks Baxter:

> Tell me all the policy considerations that go in? Or was it that from day one you were saying legally not possible? Because it sure looks like there's a heck of a lot of debate, a hell of a lot of debate here, about whether or not to rescue, whether or not to provide for an orderly transition, and none of this was cut off by a legal opinion and said not possible.

Baxter replies:[43]

> I think it's important to understand the framework that we went into Lehman weekend with. And our principal plan, our Plan A, if you will, was to facilitate a merger between a strong merger partner and Lehman. That was Plan A. And rest assured, Commissioners, we worked night and day to try to make that plan happen.

Baxter describes the failure of the Barclays acquisition, and then continues:

> So Plan A couldn't be executed. Now Secretary Geithner, when I worked for him when he was president of the New York Federal Reserve Bank, used to say to the staff, and sometimes in an animated way, "plan beats no plan." So he was not going to allow us to be in a position where we had no contingency plan. So our contingency plan for the facilitated merger-acquisition of Lehman, was the following: The parent would file a Chapter 11 petition. The U.S. broker-dealer would stay in operation with the benefit of Federal Reserve liquidity until such time as a proceeding could be commenced under the Securities Investor Protection Act. That was the contingency plan. The Plan B if you will.

Later in the hearing, Commissioner Wallison presses Baxter on why the Fed did not provide liquidity assistance to LBHI.[44] Baxter replies that such an action "was inconsistent with the contingency plan that we were executing after Plan A fell apart and we couldn't find a merger partner."

In this exchange, Baxter also says *why* a loan to LBHI was neither Plan A nor Plan B: it would have been futile for resolving Lehman's crisis. Lehman CEO Fuld, testifying alongside Baxter, had said that Lehman needed a "bridge loan" to keep the firm in operation while it addressed its problems. Baxter tells Wallison:[45]

> It was felt that that kind of bridge loan was a bridge loan to nowhere, because the management of Lehman had worked, I think as diligently as possible, to find a solution to their problems in the run-up to Lehman weekend. We had worked through Lehman weekend to find a solution to those problems. The market no longer had confidence in Lehman. The market was no longer willing to trade with Lehman.

Baxter also calls assistance to LBHI "a bridge to nowhere" at two other points in his testimony.[46] He elaborates on this idea in his follow-up letter to the FCIC, discussed below.

Baxter's argument, it appears, is that Fed liquidity support could not have improved the outcome of the Lehman crisis. That claim is dubious. As detailed in Chapter 6, liquidity support could have kept Lehman in operation for weeks or months. Given this time, policymakers and Lehman executives probably would have found a resolution of the crisis that was less damaging to the financial system than the September 15 bankruptcy. (Some possible resolutions are discussed in Chapter 9.)

In any case, Baxter's account of policy deliberations does not fit well with Chairman Bernanke's testimony the next day. Bernanke says the New York Fed staff intensively analyzed Lehman's collateral over its final weekend, and "I would refer you to them" for details. According to Bernanke, Fed officials determined that Lehman's collateral was inadequate, and that was the reason for denying assistance to LBHI. This account makes sense only if officials seriously considered such assistance during the weekend – not if they dismissed the possibility before the weekend, as Baxter claims.

On this point, the record supports Bernanke's account more than Baxter's. As detailed earlier, there was intensive discussion of support for LBHI among New York Fed staff from Wednesday, September 10 through Saturday, September 13. This discussion included the "gameplan" memo prepared for the weekend meetings at the Fed. That memo, which Baxter received, suggested liquidity support for two months to a year.

Baxter's Follow-Up Letter

The FCIC sent Baxter a follow-up letter on October 1, 2010, which includes a question that it also posed to Ben Bernanke:

> Please report the dollar value of the shortfall of Lehman collateral relative to the collateral necessary to issue a bridge loan or other secured assistance to Lehman on September 14, 2008.

In replying to the FCIC on October 15, 2010, Baxter restates the question and then gives this response:[47]

> As far as I am aware, the possibility of extending a so-called "bridge loan" to LBHI on September 14 was never seriously considered by the Federal Reserve because such a loan, as I said during the Commission's September 1, 2010 hearing, would have been a bridge to nowhere. This view was not simply my own, but rather at the time was held throughout the U.S. government, broadly among Lehman's counterparties, and even by Lehman itself. As noted above, by September 14, 2008, LBHI's own board had concluded that bankruptcy was an "ultimate inevitability." Of course, after LBHI filed for bankruptcy, the FRBNY did extend on September 15 an aggregate amount of credit of approximately $60 billion to LBI, which enabled LBI to continue in business. This extension of credit

was secured by a pledge of collateral that we valued at more than $60 billion. To keep all of Lehman operating as a going concern, rather than only the U.S. broker dealer, would have required a vastly greater amount of credit and collateral.

This statement largely repeats claims from Baxter's earlier testimony, but two details are noteworthy:

First, recall Baxter's testimony that LBHI might have needed $40 billion in credit to stay in operation, in addition to the $60 billion actually lent to LBI. In his follow-up letter, Baxter says that LBHI needed an amount "vastly greater" than $60 billion. "Vastly greater" is imprecise, but it sounds larger than $40 billion added to $60 billion.

Second, Baxter says that his view about a "bridge to nowhere" was shared "by Lehman itself." This claim is absurd. By all accounts, Lehman's executives tried desperately to borrow from the Fed because they believed that would lead to a better outcome for the firm. As in his comments on solvency discussed in Chapter 4, Baxter misinterprets the reference to the "ultimate inevitability" of bankruptcy in the minutes of the Lehman board meeting. The board believed that bankruptcy was inevitable because the Fed had refused to assist LBHI, not because assistance would have been futile.

Alvarez's Testimony and Interview

Scott Alvarez, the General Counsel of the Board of Governors, also appeared before the FCIC on September 1, 2010. His testimony focused primarily on the acquisition of Wachovia by Wells Fargo, but he commented briefly on Lehman:[48]

> [W]e didn't have the tools to do anything other than what we did. Lehman needed far more liquidity than the Federal Reserve could provide on a secured basis. And without that security, we are not authorized to provide lending.

Once again, FCIC Chairman Angelides pressed for details about Lehman's collateral, leading to the following exchange:[49]

CHAIRMAN ANGELIDES: Just kind of yes or no, did the Fed ever do a collateral analysis? Did anyone in the federal government? I've never seen a collateral analysis.

WITNESS ALVAREZ: A written report on the value –

CHAIRMAN ANGELIDES: Yes.

WITNESS ALVAREZ: – of the collateral? No. There was no time for that ...

Like the other witnesses at the FCIC hearing, Alvarez had previously been interviewed by FCIC staff. His interview on July 29, 2010 is more interesting than most because the staff questioned him somewhat aggressively. Alvarez says that his office wrote a memo about each of the Fed's loans under Section 13(3), which discussed the collateral for the loans. That statement leads to the following exchange:[50]

INTERVIEWER: Does that same document exist for Lehman, taking the assets, assessing that their value wouldn't support the collateral?

ALVAREZ: Nope. No.

INTERVIEWER: Then how do you know you couldn't make a loan under 13(3)?

ALVARAREZ: Folks had a pretty good feeling for the value of Lehman during that weekend, and so there was no memo prepared that documented why it is we didn't lend. It was just the thought that we are not going to lend because the decision makers who were involved in the negotiations, who were on the scene, who were talking to the Bank Americas complaining about the size of the hole, and talking to the industry saying we're not going to put up any money to solve this, and talking to the Lehman people who are saying, "My God, how are we going to open on Monday," they understood from all of that that there wasn't enough there for us to lend against and so they weren't willing to go forward.

Here, Alvarez says policymakers "understood" that Lehman had insufficient collateral despite an absence of documentation. He cites three pieces of evidence: Lehman had a "hole"; the private sector would not rescue the firm; and it could not open on September 15. None of these points is responsive to the interviewer's question about collateral.

- The term "hole," as used by Bank of America executives and others, refers to Lehman's overvaluation of assets and possible insolvency.[51] The available evidence suggests that Lehman was near the border of solvency based on market values of assets, and solvent based on fundamental values. In any case, as stressed throughout this book, the adequacy of Lehman's collateral for a Fed loan does not turn on the question of solvency.
- The point about "the industry" is confused in two ways. First, the analysis by the private sector consortium, like the discussion of holes, concerned asset valuation and solvency, not liquidity and collateral. Second, the consortium did *not* refuse to put up any money. It agreed to finance some of Lehman's assets to facilitate a Barclays deal.
- Finally, as we have seen again and again, the reason that Lehman could not open on Monday, September 15 was its liquidity crisis: it could not borrow enough from the private sector to meet its obligations. Under Section 13(3), such a predicament does not rule out a Fed loan; to the contrary, it is one of the requirements for a loan. Thus Alvarez, the top lawyer for the Fed's Board of Governors, joins Thomas Baxter, the top lawyer for the New York Fed, in nonsensically citing the fact that Lehman satisfied a requirement for 13(3) lending to explain why the Fed did not lend.[52]

DID LEHMAN NEED A "NAKED GUARANTEE?"

Fed officials have sometimes put forward a variation on their claims about collateral and legal authority. They have argued that a Lehman rescue required an unsecured guarantee of all the firm's obligations, which the Fed could not legally provide. In fact, Lehman did not need such a guarantee to stay in operation.

Recall that a dispute about a guarantee derailed the Barclays acquisition of LBHI. The Fed demanded that Barclays guarantee all of Lehman's obligations between the initial deal and final approval by Barclays and Lehman shareholders. Under UK law, however, such a guarantee itself required a shareholder vote, which could not happen quickly, and the United Kingdom's Financial Services Authority (FSA) refused to waive this requirement.

One possible resolution of this impasse was for the New York Fed to guarantee Lehman's obligations, rather than Barclays, and the FSA suggested this option.[53] Fed officials have argued, however, that Section 13(3) did not allow them to issue an unlimited and unsecured guarantee. On this point, their argument about legal authority appears sound.

However, a number of Fed statements about this issue are misleading because they suggest that an unlimited guarantee was the only way to avert Lehman's bankruptcy. In fact, as we have seen, the firm could have survived with a finite amount of well-secured lending. Secured lending through the PDCF allowed LBI to operate after LBHI's bankruptcy, and similar lending could have supported all of LBHI rather than LBI alone.

General Counsel Baxter emphasizes the unlimited guarantee issue in his FCIC testimony. In his written testimony, he describes how the issue derailed the Barclays deal, and then says:[54]

> Many have asked why, when the Barclays guarantee problem presented itself, the Federal Reserve did not step forward and guarantee the trading obligations of Lehman pending its merger with Barclays . . .. Under the law, the New York Fed does not have the authority to provide what I would characterize as a "naked" guarantee – one that would be unsecured and not limited in amount, and would put the U.S. taxpayers at risk for the *entirety* of Lehman's trading obligations.

In his opening statement at the FCIC hearing, Baxter describes what was needed to avert Lehman's bankruptcy:[55]

First, we needed a suitable merger partner for Lehman. Second, we needed that merger partner to provide a guarantee similar to the one that JPMorgan Chase provided in its acquisition of Bear Stearns wherein the acquiring institution agreed to backstop Lehman's trading obligations between the signing of the merger agreement and the merger closing . . . .This guarantee was indispensable to Lehman's rescue.

Baxter returns to the guarantee issue at several points in his testimony, reiterating that the Fed could not provide a guarantee:[56]

The Fed has no such legal authority. And the reason is that in Section 13(3) of the Federal Reserve Act there's a requirement that we're secured to our satisfaction. A naked guarantee of unlimited amount, unsecured, does not meet that statutory requirement. Full stop.

Baxter contrasts a guarantee for LBHI with the Fed's "fully secured" lending to LBI, which was legal.[57]

Ben Bernanke does not discuss the guarantee issue in his FCIC testimony, but he raises it in earlier testimony before the House Financial Services Committee on April 20, 2010. On that occasion, Bernanke says that Lehman needed an unlimited guarantee to survive:

Lehman needed both substantial capital and an open-ended guarantee of its obligations to open for business on Monday, September 15. At that time, neither the Federal Reserve nor any other agency had the authority to provide capital or an unsecured guarantee, and thus no means of preventing Lehman's failure existed.

Finally, Board General Counsel Alvarez makes a relevant comment in his FCIC interview. An interviewer asks how much Lehman needed to borrow, and Alvarez replies:[58]

We were faced with having to give an open-ended guarantee. Lehman didn't come to us and say, "can we borrow $10 billion?"

It was, "will you guarantee our operations tomorrow?" How big is that loan?

Alvarez goes beyond Baxter and Bernanke in claiming that Lehman executives asked for an unlimited guarantee from the Fed. The record does not support that claim. What Lehman asked for was secured funding from the PDCF, as detailed in the next chapter.

8 Fed Actions That Ensured Lehman's Bankruptcy

Preceding chapters have shown that the Fed could have averted Lehman's bankruptcy with a well-collateralized loan if it had chosen to do so. In this chapter, we see that Fed officials did not merely stand by and allow Lehman to fail but intentionally took actions to force LBHI into filing a bankruptcy petition. As General Counsel Thomas Baxter told the FCIC, the LBHI bankruptcy was the Fed's "Plan B." Officials pushed for bankruptcy once they saw that "Plan A," the Barclays acquisition, was not going to work.

AN OVERVIEW OF THE FED'S ACTIONS

To force the Lehman bankruptcy, Fed officials took two kinds of actions. First, they instructed Lehman's executives and attorneys to file a bankruptcy petition before markets opened on Monday, September 15. Baxter delivered this instruction at a meeting at the New York Fed on the afternoon of Sunday, September 14. It was reiterated in thinly veiled language in a phone call from Fed and SEC officials to Lehman's board on Sunday evening.

Neither the Fed nor the US government has the authority to order a private corporation to file for bankruptcy. Therefore, Fed officials had to back up their instructions with a second kind of action that would force the hand of Lehman's board. Specifically, they acted to ensure that Lehman would not have sufficient cash to operate on September 15.

Fed policymakers faced a tricky problem on September 14. Hoping to avoid a financial disaster, they wanted to ensure that all the Wall Street firms *except* Lehman had adequate liquidity, so they expanded the range of collateral accepted by the Primary Dealer Credit Facility. They also wanted LBI to stay in business, so they gave it access to the PDCF and accepted assets of questionable value ("goat poo") as LBI's collateral.

At the same time, officials did not want Lehman to be able to borrow enough from the PDCF to keep all of LBHI in operation. As detailed in Chapter 6, Lehman had enough collateral to do so, but the Fed prevented this outcome by restricting the firm's access to the PDCF.

The restrictions on Lehman's PDCF access are one of the murkier aspects of the firm's crisis. Lehman executives told the FCIC that the Fed refused to broaden the range of acceptable collateral for their firm as it did for others. But General Counsel Baxter has denied this claim, and the real-time evidence is ambiguous.

On the other hand, there is clear evidence of a different kind of limit on Lehman's PDCF access – a restriction on which parts of the firm received assistance from the facility. In particular, the Fed prevented LBIE, Lehman's broker-dealer in London, from receiving the cash that it needed to make payments on September 15. As a result, LBIE defaulted, and that default implied that LBHI also defaulted because it guaranteed LBIE's payments.

The Fed made two policy decisions that denied cash to LBIE. First, it lent to LBI but refused a request for a similar loan to LBIE. This action contrasts starkly with the Fed's decision seven days later to lend to the London broker-dealers of Morgan Stanley and Goldman Sachs.

By itself, it probably would not have mattered that the Fed lent to LBI and not LBIE. LBI could have borrowed enough cash to meet both its own *and* LBIE's liquidity needs, using routine transfers of cash and collateral among Lehman subsidiaries. If that had happened, LBIE would have avoided the defaults on payments that triggered the defaults on guarantees by its parent LBHI. At one point on September 14, Lehman executives had planned such an arrangement, but this plan was thwarted by another Fed action: the "Friday criterion." This rule limited the collateral that LBI could pledge to the PDCF to assets on LBI's balance sheet on Friday,

September 12. This restriction prevented other Lehman subsidiaries from transferring assets to LBI that it could use as collateral. As a result, LBI could not borrow enough cash to keep all of Lehman in operation.

The remainder of this chapter provides details and documentation for the Fed's decisions and actions.

THE FED TELLS LEHMAN TO FILE FOR BANKRUPTCY

Fed officials discussed bankruptcy with Lehman's executives, attorneys, and board at two points on Sunday, September 14: in an afternoon meeting at the New York Fed, and in an evening phone call to the board.

The Sunday Afternoon Meeting

Fed officials invited Lehman executives and attorneys to the afternoon meeting, which began around 1:00 PM. General Counsel Baxter ran the meeting, which included about twenty-five people from the Fed and SEC. Attorney Harvey Miller led the Lehman representatives, including several of Miller's law partners, Lehman President Bart McDade, and Alex Kirk, Lehman's Global Head of Principal Investing.

Several of the Lehman representatives subsequently described the meeting in FCIC interviews, and their accounts are similar. Other similar accounts appear in Miller's written testimony to the FCIC, in the Valukas Report, and in Sorkin's *Too Big to Fail*. To my knowledge, nobody from the Fed has mentioned the meeting in any interview, testimony or writing.

By all accounts, General Counsel Baxter firmly instructed LBHI to file for bankruptcy, and he rebuffed questions about this order from Lehman's representatives.

The Valukas Report summarizes the meeting in its chronology of Lehman's final week, under the heading, "The FRBNY directed Lehman to file for bankruptcy."[1] The Report cites attorney Miller and Lehman CEO Fuld as sources. It says:

[Lehman President] McDade called Fuld from the meeting at the FRBNY to tell him that "the Fed has just mandated that we file for bankruptcy." At the FRBNY, Baxter said that Lehman needed to file by midnight that night. Miller responded to Baxter's statement by asking why and objecting that the filing could not happen by midnight. Miller said that a Lehman bankruptcy would "bring great destabilization in the market," "bring trading to a halt," and result in financial "Armageddon." The Government representatives' reply was that the issue had been decided and there were cars available to take the Lehman people back to their offices.

The most detailed account of the meeting is given by Harvey Miller in his written testimony to the FCIC:[2]

> In substance, the Lehman representatives were advised that a transaction with Barclays was not going to occur and, further, that there would be no federal assistance provided to save or support Lehman. Despite requests for elucidation as to the basis of the decision, Lehman's representatives were instructed that there would be no further information provided as to the basis of the decision to refrain from providing Lehman with financial support or other assistance.

Miller's account continues for two pages: Fed officials say they will provide liquidity to LBI but not the rest of LBHI. Lehman's representatives stress the disastrous consequences if LBHI fails, ask again for an explanation for the Fed's decision, and receive responses that are "not illuminating."

At one point there is a break in the meeting. According to Miller:

> After listening to comments from Lehman and Weil [Miller's law firm], Mr. Baxter stated that the government representatives would caucus to consider Lehman's comments. The government representatives then left the conference room for approximately one hour. When they returned, Mr. Baxter reported that after consideration of all of the contentions made on behalf of Lehman,

the decision not to support Lehman had been reaffirmed. Accordingly, he stated that the only alternative was that Lehman had to fail. Mr. Baxter then directed that the Lehman and Weil teams should promptly return to Lehman's headquarters and arrange for a meeting of Lehman's Board of Directors to be convened for the purpose of adopting a resolution authorizing and directing LBHI to commence a bankruptcy case before 12:00 midnight of that day.

The meeting continues in the same vein, with Lehman's representatives *again* requesting an explanation and Fed officials replying that "there existed no obligation or duty to provide such information or to substantiate the basis for the decision not to aid or support Lehman." At the end of the meeting:

> The direction to return to the Lehman headquarters was repeated. The Lehman and Weil teams were encouraged to promptly leave the premises and did so.

Sorkin's *Too Big to Fail* gives essentially the same account of the Sunday afternoon meeting, but with a more dramatic tone.[3] Baxter tells Miller, "We've come to the conclusion that Lehman has to go into bankruptcy," leading to an argument in which Miller "bellows" and Baxter responds "sheepishly" and "uneasily."

The Evening Phone Call to the Board

On the evening of Sunday, September 14, the LBHI board of directors convened at 5:00 PM, adjourned at 6:10, and reconvened at 7:55. At some point after that, Fed and SEC officials called Lehman and asked to address the board by speakerphone. After some discussion, the board agreed to take the call.

This phone call, like the afternoon meeting at the New York Fed, is described consistently by numerous Lehman sources and by Sorkin. The top officials on the call were General Counsel Baxter and Christopher Cox, the Chairman of the SEC. By all accounts, Baxter and Cox wanted LBHI to file for bankruptcy, but hesitated to give an explicit order to the board. According to Harvey Miller's testimony:[4]

> In substance, Messrs. Cox and Baxter stated that it was in the best interests of the financial system and the United States economy for Lehman's Board of Directors to pass a resolution approving the commencement of a bankruptcy case prior to 12:00 midnight of that day. Several Directors asked Messrs. Cox and Baxter whether they, on behalf of the NY Fed and the SEC, were directing the Board of Directors to adopt a bankruptcy resolution. In response, Mr. Cox hesitated, and Mr. Baxter suggested they hold an offline caucus. After five or ten minutes, Messrs. Cox and Baxter rejoined the conference call with the Directors.
>
> Mr. Cox stated that he and Mr. Baxter were not issuing a direction to the Lehman Board of Directors to pass a resolution authorizing the commencement of a bankruptcy case. Rather, he indicated that the decision was for Lehman's Directors to make in the exercise of their business judgment and discretion. Such response notwithstanding, Lehman's Directors persisted in asking for a clear and definitive answer to the question of whether the NY Fed and SEC were directing the passage of a bankruptcy resolution. These questions precipitated another caucus that extended for another five to ten minutes. When Messrs. Cox and Baxter rejoined the conference call, they reiterated that the decision of whether to adopt a bankruptcy resolution was a decision for Lehman's Board of Directors to make and, further, that neither the SEC nor the NY Fed was directing the adoption of such a resolution. However, Mr. Cox stated that he believed that the preferences of the NY Fed and the SEC had been made unequivocally clear to Messrs. McDade, Kirk, and others at the meeting that had been held earlier that day at the NY Fed.

Treasury Secretary Henry Paulson mentions this phone call in his memoir. He says:[5]

> [S]haring the line with Tom Baxter, the general counsel of the New York Fed, and other Fed and SEC staffers, Cox called Fuld shortly after 8:00 PM to reiterate that there would be no government rescue. Lehman had no alternative to bankruptcy. Fuld connected Cox to Lehman's board. "I can't tell you what to do," Cox told them. "I can only tell you to make a quick decision."

Paulson says he encouraged Cox to call Lehman even though "I understood that it was awkward and unusual for a regulator to push a private-sector firm to declare bankruptcy."

The minutes of the Lehman board meeting list a number of reasons for the decision to file for bankruptcy. Reflecting the discussions with policymakers, these reasons include "the clear preference of the Federal government that the Corporation file for bankruptcy that evening" and "the potential goodwill that may be generated by a filing." Other factors include "the potential difficulty in meeting all payment obligations the next day" and "the ultimate inevitability of a bankruptcy filing under the circumstances" (where "the circumstances" refers to the firm's liquidity crisis).[6]

CONFUSION ABOUT THE PDCF RESTRICTIONS

The Fed prevented Lehman from borrowing the cash it needed by restricting its access to the PDCF, but the nature of the restrictions is not completely clear. Lehman executives say the broadening of PDCF collateral on September 14 was not extended to their firm, but General Counsel Baxter flatly denies this claim. The real-time evidence is ambiguous. This issue produced a long and confusing debate among Baxter, CEO Fuld, and several FCIC Commissioners at the hearing on September 1, 2010.

Claims by Lehman Executives

In his opening statement to the FCIC, CEO Fuld describes the events of Sunday, September 14. He says:[7]

Notably, on that same Sunday the Fed expanded for investment banks the types of collateral that would qualify for borrowings from its Primary Dealer Credit Facility. Only Lehman was denied that expanded access. I submit that, had Lehman been granted that same access as its competitors, even as late as that Sunday evening, Lehman would have had time for at least an orderly wind down or an acquisition, either of which would have alleviated the crisis that followed.

Later in the hearing, FCIC Chairman Angelides asks Fuld, "What do you think was at the nub of the decision not to rescue or provide liquidity for an orderly wind down?" In reply, Fuld says in part:[8]

> I really cannot answer you, sir, as to why the Federal Reserve and the Treasury and the SEC together chose not to not only provide support for liquidity, but also not to have opened the window to Lehman that Sunday night as it did to all of our competitors. And I must tell you that when I first heard about the fact that the window was open for expanded collateral, a number of my finance and treasury team came into my office and said we're fine. We have the collateral. We can pledge it. We're fine. Forty-five minutes later, they came back and said: That window is not open to Lehman Brothers.

Fuld repeats this account when he is questioned later by FCIC Commissioner Holtz-Eakin.[9]

Lehman President Bart McDade did not appear at the FCIC hearing, but he gave a similar account in an interview with FCIC staff on August 9, 2010. He says that Fed officials described the terms on which Lehman could borrow from the PDCF at the Sunday afternoon meeting at the New York Fed, and the following exchange occurs:[10]

INTERVIEWER: How were the terms that Lehman would get different from what other participants would get, and what was the explanation of why?

MCDADE: The terms were just different. Lehman would have access to the old terms. All the other banks would have access to the new terms –

INTERVIEWER: Let me stop you for a minute if I can. In terms of the old terms, does that primarily or even exclusively mean not as broad based of collateral types being accepted?

MCDADE: Yes.

McDade goes on to say the reasons given by the Fed were "vague." Asked about the impact of the collateral restriction on Lehman, he says:

> It made the difference between being able to be open the next day and still have a chance for an orderly unwind.

Lehman CFO Ian Lowitt was also asked by FCIC staff about Lehman's access to the PDCF. Lowitt, like Fuld, says that Lehman initially believed it could pledge the broader types of collateral, but then learned it could not:[11]

> On clarification ... it was determined that actually [the PDCF] wouldn't be open to us for more collateral types, but that it would be open to the broker-dealer on the Monday for the normal liquid securities that LBI held.

Baxter's Account

General Counsel Baxter testified alongside CEO Fuld at the FCIC hearing. Baxter repeatedly contradicts Fuld about Lehman's PDCF access, saying at one point, "Mr. Fuld is simply incorrect."[12] He says, "Lehman had access to the PDCF with the expanded collateral, but with a higher haircut." Asked whether that was true before LBHI's bankruptcy filing, Baxter says, "Prior to filing, exact same terms for Lehman as for all other primary dealers."[13]

Later, Baxter has an exchange with Chairman Angelides:[14]

CHAIRMAN ANGELIDES: [I]n our staff interviews of Mr. McDade and Mr. Lowitt, what the chronology we put out today indicates is, it says Baxter tells them that Lehman cannot access the expanded window and had to file for bankruptcy. So you dispute that? You said you never told that to nobody?

WITNESS BAXTER: Correct.

CHAIRMAN ANGELIDES: So how did all these people infer all this? Why did they come to this conclusion? I mean, how does that happen?

WITNESS BAXTER: I think you'll have to ask them that, Mr. Chairman.

Several times, Baxter supports his position by citing a letter to Lehman dated September 14 from Christopher Burke, a New York Fed Vice President. This letter includes a detailed list of acceptable PDCF collateral, and it reflects the expansion that had just occurred. At one point Commissioner Holtz-Eakin asks, "Could the broker dealer [LBI] have accessed [the PDCF] on Sunday night on the same terms as everyone else?," and Baxter replies:[15]

> There's a letter from Chris Burke who is an officer of the New York Fed to Lehman Brothers. You have it in the record, and you can look at that and see what we said in plain terms. There shouldn't be doubt about this. You have it in writing.

Baxter also cites the Burke letter in his follow-up letter to the FCIC.

The Real-Time Evidence

From September 15 to 18 (after the LBHI bankruptcy), the broker-dealer LBI borrowed from the PDCF. Over that period, the PDCF *did* accept the expanded range of collateral from LBI. Indeed, it accepted securities from LBI that Lehman employees had denigrated as "very toxic."

However, what is relevant for understanding LBHI's bankruptcy is what happened *before* the filing, not after. What did the Fed tell

Lehman on September 14 about its access to the PDCF and the collateral it was allowed to pledge?

The evidence on this point is mixed. General Counsel Baxter, in his letter to the FCIC, cites an email from New York Fed official James Bergin to his colleague William Dudley at 2:15 PM on September 14.[16] This email says, "We informed Weil [Harvey Miller's law firm] of the expansion of the PDCF collateral." But this news apparently did not reach everyone at Lehman. At 8:35 PM, Lehman's Timothy Lyons emailed CFO Lowitt to say, "The fed is letting the other eighteen broker dealers fund a much broader range of collateral than us."[17]

Some Fed officials were also confused about Lehman's access to the PDCF – including William Dudley, the recipient of the email cited by Baxter. On September 16, when Dudley reported to the Federal Open Market Committee on developments in financial markets, Philadelphia Fed President Plosser asked him whether the expansion of PDCF collateral applied to LBI. Dudley answered incorrectly:[18]

> In terms of the Lehman collateral, they are not allowed to broaden the PDCF – they are basically bringing us the stuff they had on Friday.

Baxter emphasizes the letter from Christopher Burke, but its relevance is dubious. The letter is dated September 14, but it was emailed to Lehman at 2:24 AM on September 15, which was after the bankruptcy filing.[19]

In his letter to the FCIC, Baxter says that Burke's letter "formalized and memorialized conversations that the FRBNY had with Lehman throughout that Sunday, September 14."[20] However, he cites only one specific conversation: a call from Burke to "all of the primary dealers to explain the newly expanded access to the PDCF." Based on New York Fed emails discussing the call, we can tell that it occurred between 8:40 and 11:48 PM on Sunday, September 14.[21] The LBHI board convened for the final time at 7:55 PM, so it is unlikely the board knew of Burke's call when it decided on bankruptcy.[22]

While it is not clear what the Fed told Lehman about the collateral it could pledge to the PDCF, it *is* clear that the Fed restricted Lehman's PDCF access along a different dimension: The facility would lend only to LBI, Lehman's New York broker-dealer. LBIE, the London broker-dealer, was not allowed to borrow from the PDCF on any terms.

The Restriction and Its Impact

The Lehman board meeting at 5:00 PM on September 14 began with a situation report by Thomas Russo, Lehman's in-house general counsel. Russo described LBIE's predicament and the Fed's unwillingness to help. According to the minutes:[23]

> Mr. Russo reported that a failure to fund Lehman Brothers (International) Europe ("LBIE") would obligate the LBIE directors to initiate administration [bankruptcy] proceedings under UK insolvency laws, which would trigger cross-defaults to the Firm's [LBHI's] swaps book. Mr. Russo described these cross-defaults as representing a massive systemic risk that may require the Corporation [LBHI] and certain subsidiaries to seek protection under Chapter 11 [of the US bankruptcy code]. The Board discussed the use of the Fed window to fund LBIE and it was explained that despite the efforts of management to convince the Fed on this point, should the Fed not change its position on the use of the expanded window, the Board of Directors of LBIE would have to initiate the UK administration process.

The Fed's treatment of LBIE was subsequently confirmed by the United Kingdom's Financial Services Authority (FSA). In March 2010, the FSA prepared a chronology of its actions during the Lehman crisis for Bankruptcy Examiner Valukas.[24] One item in the chronology is:

> Later that evening [September 14] a conference call took place between the FSA and the FRBNY. The FRBNY explained that Lehman would shortly file for Chapter 11, but that Lehman

Brothers Inc. would be kept afloat using FRBNY financing. The FSA asked if this funding would be made available to LBIE and was told that this was not possible.

According to the FSA chronology, this call took place before 7:00 PM New York time (midnight in London). Therefore, despite the Fed's statement that "Lehman would shortly file," the FSA/FRBNY conversation occurred before the Lehman board convened for the final time at 7:55. It was after 7:55 when the board received the phone call from Baxter and Cox and finally decided on bankruptcy.

Could the Fed Have Lent to LBIE?

On September 14, the entities eligible to borrow from the PDCF were the nineteen primary dealers in Treasury securities. These dealers were New York-based subsidiaries of global financial firms, and included LBI but not LBIE or LBHI. A loan to LBIE would not have been a routine transaction for the PDCF.

However, the Fed could have changed the rules on September 14 to give LBIE access to the PDCF or a similar facility. The Board of Governors could have authorized this action under Section 13(3).

We can see that this action was feasible from what happened after September 14. In the wake of the Lehman bankruptcy, Goldman Sachs and Morgan Stanley, the last two of the Big Five investment banks, experienced liquidity crises. These firms, like Lehman, had broker-dealer subsidiaries in both New York and London, and liquidity drains occurred in both places. The Fed took several steps to keep Goldman and Morgan in business, one of which was the extension of PDCF access to their London broker-dealers.

This action was one of several announced in a Fed press release at 9:30 PM on Sunday, September 21. The relevant part of the press release is the last sentence:

> In addition, the Board also authorized the Federal Reserve Bank of New York to extend credit to the London-based broker-dealer

subsidiaries of Goldman Sachs, Morgan Stanley, and Merrill Lynch against collateral that would be eligible to be pledged at the PDCF.

This action received little attention at the time, and there have been few mentions of it in previous accounts of the financial crisis. It was overshadowed by the announcement, in the same press release, that the Fed had approved the applications of Goldman Sachs and Morgan Stanley to become bank holding companies (a strategy for boosting confidence in those firms discussed in Chapter 10).

It is not clear from the press release whether the Fed planned to lend to the London broker-dealers through the PDCF, or through a new facility that accepted the same types of collateral. What actually happened, it appears, is that the London broker-dealers borrowed from the PDCF in the same way their New York counterparts borrowed.

This policy change is reflected in the data on PDCF lending on the Board of Governors website.[25] On each day of the week of September 15, the PDCF lent to Goldman, Sachs & Co. and Morgan Stanley & Co. Incorporated, the New York broker-dealers of the two firms. Starting on September 22, the PDCF continued to lend to those two entities but *also* lent to Goldman, Sachs & Co.-London and Morgan Stanley & Co. Incorporated-London. At the height of the crisis, lending to the London units was a substantial fraction of PDCF support for Goldman and Morgan. On September 30, for example, Goldman-New York borrowed $10.0 billion and Goldman-London borrowed $6.5 billion. For Morgan Stanley, the corresponding figures were $34.7 billion and $25.5 billion.

THE FRIDAY CRITERION

Even with the PDCF closed to LBIE, LBI probably would have been able to borrow enough cash to keep all of Lehman in operation. As collateral, LBI could have pledged its own PDCF-eligible assets plus assets transferred from LBHI and other LBHI subsidiaries.

Indeed, there is evidence that Lehman tried to implement this strategy on September 14. It was thwarted when the Fed imposed the "Friday criterion" which limited LBI's collateral to only those assets that were on its balance sheet on Friday, September 12.

The Flow of Assets within LBHI

To understand how LBI might have borrowed more from the PDCF, it helps to understand the normal interactions among LBHI and its subsidiaries, including LBI and LBIE. Each day, large quantities of cash and securities flowed among these entities, creating payables and receivables. These items appear on the *unconsolidated* balance sheets of LBHI and its subsidiaries. For example, on May 31, 2008, LBHI's assets included $172 billion due from subsidiaries and its liabilities included $79 billion due to subsidiaries. LBI had $77 billion due from other Lehman entities and $161 billion due to them.[26]

These figures reflect a variety of complex transactions among the different parts of Lehman. The following are examples of such transactions:

- The Valukas Report emphasizes that LBHI helped manage liquidity for its subsidiaries: It was a "central banker" for the Lehman enterprise.[27] Each day LBHI received cash from subsidiaries with more liquidity than they needed, creating payables to those subsidiaries. LBHI distributed cash to other subsidiaries, creating receivables.
- Lehman entities deposited cash and securities in accounts at other Lehman entities. For example, the LBI Trustee reports, "Other Lehman entities maintained accounts at LBI to hold securities for various purposes related to their or their own customers' transactions."[28] LBI sometimes used the securities in these accounts as collateral in other transactions.
- Different parts of Lehman made repurchase agreements with each other. For example, at the time of the Lehman bankruptcy, LBIE's liabilities included $211 billion of repos and similar transactions with other Lehman entities.[29] Repos allowed different units of Lehman to help finance each other's transactions. For example, LBI could obtain cash from LBIE through a repo, and then pass the cash on to customers through reverse repos.[30]

What Might Have Happened on September 14

Given the financial flows within Lehman, it probably should not have mattered which part of the enterprise borrowed from the PDCF. As demonstrated in Chapter 6, Lehman as a whole had enough collateral to borrow the cash it needed to survive its liquidity crisis. Even with only LBI eligible to borrow, collateral could have been transferred to LBI from other Lehman units; LBI could have pledged the collateral to the PDCF; and the cash it received could have been spread around Lehman as needed.

In particular, LBIE's liquidity crisis could have been solved through the following series of transactions: LBIE sends securities to LBI, which incurs a payable; LBI pledges the securities to the PDCF in return for cash; and LBI gives the cash to LBIE, eliminating the payable.

One piece of evidence suggests that Lehman actually tried to use LBI's access to the PDCF to borrow cash for other parts of the firm. This evidence is an item in a chronology included in the LBI Trustee's Preliminary Investigation Report:[31]

> 9/14/2008 4:12 PM: LBI prepares a plan for delivering securities to the Fed pursuant to the PDCF. LBHI and LCPI [Lehman Commercial Paper Inc.] would prepare a schedule of pledged assets and deliver them to the Fed, as an amendment to the current documents, through LBI "as Agent to the Fed for LBHI and LCPI."

This item is cryptic, but it suggests that, in its final hours, Lehman was trying to overcome the restriction that only LBI could borrow from the PDCF.

One detail from the Trustee's report that makes sense is that LCPI was a potential source of PDCF collateral. According to the Valukas Report, a substantial share of Lehman's corporate debt and equity was held on the balance sheet of LCPI.[32]

What the Friday Criterion Did

The Valukas Report describes the Friday criterion as follows:[33]

> [T]he FRBNY limited the collateral LBI could use for overnight financing to the collateral that was in LBI's box at JPMorgan as of Friday, September 12, 2008. This restriction was referred to as the "Friday criterion."

LBI's "box" was an account at JPMorgan, its clearing bank, where it held its tri-party repo collateral.

General Counsel Baxter describes the Friday criterion in his follow-up letter to the FCIC:[34]

> [T]he FRBNY asked LBI to certify that the securities that LBI pledged to the PDCF on September 15 were in fact owned by LBI as of September 12 and had not since been transferred from LBI's parent LBHI.

It appears the Friday criterion ruled out transfers of assets to LBI not only from LBHI, but also from other units of Lehman. The assets that were unavailable to LBI included the debt and equity securities held by LCPI, which was a subsidiary of LBI. LBI could not use its subsidiary's assets as collateral because they were not in its repo box on September 12.

It seems that Lehman's top executives were unaware of the Friday criterion. As discussed above, CEO Fuld and President McDade told the FCIC that the Fed restricted Lehman's access to the PDCF. But they thought the restriction involved the types of assets the PDCF would accept as collateral, not the legal entities that owned the collateral.

However, at least one Lehman executive understood the Friday criterion: Alex Kirk, the Global Head of Principal Investing. Kirk participated in the September 14 afternoon meeting at the New York Fed at which officials said they would assist LBI but not LBHI. Kirk describes part of the meeting in his 2010 interview with FCIC staff:[35]

We then were told that the Fed would provide us financing against then-eligible assets to be financed by the Fed, and they were going to provide that financing for the strict purpose of paying back the financing counterparties, i.e., anybody who ran a repo line outstanding with Lehman Brothers the broker-dealer in the U.S. We then had a long series of discussions about the necessity, from our point of view, of being able to move money through the system as we normally had between the various entities, but it was explained to us that each legal entity would now be a box in and of itself, and we were prohibited from moving any money in or out of the broker-dealer ....

Later in his interview, Kirk says the Fed's policy was fatal to Lehman:[36]

Like any financial institution, the inability to move money between your various subsidiaries will shut you down very quickly .... The inability to move money between legal entities, in and of itself, would have caused us to file, certainly, within days.

It appears that LBI obeyed the Friday criterion when it borrowed from the PDCF on September 15. A JPMorgan email on the evening of the 15th describes the collateral pledged to the PDCF that day:[37]

- The assets in Lehman's [LBI's] 9/15/2008 PDCF repo of $28 billion are of comparable type to the assets that were in Lehman's tri-party book on 9/12/2008.
- The assets were all pledged by Lehman Brothers Inc. (the broker dealer).
- To the best of our knowledge, there are not any Lehman Brothers Holdings Inc. securities collateralizing this PDCF repo.

Bernanke's Comment on LBI and LBHI

In his FCIC testimony, Ben Bernanke appears confused about the relationship between LBI and LBHI. In arguing that LBHI could not be saved, Bernanke says:[38]

> [B]y the way, we didn't do anything to prevent the broker-dealer from lending to its own holding company, and it didn't seem to decide that was a smart thing to do.

This statement does not square with the facts that Lehman tried to fund LBHI with PDCF borrowing by LBI, and that the Fed's Friday criterion thwarted Lehman's plan.

Baxter's Justification for the Friday Criterion

To my knowledge, General Counsel Baxter's 2010 letter to the FCIC is the only place where a Fed official discusses the Friday criterion. After saying that LBI had to certify that its PDCF collateral was on its balance sheet on September 12, Baxter continues:[39]

> This certification was an important legal risk mitigant, and was crafted in light of LBI's unique situation as a subsidiary of a bankrupt parent. Had LBHI transferred securities to LBI, so LBI could then pledge them to the PDCF, those securities could have become subject to a preference or fraudulent conveyance claim, leaving the FRBNY, and consequently the taxpayers, undersecured. The FRBNY's need to confirm that none of the collateral that it held could be subject to a superior claim in the bankruptcy court may be what Lehman personnel referred to as the "Friday criterion," as described in the Valukas Report.

Baxter's claim, apparently, is that assets transferred from LBHI and then pledged to the PDCF might have been taken away from the Fed in LBHI's bankruptcy proceedings.

There are two problems with Baxter's reasoning. First, it is circular. Baxter says the Friday criterion was necessary because LBHI was bankrupt, but the bankruptcy was caused by the Friday criterion. If not for this restriction on PDCF access, Lehman could have borrowed enough to keep LBHI in operation, making Baxter's concern about the bankruptcy court irrelevant.

Second, Baxter's argument about legal risk is cryptic. He refers to the concepts of preference and fraudulent conveyance in bankruptcy law, but their relevance to asset transfers among LBHI and its subsidiaries is unclear at best.

According to the federal Bankruptcy Code, a preference is a payment from a bankrupt firm "for or on account of an antecedent debt" that benefits the recipient at the expense of the firm's other creditors.[40] This concept does not appear relevant to the intra-Lehman transfers at issue here, simply because these transfers would not have been payments for antecedent debts.

A fraudulent conveyance is a transfer of assets from a bankrupt firm to another entity that either (i) is made "with actual intent to hinder, delay, or defraud" the firm's creditors; or (ii) harms creditors because the firm has "received less than a reasonably equivalent value in exchange for such transfer."[41] Condition (i) seems not to apply, because the transfers that LBHI wanted to make were not intended to defraud its creditors; indeed, they would have benefitted creditors by making bankruptcy less likely. Perhaps there is some argument that condition (ii) applies, but General Counsel Baxter gives no indication of what that argument might be. Transfers of assets among LBHI and its subsidiaries, with offsetting payables and receivables, were a routine part of Lehman's liquidity management.

Previous chapters have established that there were feasible, legal actions that the Fed could have taken to rescue Lehman from its liquidity crisis, but that policymakers chose not to take them. This chapter establishes that the Fed took deliberate actions to ensure that Lehman would not survive its crisis. Fed officials bluntly told Lehman executives to file for bankruptcy, and they backed up that instruction with restrictions on the firm's access to the PDCF. Those restrictions ensured that Lehman's London subsidiary LBIE would not have enough cash to meet its obligations on Monday, September 15, thereby causing both its bankruptcy and that of its parent, LBHI.

9 Possible Long-Term Outcomes for Lehman

We have seen that Lehman Brothers had sufficient collateral for Fed liquidity support that would have averted its September 15 bankruptcy and kept the firm in operation for a considerable period of time. This period might have lasted around two months to a year, as suggested by the September 11 New York Fed "Gameplan," or it might have lasted even longer.

The Fed would not have supported Lehman forever, however. At some point, the firm would have needed to solve the problems that caused its crisis, or go out of business. Fed liquidity support would have served a purpose only if the long-term outcome of Lehman's crisis was better for the firm's stakeholders, and/or less disruptive to the broader financial system, than the September 15 bankruptcy.

Fed officials sometimes suggest that there was no hope of a benign resolution of Lehman's crisis, even with Fed assistance. General Counsel Baxter, for example, dismissed the idea of liquidity support as "a bridge to nowhere." Yet it is easy to imagine resolutions of the crisis that would have avoided much of the damage caused by Lehman's bankruptcy. These possibilities include plans that Lehman was trying to implement when the bankruptcy occurred, and plans that Fed officials had discussed. Other possibilities are suggested by the experiences of firms that the Fed chose to assist during the financial crisis, both before and after the Lehman bankruptcy.

With sensible behavior by Fed officials and Lehman executives, it is likely that the firm's crisis would eventually have been resolved in one of three ways: completion of the Barclays acquisition; long-term survival of Lehman as an independent firm; or a wind down over a period of a year or two.

It is very hard to say which of these outcomes would have occurred if the Fed had assisted Lehman. It is likely, however, that any of the possibilities would have been better for the firm and its creditors (both short-term and long-term) than the actual bankruptcy. It is also likely that the damage to the broader financial system and economy would have been smaller.[1]

POSSIBLE OUTCOME #1: COMPLETING THE BARCLAYS DEAL

On the morning of Sunday, September 14, there was a tentative deal to rescue Lehman. Barclays would purchase the bulk of LBHI, leaving behind $40 billion of real estate and private equity that a group of Wall Street firms would finance.[2] One possible resolution of Lehman's crisis would have been the completion of the Barclays deal.

The deal fell through because of a disagreement between US and British regulators about funding Lehman during the period before final approval of the deal by Barclays and Lehman shareholders. Without an arrangement for interim funding, Lehman probably could not have survived until the deal was closed. The Fed insisted that Barclays solve this problem by guaranteeing all of Lehman's obligations immediately. But under UK law, such a guarantee would itself require a shareholder vote, and the United Kingdom's Financial Services Authority (FSA) refused to waive this requirement.[3]

The Fed could have dropped its demand for a Barclays guarantee and provided funding to LBHI for the month or two needed to organize shareholder votes. As Chapter 6 documented extensively, the Fed's lending could have been well secured with Lehman collateral that met the standards of the PDCF. Claims by Fed officials that LBHI needed "unlimited and unsecured" assistance are not correct.

Some commentators (including Henry Paulson) suggest that the FSA was determined to thwart Barclays' acquisition of LBHI, believing it was too risky for the UK economy.[4] If the guarantee issue had not derailed the deal, the FSA might have found another reason to reject it. In that case, Fed liquidity assistance would not have saved the deal.

The FSA denies that it would have vetoed any Barclays-Lehman deal. In its 2010 statement to the Lehman Bankruptcy Examiner, it confirms that it rejected the Fed's request to waive a shareholder vote, which "would represent a compromise of one of the fundamental principles of the FSA's Listing Regime." The FSA also demanded that Lehman have access to the PDCF. However, FSA Chief Executive Hector Sants repeatedly told Barclays that "the FSA had no objection in principle to Barclays purchasing Lehman."[5]

POSSIBLE OUTCOME #2: SURVIVAL OF AN INDEPENDENT LEHMAN

After the Barclays deal fell through, it was unlikely that a different firm would step forward to buy Lehman. By the time Lehman failed, both the firm and policymakers had searched exhaustively for potential acquirers. The only institutions with any interest were Barclays and Bank of America, and the latter dropped out when it bought Merrill Lynch. Without a Barclays deal, therefore, it seems Lehman's only chance to avoid bankruptcy would have been to survive as an independent firm.

It is not clear whether that could have happened. The market's loss of confidence in Lehman might have proven irreversible, in which case the firm could never have funded itself privately, and thus would never have been able to be weaned from Fed support. In that case, Lehman would eventually have gone out of business.

The fundamentals of Lehman's finances did not, however, dictate that outcome. As discussed in Chapter 4, Lehman was borderline solvent based on mark-to-market prices for its assets, and clearly solvent based on their fundamental values. Lehman also operated businesses with franchise value, including its broker-dealers. Arguably, Lehman was a viable firm that could eventually have regained the market's confidence if it had been able to weather its 2008 crisis.

Lehman's crisis stemmed from the underlying problems of low capital and excessive investment in real estate. Presumably, the firm's chances of survival would have risen if these problems had been mitigated. A number of actions by Lehman or the Fed might have helped Lehman survive.

Lehman's Strategic Plan

On September 10, five days before its bankruptcy, Lehman announced a strategic restructuring. In the first quarter of 2009, it planned to spin off most of its commercial real estate assets to REI Global, a real estate investment trust (REIT). It also planned to sell a majority stake in its Investment Management Division (IMD), which included the Neuberger Berman asset management business.

As detailed in Chapter 2, Lehman's announcement of its plans failed utterly to restore confidence and ease the firm's liquidity crisis. Yet the two planned actions might have helped in the long run if Lehman had been able to stay in business. The real estate spinoff appears to have been a sound idea, because accounting rules allowed REI Global, as a REIT, to value its assets based on future cash flows. It could have assigned higher values than did Lehman, which was required to use mark-to-market accounting. Lehman's sale of its IMD would have directly increased its capital.

Ben Bernanke describes Lehman's strategic plan in his memoir, saying the firm planned to split into a "bad bank" (REI Global) and a "good bank" (the rest of the firm). Bernanke makes some mildly favorable comments:[6]

> The good bank-bad bank strategy can be successful under the right conditions. The good bank – shorn of its questionable assets – may be able to raise new capital, while the bad bank can be financed by speculative investors at high interest rates and wound down, with assets being sold off over time. Fuld said that he hoped to divest Lehman's bad assets and make up the losses by selling one of the company's most valuable subsidiaries, its asset management unit, Neuberger Berman. Some thought it could fetch $7 billion to $8 billion.

Bernanke then explains why the plan was not implemented:

> [T]he plan, even if it ultimately proved workable, would take months to complete. It was time Fuld didn't have.

Of course, the reason Fuld did not have time was because the Fed chose to deny liquidity support to Lehman. Support from the Fed would have given Lehman time to try its strategy. (Instead, on September 29, the LBHI estate sold most of IMD for the fire-sale price of $2 billion.)

A Maiden Lane for Lehman

Lehman could also have shed real estate assets if the Fed had created a special purpose vehicle (SPV) to buy them. The Fed created SPVs to help other firms during the financial crisis: it created Maiden Lane LLC and Maiden Lane II to buy mortgage assets from Bear Stearns and AIG respectively.

Fed officials discussed the possibility of "a Maiden Lane type vehicle" for Lehman during the summer of 2008. On July 15, William Dudley, then head of the Markets Group at the New York Fed (and later its President) circulated a memo titled "Lehman Good Bank / Bad Bank Proposal."[7] Dudley sent the memo to New York Fed colleagues, including President Timothy Geithner, and to officials at the Board of Governors, including Vice Chair Donald Kohn and Governor Kevin Warsh. Dudley described his proposal as "very much in the spirit of what we did with Bear," and summarized it as follows (with the caveat that his numbers were "rough guesses"):

> Separate [Lehman] into two parts:
>   Maiden Lane type vehicle: $60 billion of illiquid assets backstopped by $5 billion of Lehman equity. Fed guarantees financing or finances the $55 billion. Lehman owns this vehicle, so if assets > liabilities upon windup, accrue to Lehman shareholders.

Clean Lehman left. $600 billion of assets, $23 billion of equity. Much less risk, greater liquidity cushion (don't have to finance illiquid assets).

Fed gets equity in clean Lehman (whether warrants or some other form of equity TBD in compensation for backstop financing in SPV).

Dudley's memo goes on to describe the rationale for his proposal:

Why we want to do this. Takes illiquid assets off the market, reduces risk that forced sale of assets will generate losses that make Lehman insolvent. Preserve Lehman franchise value as a going concern. No negative externality to rest of financial system. Moral hazard considerations low given equity dilution. Clean Lehman can be sold or remain a viable concern . . .. No need for distressed sale of the entire company. Can find a medium-term solution.

If Lehman is solvent now, this preserves solvency. If Lehman is, in fact, insolvent now – even in the absence of forced asset sales – this limits degree of insolvency. Risk of not intervening early, Lehman is solvent now, becomes insolvent due to forced asset sales. Benefits of forced sale of firm under duress accrue to buyer, and large negative externalities to the broader market.

Dudley suggests that his plan would be safe for the Fed, noting: "Protections to the Fed. First loss piece, net interest margin on SPV, and equity in clean Lehman." These features of Dudley's plan are similar to protections the Fed received in the rescues of Bear Stearns and AIG. The "first loss piece" refers to the $5 billion of equity that Lehman would contribute to the SPV. This investment would protect the Fed in the same way that JPMorgan Chase's $1 billion subordinated loan to the first Maiden Lane protected the Fed. "Equity in clean Lehman" is similar to the equity in AIG that the government acquired. The "net interest margin" is the gain from the Fed charging the proposed SPV an above-market interest rate, which was also a feature of the AIG deal.

The reaction to Dudley's proposal was lukewarm. His idea was discussed in an FRBNY-Board conference call on July 14, with one participant reporting, "Kohn did not push back very hard on this proposal."[8] President Geithner replied to Dudley's memo with a brief email:[9]

> Pls add something on how we decide what assets to take. And we need a broader framework in which to place this, with high procedural hurdles.

It is not clear whether anyone followed up on these requests. There is no record that Fed officials discussed the SPV proposal between mid-July and Lehman's final week.

It does appear, however, that some version of the proposal was on the table at a late stage in Lehman's crisis. A September 10 email from Mark Van Der Weide of the Board of Governors' Legal Department says the "options laid out by Tim" included "a Fed-assisted BofA acquisition transaction."[10] In this context, "assistance" probably means long-term financing of illiquid assets, which BofA had demanded. The "gameplan" circulated before the September weekend meetings at the New York Fed suggests that the Fed might have helped the private consortium rescue Lehman. The document says, "We should have in mind a maximum number of how much we are willing to finance before the meeting starts."[11]

Since the bankruptcy, Fed officials have said that they might have financed some of Lehman's assets, but only if that action had facilitated an acquisition of the firm. For example, the Valukas Report says:[12]

> [W]hen shown the Liquidity Consortium gameplan document, Geithner confirmed that the FRBNY would have considered extending financing to Lehman, but only if a willing buyer for the firm had surfaced.

Yet Dudley's plan for an SPV did *not* depend on an acquisition of Lehman. Indeed, Dudley presumed that Lehman would remain independent and cited that as an advantage of his plan. He said the plan was "in the spirit of what we did with Bear, but better because less damage to franchise, no forced sale."

The Fed created the first Maiden Lane to facilitate JPMorgan's acquisition of Bear Stearns. However, the purpose of Maiden Lanes II and III, created during AIG's crisis, was to strengthen that firm and help it remain independent. Another Maiden Lane might have helped Lehman remain independent.

New Equity

As discussed earlier, it is unlikely that any institution besides Barclays would have bought all of Lehman Brothers. If Lehman had survived its liquidity crisis, however, it might have found investors to purchase equity stakes in the firm, just as Goldman Sachs and Morgan Stanley raised equity at the height of the financial crisis from Warren Buffett and Mitsubishi respectively.

In June 2008, Lehman raised $6 billion through a public offering of stock. After that, the firm sought investments from more than thirty institutions and wealthy individuals, but all these efforts failed.[13] The last big hope was the Korean Development Bank (KDB), which expressed interest in a $6 billion investment but ended negotiations on September 9. It might seem that, by the time of Lehman's bankruptcy, the firm had exhausted all possibilities for new equity.

However, Lehman's inability to raise equity was due, in part, to its liquidity crisis and bankruptcy risk, which scared off investors. Outcomes might have been different if the Fed had provided liquidity support to stabilize Lehman.

In particular, Fed assistance might have saved the KDB deal. Lehman set deadlines for completing a deal – first September 10 and then September 18 – and KDB ended negotiations in part because it found the deadlines too tight.[14] Presumably Lehman's insistence on a quick deal reflected its acute liquidity crisis. Fed support might have given Lehman and KDB enough time to reach an agreement.

Another potential investor, the Investment Corporation of Dubai (ICD), was deterred by the threat of bankruptcy. On September 9, when Lehman's stock price fell drastically, ICD said it needed a "time out" in negotiations about an investment.[15] Once again, negotiations might have continued if the Fed had stabilized Lehman.

If Lehman had survived past September 14, other investors probably would have emerged. By many accounts, several firms were interested in Lehman during 2008 but ultimately did not invest because Lehman demanded unreasonably high prices for its stock. After September 14, with the firm on the brink of failure, its executives would have softened their bargaining position. Indeed, they were willing to sell the entire firm to Barclays for the fire-sale price of $3 billion.

A Bank Holding Company

Finally, Lehman might have become a bank holding company (BHC). The Fed allowed Goldman Sachs and Morgan Stanley to become BHCs on September 21, and that action appears to have boosted confidence in the firms because it implied greater oversight of their activities by the Fed.

Lehman raised the idea of becoming a BHC with New York Fed officials in July 2008. The officials responded negatively: President Geithner said the idea was "gimmicky," and General Counsel Baxter suggested that markets might react negatively. Lehman never applied formally for BHC status.[16]

POSSIBLE OUTCOME #3: AN ORDERLY WIND DOWN

Even if the Fed had provided liquidity support to Lehman, it is possible that the Barclays deal would not have been consummated, and that the firm could not have survived on its own. In that case, Lehman would eventually have been forced into bankruptcy. Yet even this outcome would have differed significantly from the actual bankruptcy on September 15, because the delay would have provided time for an orderly wind down.

During a wind down, Lehman could have closed out trading positions and sold assets and subsidiaries over time. The firm's prime brokerage customers could have moved their assets elsewhere. Much of the value destruction from the bankruptcy could have been avoided, including the losses to Lehman's estate from fire sales, termination of derivatives, and disruption of investment projects. Given Lehman's solvency or near-solvency before bankruptcy, losses to the firm's creditors might have been minimal. Short-term creditors, such as holders of Lehman's commercial paper, would have been repaid fully during a wind down, and recovery rates for other creditors, including holders of Lehman's long-term debt, would have been higher than the recovery rates in the actual bankruptcy proceedings, which are projected to be well below 50 percent.[17]

In addition, an orderly wind down probably would have reduced the damage to the US financial system from Lehman's failure. There would have been less panic in financial markets after September 15. Lehman would not have defaulted on the commercial paper held by the Reserve Primary Fund, so the run on money market funds and the resulting disruption of credit flows might have been avoided.

An obvious model for a wind down of LBHI was the wind down of LBI that the Fed planned on September 14 (a plan that changed when Barclays purchased most of LBI). General Counsel Baxter told the FCIC that the Fed supported LBI "to enable the broker-dealer to wind down its trading book in an orderly manner – thereby mitigating to some degree the impact of the failure on financial markets and the economy."[18] Support for all of Lehman would have allowed wind downs of other parts of its business, including the trading book of LBIE.

At two points during Lehman's final weekend, its executives began planning for a wind down of the firm. In both cases, the planning was cut short when policymakers decided to pursue a different strategy.

The first of these incidents occurred on the morning of Saturday, September 13, when Lehman executives Alex Kirk and Bart McDade met at the New York Fed with some of the Wall Street CEOs gathered there (specifically, the CEOs of Citigroup, Merrill Lynch, and Morgan Stanley). Kirk describes the meeting in his FCIC interview:[19]

> The topic of discussion was that the government, the Fed, had asked this group of banks to put together a plan on how to wind down Lehman Brothers over a long period of time and what sort of funding would Lehman Brothers need, for what term, etc, how many people, the business plan, effectively ... We were then asked to return and work with our colleagues to put that together.

But that work was quickly aborted, says Kirk:

> When we were on our way from that meeting, we were stopped by Steve Shafran, who was working for Henry Paulson at the time, and we were asked to focus all our efforts on trying to move forward with Barclays as a potential acquirer of the firm.

The other wind down planning occurred on September 14, after the failure of the Barclays deal. The Valukas Report describes what happened under the heading, "Lehman Developed a Plan for an Orderly Liquidation":[20]

> James P. Seery, Jr., Lehman's Global Head of Fixed Income – Loan Business, and others at Lehman then started working on an "orderly" liquidation plan for Lehman. The plan contemplated that it would take six months to effect an orderly unwinding of Lehman's positions. During that time, Lehman would have to continue to employ a substantial number of people, and pay bonuses to keep them. The plan also assumed that the FRBNY would provide financing support through the wind-down process.

Once again, planning for a wind down stopped abruptly. The Valukas Report continues:

> All work on the liquidation plan came to a halt when word circulated that the Government had told Lehman that Lehman would need to file bankruptcy that evening.

10 How Risky Were the Fed's Rescues of Other Firms?

We have seen what Fed policymakers did to ensure Lehman's bankruptcy and how they might instead have rescued the firm. We can get another perspective on policymakers' treatment of Lehman by comparing it to their treatment of other financial institutions that faced liquidity crises during 2008, specifically, Bear Stearns, AIG, Morgan Stanley, and Goldman Sachs. The Fed helped these firms avoid bankruptcy with a mixture of liquidity support and long-term financing of assets.

Why did the Fed choose not to rescue Lehman but to rescue these other firms? Fed officials say that Lehman did not have adequate collateral for the loan it needed and that these other firms did. Because of this difference, a Fed rescue of Lehman would have been risky and illegal but the assistance given to others was safe enough to be legal.

Once again, the available evidence does not support the Fed's position. When the Fed lent to Morgan Stanley and Goldman Sachs, the collateral it accepted was similar to the collateral that Lehman could have pledged for the loan it needed (a range of securities accepted by the Primary Dealer Credit Facility). Therefore, the Fed's loans to Morgan and Goldman were no safer than a loan to Lehman would have been. In lending to AIG and Bear Stearns, it appears, based on the nature of the collateral and other loan terms, that the Fed took on *more* risk than it would have in rescuing Lehman – although we cannot be sure for AIG, because the Fed has refused to give a detailed accounting of AIG's collateral.

Another response of the Fed to the financial crisis was the creation of the Commercial Paper Funding Facility (CPFF) in October 2008. The CPFF bought commercial paper from many corporations at a time when the run on money market funds had disrupted the commercial paper market and made it difficult for firms to obtain working capital. It appears that the Fed's extension of credit under this program, like the Bear Stearns and AIG loans, was riskier than a Lehman rescue would have been. Fed officials have said the CPFF was protected by insurance premiums on the commercial paper it bought, but the argument behind this claim has major flaws.

LIQUIDITY SUPPORT FOR MORGAN STANLEY AND GOLDMAN SACHS

After the Lehman failure, the investment banks Morgan Stanley and Goldman Sachs experienced large losses of liquidity that threatened them with bankruptcy. The Fed kept the two firms in business with loans from the Primary Dealer Credit Facility and the Term Securities Lending Facility; support peaked in late 2008 at $107 billion for Morgan Stanley and $69 billion for Goldman Sachs. Ultimately, these firms survived with the help of their bank-holding-company status, equity injections from both private investors and the Troubled Asset Relief Program, and the general stabilization of the financial system in 2009.

The Fed facilities accepted the same types of collateral from Morgan Stanley and Goldman Sachs that they accepted from LBI after the LBHI bankruptcy. Some of this collateral was low-quality; for example, at the peak of Morgan Stanley's borrowing, about $2 billion of its PDCF collateral were securities rated CCC or lower.[1] If Lehman had faced the same collateral standards and had been given free access to the PDCF (without the restrictions on funding LBIE in London), it could have borrowed enough to avoid bankruptcy.

When the PDCF lent to LBI after the bankruptcy of LBHI, the haircuts set on LBI's collateral were larger than the typical haircuts in the tri-party repo market. By contrast, the PDCF haircuts set for Morgan Stanley and Goldman Sachs on September 14 were *smaller* than the market haircuts for most collateral types. The haircuts for speculative-grade corporate bonds, for example, were 16.7 percent for LBI, 13 percent in the market, and only 6.5 percent for Morgan Stanley and Goldman Sachs.[2]

THE BEAR STEARNS RESCUE

When Bear Stearns experienced its liquidity crisis in March 2008, the Fed first stepped in to help in the early hours of Friday, March 14. The Fed lent Bear $12.9 billion to meet its obligations that day and Bear pledged $13.8 billion of securities as collateral. That arrangement was similar to the Fed's overnight lending to investment banks through the PDCF after that facility opened on March 17.[3]

On Sunday, March 16, the Fed provided a different kind of assistance to Bear by creating Maiden Lane LLC and lending it approximately $29 billion to purchase real estate assets from Bear. Because this transaction appears riskier than the Fed's overnight lending to Bear and others, it deserves closer examination.

The Maiden Lane Deal

The Maiden Lane transaction is described in a June 2008 report prepared for the New York Fed by the accounting firm of Ernst and Young.[4] Maiden Lane purchased $30 billion of assets from Bear, based on Bear's valuations. The assets were selected by agreement of the Fed and JPMorgan Chase. The Fed retained BlackRock Financial Management to manage Maiden Lane's portfolio, instructing BlackRock to sell the Bear assets over time to maximize returns. It took BlackRock about four years to sell all the assets.

The $30 billion paid by Maiden Lane came from a non-recourse loan of $28.8 billion from the Fed and a subordinated loan of $1.2 billion from JPMorgan Chase. Under this arrangement, JPMorgan would absorb the first $1.2 billion of any losses on Maiden Lane's assets, and the Fed would absorb the rest. The interest rate on the Fed's loan was 2.5 percent, which was the discount rate at the time. In June 2012, the Fed reported that its loan had been repaid in full.

According to the Ernst and Young report, the $30 billion of assets purchased by Maiden Lane included $16.8 billion of mortgage-backed securities [MBSs], $8.2 billion of commercial mortgages, $1.6 billion of residential mortgages, and $3.3 billion of credit and interest-rate derivatives. Virtually all the MBSs were investment-grade, and all the mortgages were classified as performing.

In 2010, the New York Fed released a financial statement for Maiden Lane as of December 31, 2008.[5] This statement broke down Maiden Lane's assets by the method used to value them. A total of $11.4 billion of assets were valued based on Level 3 inputs, the most subjective method in the hierarchy of the Financial Standards Accounting Board. Maiden Lane's Level 3 assets included all its holdings of commercial and residential mortgages, and about $2 billion of its mortgage-backed securities.

An Adequate Haircut?

How well-secured was the Fed's loan to Maiden Lane? Under the deal with JPMorgan, the Fed lent $28.8 billion and received a senior claim on $30 billion in assets. Essentially, the Fed lent to Maiden Lane against $30 billion of collateral with a haircut of $1.2 billion, or 4 percent.

This haircut was significantly lower than those for other Fed loans during the financial crisis. The PDCF, which did most of the Fed's lending against mortgage assets, imposed haircuts of 6.5 percent on investment grade MBSs and 8.3 percent on whole mortgages.[6]

Moreover, the indefinite term of the Maiden Lane loan made it substantially riskier than PDCF loans, which were overnight. Haircuts for overnight repos are chosen to cover the costs to cash lenders of liquidating collateral and to protect them from *one-day* changes in collateral values. If collateral depreciates over time, a lender reduces the daily cash it provides to maintain the haircut and avoid losses. In the Maiden Lane deal, by contrast, the Fed's commitment of $28.8 billion left it exposed to the risk of falling collateral values.

In sum, because of its indefinite term, the Maiden Lane loan was riskier than PDCF lending to Lehman would have been even if the haircuts had been the same. The riskiness of the Maiden Lane loan was increased further by the small haircut set by the Fed.

The Performance of the Maiden Lane Portfolio

The previous section assesses the riskiness of the Maiden Lane loan when the Fed made it, based on the terms of the loan. Another perspective on the risk to the Fed comes from examining what actually happened *after* the loan was made.

As the financial crisis worsened, default rates on mortgages rose and Maiden Lane's assets became much riskier. In 2010, the *Financial Times* produced evidence on this point by analyzing a large sample of MBSs from Maiden Lane's portfolio.[7] In April 2008, just after Maiden Lane was created, 93 percent of the MBSs by value were rated AAA, and 99.9 percent were investment grade (BBB or higher). Two years later, only 19 percent were AAA and 28 percent were investment grade. Forty-eight percent were CCC or lower.

As Maiden Lane's assets became riskier, their values were marked down, and the Fed's loan became undercollateralized. The Board of Governors website gives weekly figures for Maiden Lane's assets and for the balance on its loan from the Fed.[8] Total assets first fell below the loan balance on October 22, 2008. The gap between assets and the debt to the Fed peaked at $3.1 billion on May 6, 2009, when assets were $25.7 billion and the debt was $28.8 billion.

Eventually the financial crisis eased, Maiden Lane's assets appreciated, and it fully repaid the Fed's loan in 2012. This outcome does not mean, however, that the loan was safe. The Fed had lost $3.1 billion as of May 2009, and its final loss could have been that much or more if the financial crisis had worsened.

THE AIG RESCUE

At the insurance conglomerate AIG, as at the big investment banks, losses related to real estate produced a collapse of confidence and a liquidity crisis. The Fed first assisted AIG with an $85 billion line of credit on September 16, just one day after the Lehman bankruptcy. In the following months, the Fed took several other actions to stabilize AIG, including additional loans and the creation of Maiden Lane II and Maiden Lane III.[9]

Fed officials have asserted that their lending to AIG, like all their lending under Section 13(3), was well-secured. However, much of AIG's collateral consisted of equity shares in the firm's insurance subsidiaries. These subsidiaries were private companies, which are difficult to value because share prices cannot be observed in financial markets. Fed officials have never presented any evidence on the value of AIG's collateral relative to the credit extended to the firm. Indeed, they explicitly refused to provide estimates of AIG's collateral values to the Fed's Congressional oversight committees, despite a legal mandate to do so.

Under these circumstances, it is difficult to determine the adequacy of AIG's collateral, but there are pieces of evidence that allow an analysis of this issue.

The Details of the September 16 Line of Credit

In the AIG crisis, as with Lehman, the Fed and the Treasury department initially tried to broker a private-sector rescue. A consortium led by JPMorgan Chase and Goldman Sachs met at the New York Fed on September 15 and prepared a term sheet for a $75 billion line of credit for AIG. The fact that the consortium produced such a document shows that the private sector was close to rescuing the firm. On the morning of September 16, however, the consortium members decided not to go through with the deal. By that point, AIG had run out of cash and faced imminent bankruptcy.

On the evening of September 16, the Board of Governors authorized the $85 billion line of credit from the New York Fed to AIG.

The terms were similar to the deal considered by the private-sector consortium, with $10 billion added "as a cushion."[10] The line of credit had a term of two years and an interest rate of LIBOR plus 850 basis points, a rate much higher than the rates the Fed was charging other financial institutions at the time. In addition, AIG was required to give the Treasury department a 79.9 percent equity interest in the firm. (In the private-sector deal, this equity interest would have gone to the consortium of lenders.)

The collateral pledged by AIG was quite different from the collateral pledged to the Fed for other loans it made. Loans from the PDCF and loans to the Maiden Lane facilities, for example, were collateralized by specific securities and whole loans, and the cash provided by the Fed was based on the value of the collateral and on haircuts it deemed prudent. By contrast, when the Fed announced the September 16 loan to AIG, it said simply:

> The loan is collateralized by all the assets of AIG, and of its primary non-regulated subsidiaries. These assets include the stock of substantially all of the regulated subsidiaries.

The "regulated subsidiaries" were primarily insurance companies, such as American Life Insurance Company. Under state insurance laws, AIG could not pledge the assets of these companies, but it could pledge AIG's equity in the companies themselves. On September 16, New York Fed security personnel went to AIG headquarters and took possession of paper stock certificates for the companies.

The exact structure of the AIG deal was complex. Some of AIG's subsidiaries (not the ones whose stock was pledged as collateral) guaranteed its obligation to the Fed. Some assets of these subsidiaries were designated as collateral for the $85 billion loan, and other assets were pledged as collateral for the guarantees.

The Safety of the AIG Loan: Policymakers' 2010 Testimony

In the years following the AIG loan, Fed officials often asserted that the loan was well secured, so there was little risk to the Fed. On this point, as on others, the most detailed discussions appear in the 2010 FCIC testimony of Chairman Bernanke and New York Fed General Counsel Baxter. Both of them emphasized that the loan was collateralized by stock in the insurance companies owned by AIG.

According to Bernanke:[11]

> Unlike Lehman, which was a financial firm whose entire going-concern value was in its financial operations, AIG was the largest insurance company in America. And the Financial Products Division, which got into the trouble, was just one outpost of this very large and valuable insurance company .... So unlike Lehman, which didn't have any going-concern value, or not very much, AIG had a very substantial business, a huge business, more than a trillion dollars in assets and a large insurance business that could be used as collateral to borrow the cash needed to meet Financial Products' liquidity demands. So that's a very big difference. And indeed, the Federal Reserve will absolutely be paid back by AIG.

Later in his testimony, Bernanke reiterates:[12]

> [I]t was our assessment that they had plenty of collateral to repay our loan .... [T]he problems with AIG didn't relate to weaknesses in their insurance businesses, it related very specifically to the losses of the Financial Products Division. The rest of the company was, as far as we could tell, an effective, sound company with a lot of value, and that was the basis on which we made the loan.

In his written FCIC testimony, Baxter supports Bernanke's view:[13]

> Unlike the naked guarantee needed to facilitate the merger of Barclays and Lehman, our committed credit to AIG on September 16, 2008 was fully secured by good collateral, namely, AIG's sound retail insurance businesses. In fact, before any money was disbursed to AIG on September 16, AIG delivered share certificates to the

New York Fed that we continue to hold as collateral in our vaults. These shares fully secured every penny we lent to AIG on September 16, 2008.

The Safety of the AIG Loan: Policymakers' Statements in 2014–2015

More recently, both Timothy Geithner (who did not testify before the FCIC) and Ben Bernanke have discussed the AIG rescue. Both of them discuss AIG in their memoirs, and in their 2014 testimony in *Starr International Co. v. U.S.* The *Starr* case was a lawsuit brought by AIG stockholders claiming that the Fed's terms for the AIG loan were unduly harsh. (In 2017, a federal Appeals Court ruled against the plaintiffs.)

These assessments of the AIG loan are more equivocal than the FCIC testimony of Bernanke and Baxter. Geithner says in his 2014 memoir that AIG's insurance companies were "reasonably solid collateral."[14] In elaborating on this point, he says:

> Those insurance businesses would have a good chance of retaining their value *if their parent company didn't go down* [emphasis added].

This statement suggests implicitly that the AIG loan would not have been well secured if the company had entered bankruptcy.

At one point Geithner says, "I believed we had gotten taxpayers a reasonable deal," but elsewhere he says:[15]

> We would be exposing the Fed to the risk of an imploding insurance company, and there was a real possibility that our loan would simply buy the world time to prepare for a horrific default.

In the *Starr* lawsuit, the plaintiff's counsel challenged Geithner to justify the harsh terms of the AIG loan: the high interest rate and the demand for 80 percent equity in the company. In response, Geithner said:[16]

> I thought we were taking enormous, unprecedented risks, and that there was substantial risk that we would lose billions of dollars, if not tens of billions of dollars.

Geithner also testified, however:

> I also believed that there was a reasonable prospect that over time, over a longer period of time, if we were successful in preventing AIG's failure and if we were successful in averting another global depression, that we had a reasonable chance of recovering our assistance.

In his 2015 memoir, Bernanke restates his 2010 view that AIG had adequate collateral:[17]

> Unlike Lehman, AIG appeared to have sufficiently valuable assets – namely, its domestic and foreign insurance subsidiaries, plus other financial services companies – to serve as collateral and to meet the legal requirement that the loan be "secured to the satisfaction" of the lending Reserve Bank.

At the same time, Bernanke echoes Geithner in citing risk to justify the terms of AIG's loan:

> Tough terms were appropriate. Given our relative unfamiliarity with the company, the difficulty of valuing AIG FP's [Financial Products'] complex derivatives positions, and the extreme conditions we were seeing in financial markets, lending such a large amount inevitably entailed significant risk. Evidently, it was risk that no private-sector firm had been willing to undertake. Taxpayers deserved adequate compensation for bearing that risk. In particular, the requirement that AIG cede a substantial part of its ownership was intended to ensure that taxpayers shared in the gains if the company recovered.

Bernanke also says:[18]

If the loan to AIG helped stabilize financial markets, then AIG's companies and assets would likely retain enough value to help repay the loan over time. But if financial conditions went from bad to worse, driving the economy deeper into recession, then the value of AIG's assets would suffer as well. And, in that case, all bets on being repaid would be off. We had to count on achieving the better outcome.

The tone of these comments differs from Bernanke's FCIC testimony (AIG "had plenty of collateral") and Baxter's (the collateral "fully secured every penny we lent"). Why the difference? One possible factor is the contexts in which statements were made. In their FCIC testimony, Bernanke and Baxter were defending the Fed against charges that the AIG loan was excessively risky, so they had an incentive to minimize the risk. By contrast, in his *Starr* testimony, Geithner was replying to the plaintiff's claim that the Fed had imposed "extortionary" terms on AIG. He needed to emphasize the risks to the Fed to justify the terms. *Starr* may also have influenced the discussions of AIG in Geithner's and Bernanke's memoirs.

The Fed's Opacity about Collateral Values

How well secured was the AIG loan? We could better answer that question if we knew the value of the firm's collateral. Unfortunately, we know little about AIG's collateral, in part because the Fed has resisted requests for information about it.

Under Section 129 of the Emergency Economic Stabilization Act of 2008, the Fed's Board of Governors must report to its Congressional oversight committees each time it invokes its Section 13(3) authority to make a loan. Each report must include a justification for the loan, a description of its terms, and "available information concerning the value of any collateral held with respect to such a loan."

The report for the September 16 loan to AIG says, "the Board does not believe the authorization of the Credit Facility will result in any net cost to taxpayers."[19] The report does *not*, however, provide any information about the value of AIG's collateral, despite the law saying it must do so. Indeed, the report explicitly declines to estimate the collateral's value, based on an unusual argument that doing so could impede repayment of the loan:[20]

> In light of the complexities involved in valuing the extremely broad range of collateral and guarantees securing all advances under the Credit Facility [AIG's line of credit], the Board believes any estimate at this time of the aggregate value that ultimately will or may be received from the sale of collateral or the enforcement of the guarantees in the future would be speculative and could interfere with the goal of maximizing value through the company's global divestiture program and, consequently, the proceeds available to repay the Credit Facility.

In 2012, I submitted a Freedom of Information Act (FOIA) request to the Board of Governors for several documents, including "a list of the specific assets pledged as collateral for the September 2008 loan to AIG and the value of each asset as determined by the Federal Reserve." The Board searched its records and found a document "responsive to the request," but declined to release it. The Board cited Exemption 8 of FOIA, which covers documents related to "the regulation or supervision of financial institutions."

I appealed this decision to federal district court, where I was represented by the Public Citizen Litigation Group.[21] In the course of this litigation, the Board described the document responsive to my FOIA request as follows:

> Spreadsheet listing specific certificated and uncertificated securities and instruments, in particular, stock, promissory notes, and membership interests issued by certain AIG subsidiaries, delivered by AIG to the FRBNY as a portion of the collateral for the FRBNY's extension of up to $85 billion in credit to AIG (the AIG Revolving Credit Facility).

Unfortunately, the judge in the case upheld the Board's decision to withhold this document under Exemption 8.[22]

Evidence on the Security of the September 16 Loan

I have not found an estimate of the value of AIG's collateral in any public source. I have, however, found fragments of evidence concerning the adequacy of the collateral for securing the Fed's $85 billion loan. This evidence is far from conclusive, but it casts doubt on the security of the loan.

The Views of Financial Institutions The consortium led by JPMorgan Chase and Goldman Sachs decided not to lend $75 billion to AIG, even with the high interest rate and equity stake that the Fed received. One possible reason is that consortium members thought AIG's collateral was inadequate.

There is some evidence to support this conjecture. Two official documents report the views of consortium members: a 2009 report of the Special Inspector General for TARP (SIGTARP), and a 2010 report of the Congressional Oversight Panel (COP) for TARP. The SIGTARP report cites "a JPMorgan vice chairman" as reporting:[23]

> The group developed a loan term sheet, but an analysis of AIG's financial condition revealed that liquidity needs exceeded the valuation of the company's assets, thus making the private participants unwilling to fund the transaction.

The COP report says:[24]

> One bank that participated in the private-sector rescue effort told the Panel that the banks also concluded that AIG did not have adequate collateral to support the necessary loan.

Fed officials have disputed these accounts. The SIGTARP report, after relating the view of the JP Morgan executive, continues:

> FRBNY officials told SIGTARP that, in their view, the private participants declined to provide funding not because AIG's assets

were insufficient to meet its needs, but because AIG's liquidity needs quickly mounted in the wake of the Lehman bankruptcy and the other major banks decided they needed to conserve capital to deal with adverse market conditions.

The COP report includes a similar claim by Fed staff.[25] It is difficult to know who is right without more information.

Analysis at the New York Fed It appears that New York Fed staff analyzed the value of AIG's collateral in the days before the loan. On September 14, Assistant Vice President Alejandro LaTorre circulated a memo titled "Pros and Cons of Lending to AIG" to colleagues including President Geithner.[26] Attached to the memo was a presentation about AIG's insurance companies prepared on September 13 by the New York Fed's Bank Supervision Group. In these documents, discussions of AIG's collateral are cryptic, but the tone is negative.

LaTorre's memo lists "pros" of lending to AIG, which include various financial disruptions that would occur if the firm failed, and "cons" including moral hazard and concern that "lending to AIG could be perceived as inconsistent with treatment of Lehman." Point 5 in the list of cons concerns AIG's insurance companies:

5. Assets available from Ins. Co. subs [subsidiaries] may not be sufficient to cover potential liquidity shortfalls as many of the subs do not appear to be sources of strength.

   → Life Ins. Co. subs have significant unrealized losses on investments.
   → P&C [property and casualty] could be source of strength; paid $1.4B dividends, but amounts small relative to size of hole.

The presentation from the Bank Supervision group is titled, "AIG Subsidiaries: Are they a Source of Strength?" The first slide after the title is headed "Ability to support has weakened," and appears to be the source of LaTorre's comments. The slide mentions unrealized losses on investments and says "dividends to parent down sharply overall," giving figures of $4.9 billion for 2007 and $1.4 billion for 2008 year-to-date.

Another slide in the presentation, titled "What happens in a sale?," mentions risks to the solvency of AIG's insurance companies:

> Using a weighted average, all the subsidiaries shocked would wipe out their capital in a liquidation if assets are sold at a 12 percent loss or greater.

Maiden Lanes II and III

Following the September 16 $85 billion loan, the Fed took several other actions to assist AIG. On October 6, it lent $38 billion to the firm through a Securities Borrowing Facility. The Commercial Paper Funding Facility created on October 7 (discussed below) bought $16 billion of AIG's commercial paper. On November 10, the Fed aided AIG by creating Maiden Lane II and Maiden Lane III and lending them $20 billion and $24 billion respectively. The total of all these commitments was $183 billion.[27]

This section focuses on the loans to the two new Maiden Lanes, which helped AIG increase its liquidity and decrease risk. Maiden Lane II bought $21 billion of AIG's illiquid mortgage-backed securities, using the $20 billion loan from the Fed and a $1 billion subordinated loan from AIG. Maiden Lane III bought $29 billion of collateralized debt obligations (CDOs) from counterparties of AIG, using the $24 billion Fed loan and $5 billion from AIG. The purchases by Maiden Lane III allowed AIG to terminate credit default swaps tied to the CDOs, which were risky derivatives positions.

We can interpret these two arrangements, like the first Maiden Lane that assisted Bear Stearns, as long-term loans from the Fed against illiquid collateral. The subordinated loans from AIG were equivalent to haircuts on the collateral: about 5 percent for Maiden Lane II and 17 percent for Maiden Lane III. Despite these haircuts, falling asset prices meant the Fed's loans eventually became under-collateralized when the assets of Maiden Lanes II and III fell below their debts to the Fed. These shortfalls peaked in mid-2009 at $2.1 billion for Maiden Lane II and $2.7 billion for Maiden Lane III.[28]

Once again, however, the assets' prices recovered as the financial crisis eased and the Fed's loans were repaid in full in 2012.

THE COMMERCIAL PAPER FUNDING FACILITY

After the Lehman bankruptcy caused the run on money market funds on September 17–18, US corporations found it difficult to issue commercial paper. To address this problem, the Fed established the Commercial Paper Funding Facility (CPFF) on October 7. In this case (unlike any other credit extension under Section 13(3)), the public record includes a memo from the Board's General Counsel, Scott Alvarez, on the legal justification for the action.[29] The memo argues that lending through the CPFF met the legal requirement for satisfactory security, but once again the reasoning of Fed officials is unsound.

The CPFF borrowed money from the New York Fed and used it to purchase commercial paper from corporations around the country. The purchased commercial paper served as the CPFF's collateral for its loan from the Fed. This arrangement was economically equivalent to direct purchases of commercial paper by the Fed, as Alvarez's memo acknowledges.[30] At the end of 2008, the CPFF owned $335 billion of commercial paper, about 20 percent of all commercial paper issued by US corporations.[31]

The CPFF purchased only commercial paper with the highest rating, A1/P1/F1. That rule was not very restrictive, however, because 90 percent of commercial paper had that rating. In fact, LBHI's commercial paper had that highest rating until its bankruptcy. About a third of the commercial paper bought by the CPFF was asset-backed and the rest was unsecured, and most of the unsecured commercial paper was issued by financial institutions.[32] I focus on the Fed's financing of unsecured commercial paper, which is relatively easy to analyze.

When the CPFF purchased unsecured commercial paper, it required the issuer to pay an "insurance fee," in addition to the interest on the commercial paper. The fee was fixed at 100 basis points per year. For ninety-day commercial paper, the fee was approximately 0.25 percent of the security's face value. General Counsel Alvarez's memo argues that an insurance fee is one acceptable form of security under Section 13(3). It also argues that a 100 basis point fee was adequate to protect the CPFF from losses. I will not question the general point about insurance fees, but the justification for the level of the fee is weak.

The memo says the 100 basis point fee "is designed to be an insurance premium based on historical loss rates for A1/P1/F1 CP." It argues:[33]

> Like an insurance company or fund, these premiums (along with any earnings on the CP in the CPFF SPV [special purpose vehicle]) would serve as a source of funds to repay the CPFF SPV's extension of credit from the Reserve Bank if losses result from the CP. Also, like an insurance company or fund, the pool of premiums would be available to offset <u>any</u> losses, that is, the premium paid by one issuer would be available to offset losses of other issuers, not just losses from the issuer paying the premium. Mutualization of losses is an important and defining characteristic of an insurance company or fund. Moreover, the aggregate premiums retained in the CPFF SPV were computed to cover those expected losses over the expected life of the facility. Historically, the default rate of A1/P1/F1-rated CP is very low.

The flaws in this reasoning are egregious. In October 2008, when the CPFF was established, the level of distress in financial markets was far greater than at any other time since the 1930s. Historical loss rates surely understated the risk on commercial paper, especially commercial paper issued by financial institutions.

In addition, the analogy to mutualization in insurance is inappropriate because of the correlation of risk across different commercial paper issuers. In their 2010 article on commercial paper during the financial crisis, Marcin Kacperczyk and Philipp Schnabl state the obvious: "diversification reduces exposure to idiosyncratic risk but cannot reduce exposure to systematic risk which affects all commercial paper issuers at the same time."[34] A worsening of the financial crisis might have produced defaults on a significant fraction of commercial paper, with losses to the CPFF that greatly exceeded the insurance fees it received.

In justifying the CPFF and the rescues of Bear Stearns and AIG, Fed officials stretched to portray their lending as well secured. They made claims that are not supported by the available evidence, and their economic reasoning was unsound. The loans that officials chose to make carried significant risk, contrary to their denials.

In important respects, officials' actions and arguments in these cases are the opposite of their treatment of Lehman Brothers. The top Fed officials have stretched to make the case that a loan to Lehman could *not* have been well secured, despite clear evidence that this position is wrong. The next two chapters ask why Lehman was treated so differently from other financial institutions, including one (Bear Stearns) that needed a rescue before Lehman did and others (such as AIG) that needed rescues after Lehman did.

11 Who Decided that Lehman Should Fail?

Throughout this book, it has become clear that lack of legal authority was *not* the reason that the Fed let Lehman Brothers fail. If we accept this conclusion, it is natural to ask: What *were* the real reasons for the Fed's decision? To address that question, we must first understand who made the decision.

Under the Federal Reserve Act as it stood in 2008, the authority to lend or not lend to Lehman rested solely with the Federal Reserve. The Board of Governors could have invoked Section 13(3) to authorize a loan from the New York Fed. Alternatively, Lehman probably could have survived if the Fed had merely not acted to limit the firm's access to the PDCF.

Despite these facts, the decision that Lehman should fail was made primarily by Treasury Secretary Henry Paulson, a government official with no legal authority in the matter. From September 12 to 14, Paulson directed the negotiations about Lehman's fate at the New York Fed. He tried to broker an acquisition of Lehman, and when that failed he decided the firm should file for bankruptcy. Fed officials including New York Fed President Geithner followed Paulson's directions, and then reported what was happening to Ben Bernanke in Washington.

Why did Henry Paulson take charge of the Lehman decision, and why did Fed officials let him? We cannot know for sure, but two factors appear relevant. One is that Fed policymakers wanted political support from the Treasury for their controversial actions during the financial crisis. The other is the frequently noted difference in personalities between Henry Paulson and Ben Bernanke, who Geithner, for example, characterizes as "imposing and action-oriented" (Paulson) and "deferential" (Bernanke).[1]

THE FED AND THE TREASURY IN 2008

Secretary Paulson's decisions about Lehman were part of his broader role in Fed policymaking. Paulson was involved to varying degrees in many of the Fed's actions during the financial crisis.

One example is the resolution of the Bear Stearns crisis over the weekend of March 14–16. Several sources give similar accounts of this episode, including Paulson's memoir, Geithner's memoir, and *In Fed We Trust: Ben Bernanke's War on the Great Panic* by journalist David Wessel.[2] The effort to rescue Bear was led by Paulson in Washington and Geithner in New York, who talked repeatedly with each other and with Bear CEO Alan Schwarz and JPMorgan CEO Jamie Dimon. Paulson estimates that he and Geithner had two dozen phone calls over the weekend.

Geithner also talked to Ben Bernanke several times over the weekend to brief him on developments, and ultimately Bernanke approved the plan for the New York Fed to create the Maiden Lane facility and lend it $29 billion. On Sunday, March 16, Bernanke convened the Board of Governors and it voted to authorize the loan under Section 13(3).

Throughout the financial crisis, when Fed officials discussed controversial actions such as the Maiden Lane and AIG loans, they stressed the involvement of the Treasury department. The phrases "with the full support of the Treasury department" and "in close consultation with the Treasury department" became standard language in Fed press releases and in Congressional testimony by Bernanke and others.

An incident from the Bear Stearns crisis illustrates the importance of Treasury support to Fed officials. Geithner told Paulson that the Fed would lend to Maiden Lane only if Treasury indemnified the Fed from any losses on the loan. Paulson replied that Treasury could not do that without Congressional approval, and an argument ensued. Eventually Geithner and Paulson reached a compromise: Paulson wrote a letter expressing support for the loan and noting that any losses would reduce the earnings on Fed assets that the Fed remitted to Treasury.

Why did the Fed want the Treasury's support? One likely factor was a desire to deflect political criticism of the Fed's actions. In his memoir, Geithner acknowledges this motive in discussing Paulson's letter about Maiden Lane: "[W]hile it merely stated fiscal facts, I thought it gave us some cover, implicating Treasury in the risks we were taking."[3]

HENRY PAULSON'S ROLE IN THE LEHMAN CRISIS

During the Lehman crisis, Secretary Paulson was clearly in charge of policy deliberations. This situation contrasts with other phases of the financial crisis, during which he and Geithner were more equal partners. On Lehman's final weekend, Paulson traveled to New York to manage policy at the New York Fed. He announced that Lehman would receive no public assistance, rejecting Geithner's concerns about that policy. On September 14, Paulson decided that Lehman should declare bankruptcy and dictated that decision to Fed officials.

For this part of the analysis of Lehman's final weekend, one important source is Andrew Ross Sorkin's popular book, *Too Big to Fail*. Sorkin's account is based on anonymous sources, but many parts are corroborated by Paulson's and Geithner's memoirs, or by documentary evidence. To my knowledge, nobody has pointed out significant inaccuracies in Sorkin's account of the Lehman crisis.

Before the Final Weekend

After the Bear Stearns crisis in March, policymakers worried that a run on Lehman could drive it into bankruptcy. Paulson tried hard to avert that outcome by brokering an acquisition by a stronger firm. Between March and September, Paulson discussed potential acquisition deals with Lehman CEO Richard Fuld on almost fifty occasions.[4]

During the week of September 8, Paulson negotiated with the CEOs of Bank of America and Barclays, the two firms still interested in Lehman. Both CEOs said they might buy Lehman if the Fed financed some of Lehman's illiquid assets, citing the Bear Stearns precedent. Paulson ruled out such a deal, but suggested that financing might come from a private consortium. He took this position with Fed officials as well.[5]

On Thursday, September 11, Lehman's liquidity crisis was acute. That evening, Paulson participated in a conference call with Geithner, Bernanke, SEC Chair Christopher Cox, and members of their staffs. By all accounts, Paulson stated forcefully that Lehman would receive no public assistance. Paulson himself says:[6]

> [R]ealizing that I was speaking to a large group, I again emphasized that there would be no public assistance for a Lehman bailout and that we would be looking to the private sector to help the buyer complete the acquisition.

Geithner relates:[7]

> By Thursday night, when Hank [Paulson] forcefully repeated his no-public-money stand during a conference call with Ben and SEC Chairman Chris Cox, I began to worry that he actually meant it. He declared that he didn't want to be known as "Mr. Bailout," that he couldn't support another Bear Stearns solution. I could hear the influence of his political advisers, who had been trying to steer Hank away from supporting any Fed role, urging him not to let me talk him into another Bear.

Sorkin also quotes Paulson as insisting, "I can't be Mr. Bailout."[8] Sorkin adds, "Geithner was a bit hesitant about taking such a severe stance in public," but "he quickly fell in line." The policymakers agreed to convene a meeting of Wall Street CEOs the next evening. "In the meantime, Paulson instructed them, the message should be clear: *No bailouts.*"

In all these accounts, Paulson unequivocally dictates policy about Fed lending. He "instructs" Fed officials, and it seems they accept his instructions with little debate. Geithner's suggestion that he might "talk [Paulson] into another Bear" implies that the Fed needed Paulson's approval to assist Lehman.

Sorkin describes an incident on Friday, September 12 that also suggests Paulson was in charge. Geithner had a conversation with Rodgin Cohen, an attorney advising Lehman:[9]

> "I don't think this deal can get done without government assistance," Cohen stressed to Geithner. "They [Bank of America] may be bluffing us, and they may be bluffing you. But we can't afford to call that bluff."
>
> Geithner, who had expressed similar worries to Paulson the day before but had been told to stand down, was succinct in his response: "You can't count on government assistance."

On Thursday night, Paulson told his press secretary, Michele Davis, to leak his position to the press. A typical headline on Friday morning (this one from Bloomberg News[10]) was "Paulson Adamant No Money for Lehman."[11]

September 12–13

On Friday, September 12, Paulson discussed the Lehman crisis at breakfast with Ben Bernanke, and then flew from Washington to New York. Traveling from the airport to the Fed, Paulson discussed possible deals on the phone with Geithner, Lehman CEO Fuld, and Bank of America CEO Kenneth Lewis.[12]

On Friday evening, Paulson opened the meeting of Wall Street CEOs at the Fed, and immediately ruled out Fed assistance for Lehman. General Counsel Thomas Baxter told the FCIC, "Secretary Paulson opened the meeting with a short and plain declaration that there would be no public money to support Lehman."[13] Wessel quotes Paulson as saying, "We did the last one [Bear Stearns]. You're doing this one."[14] Geithner and Sorkin give similar accounts of Paulson's remarks.

Paulson then turned the meeting over to President Geithner, who says, "I echoed [Paulson's] no-public-money stance."[15] Geithner divided the CEOs into three groups and assigned them to analyze different aspects of Lehman's crisis.[16]

On Saturday, September 13, Paulson was at the New York Fed from about 7:00 AM to 9:00 PM. He negotiated with Barclays and Bank of America, Lehman CEO Fuld, and the Wall Street CEOs gathered at the Fed.[17] Geithner joined Paulson in some but not all of these discussions. By the end of the day, there was a tentative deal for Barclays to purchase Lehman, but leave behind some illiquid assets that the Wall Street consortium would finance. Paulson left the Fed feeling "optimistic about the prospects for a deal."[18]

September 14–15

On the morning of Sunday, September 14, Geithner and SEC Chair Cox spoke on the phone with Callum McCarthy, the head of the UK Financial Services Authority (FSA). McCarthy said that the FSA would not allow Barclays to guarantee Lehman's obligations without a shareholder vote, and it was that requirement that derailed the Barclays acquisition. At about 11:00 AM, Paulson called Alistair Darling, the United Kingdom's Chancellor of the Exchequer, and asked him to overrule McCarthy. Darling said no.[19]

After that conversation, Paulson reports, he told Geithner, "Darling's not going to help. It's over." According to Sorkin, Geithner replied, "Okay, let's go to Plan B," which was bankruptcy.[20]

Paulson and Geithner told the CEOs at the Fed that the Barclays deal was off and that they should prepare for Lehman's bankruptcy. Paulson called Lehman CEO Fuld and told him, "Dick, I feel terrible. We've come up with no options."[21] Lehman's executives and lawyers were summoned to the meeting at which General Counsel Baxter told them to file for bankruptcy. It is not clear who planned that meeting and gave instructions to Baxter.

On Sunday afternoon, Lehman executives learned of the expansion of PDCF collateral, and initially thought that action might save their firm.[22] Sorkin reports Paulson's reaction to the PDCF expansion:[23]

"Lehman's got to file immediately," Paulson, leaning back in his chair, instructed Geithner and Cox. He made it clear that he didn't want Lehman adding to the uncertainty in the marketplace by dragging the situation out any longer.

Paulson had another reason for insisting that Lehman file: If the Fed was going to open its discount window even wider to the remaining broker-dealers, he didn't intend that Lehman be granted that access; doing so would represent another opportunity for moral hazard.

By this account, Paulson was behind the decision to limit Lehman's access to the PDCF, which ensured its bankruptcy. Once again, Paulson "instructs" other policymakers and "insists" on his position.

On Sunday evening September 14, Paulson pushed SEC Chair Cox to call Lehman's board of directors and tell them to file for bankruptcy. (This part of the story is described in more detail later in this chapter.)

On Monday, September 15, after Lehman filed, Paulson returned to Washington and held a news conference at the White House. He took responsibility for letting Lehman fail, saying, "I never once considered it appropriate to put taxpayer money on the line in resolving Lehman Brothers."[24]

Paulson and the White House

Because Paulson was an official in President George W. Bush's administration, it is natural to suppose that he acted in consultation with the President or senior White House staff, and some fragments of evidence support this conjecture. One piece of evidence is an email from Paulson's chief of staff, Jim Wilkinson, who accompanied Paulson to New York. Wilkinson wrote to an executive at JPMorgan Chase at 9:00 AM on Sunday, September 14, after learning of the FSA's objection to the Barclays deal:[25]

> No way govt money is coming in ... I'm here writing the usg coms [United States government communications] plan for orderly unwind ... also just did a call with the WH [White House] and usg is

united behind no money. No way in hell paulson could blink now ... [ellipses in original]

Paulson says that he called Josh Bolten, President Bush's chief of staff, to report the problem with the FSA:[26]

"You've got Presidential approval to settle on a wind-down that doesn't commit federal resources," Josh told me. "Anything else, you should come back to the president and tell him what you're planning."

BEN BERNANKE'S ROLE IN THE LEHMAN CRISIS

After Chairman Bernanke and Secretary Paulson had breakfast on Friday, September 12, Paulson left for New York and Bernanke spent most of the weekend in his Washington office. In his memoir, Bernanke says, "We used frequent conference calls to keep the Treasury, the Fed, and the SEC on the same page."[27] Here I review the evidence on Bernanke's communications with the policymakers in New York.

My sources are accounts of Lehman's final weekend from the FCIC, Sorkin, and the memoirs of Bernanke, Geithner, and Paulson. According to these sources, Geithner spoke to Bernanke at several points, mostly to report developments after the fact. As far as I can tell, Bernanke did not talk directly to Paulson between the Friday breakfast and 5:00 PM on Sunday, well after Lehman's fate was sealed.

A Fed Governor, Kevin Warsh, spent the weekend at the New York Fed. Some accounts, such as Wessel's, portray Warsh as Bernanke's representative, but it does not appear that Warsh had an important role in policy deliberations about Lehman. In addition, there is little evidence of communication between Warsh and Bernanke.

Bernanke's Communications with Geithner and Paulson

I have looked for evidence of communications between Bernanke and either Geithner or Paulson in the memoirs of the three men; in the 76 pages on the September 12–14 weekend in Sorkin's book; and in the Lehman Chronology prepared by the FCIC.[28] These sources report the following handful of phone calls. It is possible that other communications occurred, but it seems unlikely that all of the sources would leave out something important.

- Bernanke says that he received "discouraging reports" from Geithner on Friday evening and/or Saturday morning.[29] Geithner reported that Bank of America, Barclays, and the consortium at the New York Fed all believed that Lehman had significantly overvalued some of its assets. Bank of America and Barclays were demanding government assistance for a Lehman deal.
- At 7:00 PM on Saturday, Bernanke and Geithner participated in a conference call with others at the New York Fed and the Board of Governors. According to an email from Bernanke before the call, the agenda included a "briefing/update on Lehman."[30] Nobody reports the details of this briefing. At the time of the call, policymakers were optimistic that Barclays would acquire Lehman.
- On Sunday morning, Geithner called Bernanke to report the failure of the Barclays deal and the plan for Lehman to file for bankruptcy. In Sorkin's narrative, Paulson and Geithner announce the bankruptcy plan to the Wall Street executives at the Fed, and later Geithner leaves Paulson "to brief Bernanke."[31] Bernanke says, "A call from Tim dashed my remaining hopes" for rescuing Lehman. He goes on to say, "It seemed the next step would be to prepare for a bankruptcy."[32]

  In the same call, says Bernanke, he raised the possibility of Fed assistance to Lehman, and Geithner rejected the idea:

  > I asked Tim whether it would work for us to lend to Lehman on the broadest possible collateral to try to keep the firm afloat. "No," Tim said. "We would only be lending into an unstoppable run" …. I pressed Tim for an alternative solution, but he had none.

- Around 5:00 PM on Sunday, Bernanke participated in a conference call with Geithner, Paulson, and others. This call occurred well after the decision that Lehman must declare bankruptcy, which policymakers originally planned to announce at 4:30. Paulson says, "We reviewed the day's dreadful events" and discussed efforts to contain the damage from the bankruptcy.[33]

Bernanke and Warsh

Fed Governor Kevin Warsh spent the September 12–14 weekend at the New York Fed. In describing Bernanke's plans for the weekend, Wessel says, "His immediate interests in New York would be represented by his lieutenant, Kevin Warsh."[34] This statement suggests that Bernanke influenced policy through Warsh, but it appears that did not actually happen, for two reasons.

First, there is no evidence that Warsh had a significant role in the decision making about Lehman at the New York Fed. He is not mentioned anywhere in Sorkin's or Geithner's accounts of the weekend. Paulson mentions Warsh only as a participant in the Sunday afternoon conference call with Bernanke and others.

Second, there is little evidence of communication between Bernanke and Warsh. Bernanke does not mention Warsh in his account of the weekend, beyond saying at the beginning that "Paulson, Geithner, [SEC Chair] Cox, and Kevin Warsh were in New York for the negotiations."[35] Besides the one conference call, the only documented interactions between Bernanke and Warsh were two emails on Sunday afternoon, after the bankruptcy plan was set.[36]

The first email was sent by Bernanke at 2:55 PM on Sunday. It was addressed to Warsh, General Counsel Scott Alvarez, Vice Chair Kohn, and Brian Madigan, Director of the Board's Division of Monetary Affairs. The message says in its entirety:

> Anything new, Kevin?
>
> Brian, Scott: Any more details on PDCF collateral, 23A details?

(Bernanke's question for Brian and Scott concerns measures to support the tri-party repo market after Lehman's failure.)

The public record does not include any direct response from Warsh to Bernanke's email. However, Bernanke heard from Warsh indirectly in an email from Vice Chair Kohn. At 3:03 PM, Kohn wrote:[37]

> Just talked to Kevin. LEH heard about the pdcf enlargement and thought it was a lifeline, but they didn't understand it was limited to triparty. KW thinks everything's on track for 430ish. SEC will go first announcing Chapt 11 for holding company. I haven't seen any details.

Bernanke sent his second email to Warsh at 4:55 PM. It said:

> Anything to report?
>
> In case I am asked: How much capital injection would have been needed to keep LEH alive as a going concern? I gather $12B or so from the private guys together with Fed liquidity support was not enough.

Bernanke's reference to a $12 billion capital injection is puzzling because such a plan was not the focus of negotiations at the New York Fed. Rather, the private consortium agreed to lend $40 billion against Lehman's illiquid assets to facilitate a Barclays acquisition.

WHY WAS PAULSON IN CHARGE?

As it stood in 2008, the Federal Reserve Act gave the Fed sole authority over its lending under Section 13(3). Legally, the Treasury Secretary had no role in approving Fed loans. Bernanke acknowledges this fact at one point in his memoir. In discussing Paulson's "no government money" position, Bernanke says:[38]

> Hank's statements were to some extent beside the point, in that Fed loans were the only government funds available. It would have been the Federal Reserve's decision – not Hank's or the Treasury Department's – whether to make a loan, had a loan of sufficient size to save the firm been judged feasible.

Geithner makes a similar comment about Paulson's opposition to rescuing Lehman: "This wasn't really Hank's decision; he couldn't tell the Fed how to use its authority."[39]

Yet, in the end, Paulson *did* tell Fed officials what to do. Why did he take charge of policy toward Lehman? And why did Fed Chair Bernanke let Paulson take charge?

Presumably one factor was the desire of Fed officials for Paulson's political support. Yet political pressures may not fully explain Paulson's and Bernanke's roles in the Lehman episode. We cannot know the inner motivations of the two men, but their basic personalities are a likely factor in how things played out that weekend. By many accounts, Paulson is a highly assertive person who often tells others what to do, and Bernanke is not. Based on these traits, we would expect Paulson to take charge in a crisis.

Many journalists and economists have described the personalities of Paulson and Bernanke, often in colorful terms. Wessel says that Paulson "had a tendency to talk more than listen." Sorkin notes Paulson's "bulldog tenacity" and mentions that he played tackle on the Dartmouth football team, "where his ferociousness in playing earned him the nicknames 'The Hammer' and 'Hammering Hank'."[40]

In contrast, as I document in a 2016 article, people typically describe Bernanke with words such as "modest," "unassuming," "shy," "introverted," "quiet," and "a nerd."[41] In naming Bernanke its 2009 Man of the Year, *Time* magazine said "he does not have a commanding presence." In 2014, Binyamin Appelbaum of the *New York Times* reported that Bernanke "did not push forcefully" for policies he supported in FOMC meetings.[42]

Several people have explicitly compared the personalities of Paulson and Bernanke. Adam Davidson of National Public Radio says:[43]

> It's easy to contrast the two men, Henry Paulson and Ben Bernanke, this kind of headstrong, tall, bold bulldog in Henry Paulson and the much softer, quieter, bookish Bernanke.

Alan Blinder, Bernanke's former colleague at Princeton, says:[44]

> [T]he chairman of the Fed had come from the cloistered halls of
> academia. But Paulson had been the head of Goldman Sachs,
> a lion of Wall Street, a King of the Universe, a man who had spent
> his entire adult life in the rough-and-tumble of the financial
> world. (He collected birds of prey as a hobby, which, some people
> claimed, told you something.)

Finally, Geithner says:[45]

> Hank was a bullet-headed former Goldman investment banker and
> CEO, as imposing and action-oriented as Ben was deferential and
> measured.

Sorkin's book relates an incident involving Paulson and SEC
Chairman Cox that illustrates Paulson's personality.[46] On the afternoon of September 14, Paulson told Cox to call Lehman's executives
and tell them to file for bankruptcy. Several hours later he learned that
Cox had not made the call, and Sorkin reports:

> After barging in and slamming the door, Paulson shouted, "What
> the hell are you doing? Why haven't you called them?"
>   Cox, who was clearly reticent about using his position in
> government to direct a company to file for bankruptcy, sheepishly
> offered that he wasn't certain if it was appropriate for him to make
> such a call.
>   "You guys are like the gang that can't shoot straight!" Paulson
> bellowed. "This is your fucking *job*. You have to make the phone
> call."

Geithner confirms that Paulson "yelled at Cox to pick up the
phone and get Lehman to move," and he also quotes the put-down
about "the gang that can't shoot straight."[47] Cox called Lehman's
board of directors shortly after this conversation.[48]

As Treasury Secretary, Paulson had no more legal authority over the SEC Chair than he had over the Fed, but he bullied Cox into following his orders. There is no account of Paulson treating Fed officials as harshly as he treated Cox. On the other hand, there are no recorded incidents in which Fed officials failed to promptly follow Paulson's instructions, as Cox did.

12 Explaining the Lehman Decision

Why didn't the Fed rescue Lehman? As we have seen again and again, the reasons given by Fed officials – inadequate collateral and lack of legal authority – are not credible. We are left, therefore, to speculate about the real reasons.

In my reading of the evidence, there are two likely factors. The first, which many others have suggested, is politics. Henry Paulson, who made the Lehman decision, feared the political firestorm that would have followed a rescue of the firm.

The second factor is that policymakers thought, or at least hoped, that Lehman's bankruptcy would not severely damage the financial system. This factor helps explain why Paulson put political considerations first, and why Fed officials did not push back against Paulson's decision.

After the fact, policymakers have said that they knew Lehman's failure would be a "catastrophe," a "calamity," a "nightmare," and "an epic disaster." But once again, the real-time record does not support the policymakers' claims.

FEAR OF POLITICAL BACKLASH

The "bailouts" of 2008 produced virulent criticism from politicians, economists, the media, and the American public, and there is evidence that this criticism influenced the decision to let Lehman fail.

The Reaction to Bear Stearns, Fannie Mae, and Freddie Mac

The Bear Stearns rescue in March provoked criticism from across the political spectrum. As Sorkin puts it, "attacking the rescue plan was one of the few completely bipartisan affairs."[1] Liberal Congressman Barney Frank said the government had paid "ransom" to financial institutions. Conservative Senator Jim Bunning said the rescue was "socialism."

Former Fed officials also questioned the rescue. Paul Volcker called it "a direct transfer of mortgages and mortgage-backed securities of questionable pedigree from an investment bank to the Federal Reserve," which took the Fed to "the very edge of its lawful and implied powers."[2]

Stinging criticism also came from an old friend of Fed officials: Vincent Reinhart, who had retired in 2007 as Director of the Board's Division of Monetary Affairs. In a speech at the American Enterprise Institute on April 28, 2008, Reinhart called the Bear rescue the "worst policy mistake in a generation," comparable to the Fed's mistakes during the 1930s Depression and the 1970s Great Inflation. The rescue, said Reinhart, "eliminated forever the possibility the Fed could serve as an honest broker" in future financial crises.[3]

Timothy Geithner describes the reaction to the Bear rescue and says, "it was jarring to be a target myself, with critics questioning not just my choices but my motives."[4]

On September 7, the government took over the Federal National Mortgage Association (Fannie Mae) and the Federal Home Loan Mortgage Corporation (Freddie Mac). Geithner says:[5]

> The reaction to Fannie and Freddie quickly made the backlash over Bear look mild. Senator Bunning, who had said the Bear deal's assault on free enterprise made him feel like he lived in France, now said he felt like he lived in China. Senator Obama and the Republican presidential nominee, John McCain, both expressed outrage about public rescues of private firms . . .

Media Coverage of the Lehman Crisis

During the week of September 8, the Lehman crisis replaced Fannie and Freddie as the top story in the financial news. The media reported intensively on the search for an acquirer, Paulson's no-public-money declaration, and the gathering of Wall Street CEOs at the New York

Fed. On September 13, the *Financial Times* reported that "Lehman Brothers is facing a weekend of desperate negotiations," with a headline saying, "solution sought before opening of markets" on September 15.[6] Paulson confirms that the press "was expecting a big announcement on Lehman before the Asian markets opened."[7]

Journalists expressed strong opposition to a public rescue of Lehman. Bernanke mentions two examples in his memoir:[8] the *Financial Times's* declaration that, after the Fannie and Freddie actions, "further such rescues should be avoided like the plague;" and the *Wall Street Journal's* view that a Lehman rescue would imply "a new de facto federal policy of underwriting Wall Street that will encourage even more reckless risk-taking."

The media presented the policy issue as a dichotomous choice between a Lehman bankruptcy and a "bailout." On September 12, the *Journal* asked, "Should the U.S. government let a big institution fail rather than stage another potentially costly bailout?"[9] When LBHI filed for bankruptcy, the media reported that policymakers had chosen the failure option, with the *Journal* saying, "the government had to draw a line somewhere."[10]

On September 14–15, the Fed responded to the Lehman crisis by lending $28 billion to Lehman's subsidiary LBI and greatly expanding its lending to other investment banks through the Primary Dealer Credit Facility. Yet these actions received little attention as the media focused on the LBHI bankruptcy filing.

The Influence of Politics on Paulson

Treasury Secretary Paulson decided that the Federal Reserve would not rescue Lehman. Was he influenced by the political opposition to bailouts? Several pieces of evidence suggest that he was.

Perhaps the most striking evidence is the "Mr. Bailout" remark in Paulson's September 11 call with Bernanke and Geithner. David Wessel's *In Fed We Trust* quotes Paulson as saying, "I'm being called Mr. Bailout. I can't do it again." Sorkin and Geithner (who was on the call) also report versions of this statement. Paulson does not report that he used the phrase "Mr. Bailout," but he does say, "I emphasized that there would be no public assistance for a Lehman bailout."[11]

Sorkin's book contains other relevant vignettes. One occurs at a meeting at the Board of Governors on September 9, two days after the Fannie Mae and Freddie Mac takeovers. During this meeting, Ben Bernanke comments on Paulson:[12]

> "The negative publicity is really getting to him," Bernanke acknowledged of Paulson, who had spoken to him yesterday morning and gotten an earful about the press coverage.

Political criticism also comes up in Paulson's September 12 remarks to the Wall Street CEOs at the New York Fed:[13]

> "There's no consensus for the government to get involved; there is no will to do this in Congress," [Paulson] said, stammering and stuttering at one point about how Nancy Pelosi had been all over him about bailouts.

The FCIC published a brief but telling email from Jim Wilkinson, Paulson's Chief of Staff, to his Press Secretary Michele Davis on September 9:[14] "I just can't stomach us bailing out lehman. Will be horrible in the press don't u think?" It is reasonable to suppose that Wilkinson's sentiment reflected Paulson's thinking, or at least influenced it.

EXPECTATIONS ABOUT THE COSTS OF LEHMAN'S FAILURE

Some commentators suggest that policymakers let Lehman fail in part because they underestimated the consequences. David Wessel, for example, says of Bernanke and Paulson:[15]

> Had they realized how much damage Lehman's bankruptcy would wreak, they might have had [another] option ready, one that showed some of the same creativity they exercised at other points in the crisis . . ..

To understand policymakers' expectations about the effects of Lehman's failure, we need to examine two types of information: retrospective accounts in which policymakers say what they expected, and the real-time evidence, which tells a different story.

Policymakers' Statements after the Bankruptcy

Ben Bernanke first addressed the Lehman bankruptcy in Congressional testimony eight days later. He downplayed the bankruptcy's effects, saying "investors and counterparties had had time to take precautionary measures." But Bernanke soon backed away from this testimony, and told the FCIC in 2010, "I regret not being more straightforward there."[16]

Except for that initial testimony, Bernanke has said consistently that he knew the effects of Lehman's failure would be dire. In his 2009 interview with the FCIC, Bernanke says:[17]

> We knew – we were very sure that the collapse of Lehman would be catastrophic. We never had any doubt about that.

Bernanke lists some effects that policymakers expected, including "huge impacts on funding markets" and "a huge loss of confidence in other financial firms." He then reiterates:

> So there was never any doubt in our minds that it would be a calamity, catastrophe, and that we should do everything we could to save it.

In his 2010 testimony to the FCIC, Bernanke says:[18]

> [L]et me just state this as unequivocally as I can. As you know, before I came to the Fed Chairmanship I was an academic, and I studied for many years the Great Depression, financial crises, and this is my bread and butter. And I believed deeply that if Lehman was allowed to fail, or did fail, that the consequences for the U.S. financial system and the U.S. economy would be catastrophic.

In his 2015 memoir, Bernanke describes his reaction when Geithner told him that Lehman would fail:[19]

> It was a terrible, almost surreal moment. We were staring into the abyss .... "All we can do," Tim said, in a classic Geithner-ism, "is put foam on the runway." The phrase itself conveyed what we all knew: Lehman's collapse, like the crash landing of a jumbo jet, would be an epic disaster, and, while we should do whatever we could, there wasn't much we could do.

Paulson and Geithner also say in their memoirs that they expected severe damage from Lehman's failure. Paulson says he "worked hard for months to ward off the nightmare we foresaw with Lehman." Geithner quotes himself as telling Bernanke, "It's going to be a calamity."[20]

However, not every official claims that the Fed foresaw a calamity. Board General Counsel Scott Alvarez gives a different account in his interview with FCIC staff in July 2010. An interviewer asks, "What did you see those downsides as being if you pulled the plug on Lehman?" Alvarez says in part:[21]

> When Bear Stearns fell, that was unexpected, really unexpected ... but once Bear Stearns did collapse and got sold off, the market was more attentive and they were looking at Lehman as the next one to fail ... The market had signs that they should protect themselves from Lehman ... [T]here was a lot more preparation, the market had an opportunity to shield itself, and I think we thought that the market was preparing itself better. And then when Lehman failed, it really did send reverberations throughout the market that were greater than I think we expected.

The statement that policymakers thought "the market had an opportunity to shield itself" is similar to Bernanke's initial testimony about Lehman in 2008. The difference is, Alvarez gave this account in 2010, after Bernanke had settled on a different story.

Real-Time Evidence

Several sources help us understand policymakers' expectations about the Lehman failure. In my reading of the evidence, Fed officials were uncertain about how this unprecedented event would affect the economy. They saw risks, but also expressed hope that the effects would be contained. They were *not* sure that the bankruptcy would be catastrophic.

Bernanke and Paulson on September 12 One bit of evidence comes from Henry Paulson's memoir.[22] Paulson describes his meeting with Ben Bernanke on the morning of Friday, September 12, and quotes Bernanke as saying, "We can only *hope* that if Lehman goes, the market will have had a lot of time to prepare for it." (Emphasis added.) If this quote is accurate, Bernanke's attitude was somewhere between confidence that markets were prepared, which he suggested in his September 23 testimony, and certainty of disaster.

After their meeting, Bernanke and Paulson had a conference call with their staffs and SEC Chair Cox. Wessel summarizes the discussion:[23]

> Paulson and Bernanke assured each other – and the others on the call – that all the companies and traders that did business with Lehman had been given time to protect themselves from a possible Lehman bankruptcy. They comforted themselves that, since the Bear Stearns bailout, the Fed had found new ways to lend to other investment houses that might be hurt by a Lehman collapse.

Wessel's report that Bernanke and Paulson "assured each other" and "comforted themselves" suggests, again, that policymakers were uncertain of the effects of a Lehman failure and hoped for the best.

The September 14 Meeting at the New York Fed Another bit of evidence comes from the meeting at which General Counsel Baxter told Lehman executives to file for bankruptcy. Challenged to defend this decision, Baxter and Alan Beller, a lawyer representing the SEC, expressed optimism about limiting the damage from the bankruptcy. Their view was based on actions the Fed was taking, including the PDCF expansion and support for LBI, and the good news that Bank of America was buying Merrill Lynch.

Similar accounts appear in Sorkin and in the FCIC testimony of Harvey Miller, Lehman's bankruptcy attorney.[24] According to Sorkin, when Miller said the bankruptcy would have dire effects, Beller replied, "We have a program to calm the markets." Baxter reiterated, "We have a program." When Miller continued to object, Beller said, "Look, we will have a series of [press] releases that we are fairly confident will calm the markets tomorrow."

The September 16 FOMC Meeting The Federal Open Market Committee held a regularly scheduled meeting on the morning of Tuesday, September 16, within the brief period between the Lehman bankruptcy on Monday, the 15th, and the AIG rescue on Tuesday evening. The transcript was released in 2014. Meeting participants included three people who were present at the New York Fed over the previous weekend: Governor Warsh, William Dudley, the head of the New York Fed's Markets Group, and Christine Cummings, the New York Fed's First Vice President.

Most of the meeting was a normal FOMC discussion of the prospects for growth and inflation, and of the federal funds rate target. There was also a broad discussion of "strains in financial markets," with general agreement that the effects were uncertain. When people mentioned Lehman Brothers, it was usually to praise the decision to let it fail. All in all, it does not seem that anyone thought that the bankruptcy was a calamity.

The following highlights of the meeting indicate that policy-makers did not think the Lehman failure would have catastrophic effects on the financial system or economy:

- Chairman Bernanke opens the meeting by saying:[25]

The markets are continuing to experience very significant stresses this morning, and there are increasing concerns about the insurance company AIG.

Bernanke also reports, "there are very significant problems with dollar funding in other jurisdictions – in Europe and elsewhere," and says he will propose currency swap lines. He does not mention Lehman Brothers.

- Dudley, in his capacity as Open Market Manager, briefs the Committee on developments in financial markets.[26] He discusses the Lehman failure along with a number of other topics. He notes several effects of the bankruptcy: "intensified pressure on Morgan Stanley and Goldman Sachs," including decreases in their share prices; withdrawals from money market funds; and disruptions in trading by LBI (despite the fact that LBI was still in business). Dudley does not discuss how the bankruptcy will affect the overall financial system or economy.
- Three Fed Presidents praise the decision to let Lehman fail: James Bullard of St. Louis, Jeffrey Lacker of Richmond, and Thomas Hoenig of Kansas City. Hoenig, for example, says:[27]

  > I think what we did with Lehman was the right thing because we did have a market beginning to play the Treasury and us, and that has some pretty negative consequences as well, which we are now coming to grips with.

  Only one person questions this view, President Eric Rosengren of Boston. He says, "I think it's too soon to know whether what we did with Lehman is right."[28]

- Governor Warsh discusses the Fed's responses to the Lehman failure, such as the PDCF expansion. His assessment is fairly upbeat:[29]

  > I think the work that was done over the past few days on Lehman Brothers should make us feel good in one respect. Market functioning seems to be working okay – by which I mean that the plumbing around their role in the tri-party repo business, due in part to the Fed's actions, seems to be working. It's ugly. The backroom offices of these places are going crazy. There's a lot of manual work being done. So they wouldn't give it high marks. But it looks as though positions are

being sorted out in a tough workmanlike way, and so that's encouraging.

Warsh also downplays the importance of the Lehman failure relative to the problems at AIG:

> Other than the CDS [credit default swap] moves and the equity moves on the other broker-dealers, Goldman Sachs and Morgan Stanley, I don't think that [the Lehman bankruptcy] is the real specter that's casting some question over broader financial institutions. I think the Lehman situation, no matter what judgment we made this past weekend about whether or not to provide official-sector money, is not what is driving markets broadly outside of the investment banks. What's driving the broader uncertainty are questions about institutions like AIG that were rated AAA, that were so strong that counterparties didn't need collateral, and that were a certain bet to be a guarantor around stable value funds and all sorts of other products.

- At the end of the meeting, Bernanke summarizes the discussion and adds his assessment of inflation and the real economy. He also discusses financial stresses:[30]

> Conditions clearly have worsened recently, despite the rescue of the GSEs [Fannie Mae and Freddie Mac], the latest stressor being the bankruptcy of Lehman Brothers and other factors such as AIG.

Bernanke mentions a number of problems, including tight credit conditions and difficulties in raising capital for financial institutions. Yet his conclusion is uncertain:

> [T]he medium-term implications of the recent increases in financial stress for the economy are difficult to assess. We may have to wait for some time to get greater clarity on the implications of the last week or so.

- Bernanke recommends no change in the federal funds rate target of 2%, and the Committee approves unanimously. In the statement accompanying its decision, the Committee gives equal weight to "the downside risks to growth" and "the upside risks to inflation."[31]

THE FED'S SHIFT ON AIG

To understand the Lehman episode fully, we must understand why policymakers abandoned their no-bailout position on September 16, only a day and a half after Lehman's bankruptcy, to rescue AIG. The explanation that AIG had better collateral than Lehman is not credible. It is challenging to discern policymakers' motives, but the available evidence points to some reasons for their actions.

Paulson and Geithner initially opposed an AIG rescue. It appears that they maintained this position until September 16, when they changed their minds. What caused this change?

Two factors appear relevant. First, policymakers decided that an AIG bankruptcy would be disastrous for the economy, in part from studying the firm and in part from observing the immediate aftermath of the Lehman bankruptcy. Second, as many commentators suggest, the chaos following the bankruptcy made it somewhat easier to justify an AIG rescue to politicians. Because of these two developments, fear of economic disaster trumped fear of political criticism when policymakers decided what to do about AIG.

The Last-Minute Change in Policy

Until the very end, AIG's crisis paralleled Lehman's in many ways. AIG was threatened by a liquidity crisis and asked the Fed for help. Policymakers refused, and worked to arrange a private-sector rescue. It appears that, until September 16, policymakers sincerely intended not to aid AIG and that their refusal of assistance was not just a bargaining position.

AIG first requested Fed assistance on September 9. In his memoir, Timothy Geithner says: "At the time, I still thought it was almost inconceivable that the Fed would ever help out a troubled insurance company."[32] Geithner maintained that position for the rest of the week. The Congressional Oversight Panel for TARP quotes Geithner as saying that, on the night of September 14, "it still seemed inconceivable that the Federal Reserve could or should play any role in preventing AIG's collapse."[33]

On Monday, September 15, Geithner organized the consortium of financial institutions that considered a private-sector rescue of AIG. According to Sorkin, Geithner told the group, "I want to be very clear: Do not assume you can use the Fed balance sheet." That evening, he reiterated, "There's no government money for this."[34]

Geithner reports that he changed his mind after a conference call with Treasury and Fed officials at 3:00 AM on September 16. He says:[35]

> A few days earlier, I thought there was no way we should help an insurance company. By early Tuesday, September 16, I had changed my mind. Letting AIG fail seemed like a formula for a second Great Depression. It was essential that we do everything in our power to try to avoid that.

On September 15, Secretary Paulson took the same position in public that Geithner was taking at the New York Fed. Reporters at Paulson's news conference asked him about efforts to rescue AIG, and he replied:[36]

> Let me say what is going on right now in New York has nothing to do with any bridge loan from the government. What's going on in New York is a private-sector effort . . . .

The next day, Geithner persuaded Paulson to change his mind. Sorkin relates:[37]

> However resistant Hank Paulson had been to the idea of a bailout, after getting off the phone at 10:30 AM with Geithner, who had walked him through the latest plan, he could see where the markets were headed, and it scared him . . . . [Chief of Staff] Jim Wilkinson

asked incredulously, "Are we really going to rescue this insurance company?" Paulson just stared at him as if to say that only a madman would just stand by and do nothing.

Paulson's acquiescence to Geithner's plan contrasts sharply with his behavior in the Lehman episode. According to Sorkin, when Geithner suggested assistance to Lehman, Paulson told him "to stand down."[38]

Fears about an AIG Failure

Policymakers say they rescued AIG because its failure would have been disastrous for the economy. In his FCIC interview, Bernanke says, "if we let it fail, the probability was 80 percent that we would have had a second depression." Paulson told a Congressional committee, "had AIG failed . . . unemployment easily could have risen to the 25% level reached in the Great Depression." Geithner says the Fed rescued AIG because "it was our only hope of avoiding unimaginable carnage."[39]

By themselves, these statements do not fully explain the different treatment of AIG and Lehman. Policymakers did not rescue Lehman even though, they say, they expected the firm's failure to be "a catastrophe" and "an epic disaster." However, the real-time evidence suggests that policymakers were more worried about AIG than about Lehman, especially on September 15–16.

One reason was that policymakers had by that time observed the immediate results of the Lehman failure. Henry Paulson and economist Alan Blinder summarize these developments with the same phrase: "All hell broke loose."[40] Stock prices fell sharply and there were upward spikes in the LIBOR-OIS spread and in CDS premiums for the remaining investment banks, two measures of the risk of financial-institution failures. According to Paulson, on the evening of September 15, he heard the "startling" news that General Electric was having trouble selling commercial paper, which led him to worry about another Great Depression. The next morning, Paulson learned that LBIE's UK bankruptcy administrator had seized assets belonging to LBIE's customers, "a completely unexpected – and potentially devastating – jolt."[41]

A complementary source of concern was information received by policymakers about AIG. Geithner says he "went into that weekend [September 13–14] with very little knowledge about the company" because the Fed did not supervise AIG.[42] He assigned a staff group to study the company's situation, and its reports were dire. At 3:16 AM on September 16, Geithner received an analysis suggesting that AIG's failure would do more damage than Lehman's, because of AIG's derivatives positions and its retail businesses, among other factors.[43]

Participants in the September 16 FOMC meeting also seem more worried about AIG than about Lehman, as seen in the earlier excerpts from the meeting's transcript. In his opening remarks, Bernanke mentions "increasing concerns about the insurance company AIG," but does not mention Lehman. Governor Warsh says that AIG, not Lehman, "is the real specter that's casting some question over broader financial institutions."

A final piece of evidence is Bernanke's Congressional testimony on September 23. On that occasion, Bernanke downplays the effects of the Lehman bankruptcy, saying "counterparties had time to take precautionary measures," but says the failure of AIG "would have severely threatened global financial stability."[44]

Political Effects of Lehman's Failure

Many commentators suggest that the Lehman bankruptcy changed policymakers' political calculations. When Congress and the public observed the panic that followed the bankruptcy, opposition to bailouts diminished somewhat, and that made policymakers more willing to rescue AIG and other firms. According to *New York Times* columnist Joe Nocera, "Lehman had to die so that the rest of Wall Street could live."[45] Some compare the Lehman failure to the attack on Pearl Harbor, which persuaded Congress to enter World War II.[46]

Fed policymakers have not discussed the politics of the AIG rescue. However, Bernanke suggests that Lehman's bankruptcy was critical to political support for another public rescue, the Troubled Asset Relief Program approved by Congress in October 2008. Bernanke writes, "It seems clear that Congress would never have acted absent the failure of *some* large firm and the associated damage to the system."[47]

Throughout 2008, concerns about financial stability competed with political opposition to bailouts as policymakers decided what to do about financial institutions on the brink of failure. Before September 15, financial stability concerns carried the day as policymakers at the Fed and Treasury committed funds to rescue Bear Stearns, Fannie Mae, and Freddie Mac. After September 15, stability concerns again trumped politics in the AIG rescue, the passage of TARP, and other policy actions. Lehman Brothers had the misfortune to run out of cash at a moment when previous rescues had produced overwhelming opposition to another one, and when policymakers had not yet learned how destructive the failure of a leading financial institution would be. Henry Paulson and Ben Bernanke knew that rescuing Lehman would produce a bitter political backlash, and they believed or hoped that the effects of Lehman's failure would be manageable.

13 Conclusion

In his 2015 memoir, Ben Bernanke says:[1]

> I do not want the notion that Lehman's failure could have been avoided, and that its failure was consequently a policy choice, to become the received wisdom, for the simple reason that it is not true.

At another point, Bernanke says:[2]

> If a means of saving Lehman did exist, given the tools then available, we were not clever enough to think of it during those frenetic days.

This book disputes Bernanke's claims and similar claims by other Fed officials. The truth is that Lehman's failure could have been avoided, and that policymakers did not need to be particularly clever to achieve that outcome. Lehman only needed the kind of well-secured liquidity support that the Fed provided liberally to other financial institutions (and to the Lehman subsidiary LBI after its parent's bankruptcy). Indeed, Lehman probably could have survived if the Fed had merely *not* taken actions to restrict its access to the Primary Dealer Credit Facility on September 14.

In his final speech as Fed Chair, Bernanke said:[3]

> Fostering transparency and accountability at the Federal Reserve was one of my principal objectives when I became Chairman in February 2006.

Bernanke goes on to discuss transparency about interest-rate policy, and then says:

As it happened, during the crisis and its aftermath the Federal Reserve's transparency and accountability proved critical in a quite different sphere – namely, in supporting the institution's democratic legitimacy.

Transparency, Bernanke says, requires "thoughtful explanations of what we are doing and why" to Congress and the public.

Yet Fed officials have not been transparent about the Lehman crisis. Their explanations for their actions rest on flawed economic and legal reasoning and dubious factual claims. The Financial Crisis Inquiry Commission pushed officials for better explanations of their decisions and for evidence to support their assertions, but to no avail.

Ben Bernanke has called Lehman's bankruptcy a "catastrophe" and a "calamity." Henry Paulson has called it a "nightmare," and Timothy Geithner an "epic disaster." This dramatic language is warranted. The bankruptcy on September 15, 2008 was the moment when growing stresses in financial markets exploded into the worst financial crisis and deepest US recession since the 1930s.

When the next financial crisis occurs, which it inevitably will one day, the Fed should not repeat its Lehman mistake. It should stand ready to perform its fundamental role as the economy's lender of last resort. When a major financial institution experiences a run, but has collateral, the Fed should lend it the cash it needs to avert a sudden and disorderly bankruptcy.

Unfortunately, even if future Fed leaders take the Lehman lesson to heart, they may not be able to act on it because of the Dodd-Frank Wall Street Reform Act of 2010. This legislation seeks to prevent destructive financial crises, and many of its provisions, such as higher capital requirements for financial institutions and restrictions on their risky investments, are steps in the right direction. But the Dodd-Frank Act also revised Section 13(3) of the Federal Reserve Act to significantly limit the Fed's lending authority. Today, the Fed cannot lend to an institution deemed "insolvent" or "failing"; any lending program must be designed for a substantial number of firms, not just one (like the rescues of Bear Stearns and AIG); and all lending must be approved by the Secretary of the Treasury. Under these rules, future Fed leaders may be helpless to counter runs on financial institutions and prevent unnecessary financial disasters.[4]

In light of the Lehman episode, the Dodd-Frank requirement that loans be approved by the Secretary of the Treasury is especially troubling. In 2008, Treasury Secretary Henry Paulson, fearful of being labeled "Mr. Bailout," was determined that Lehman should not receive public assistance. He told Fed officials not to rescue Lehman, and they acquiesced. However, Ben Bernanke and Timothy Geithner *could* have ignored Paulson's dictates, because the Federal Reserve Act before the Dodd-Frank amendments gave them full authority over their lending decisions. Going forward, even if the Fed's leaders are determined to resist political pressures, their actions to preserve financial stability may be vetoed by Treasury Secretaries motivated by politics.

The Dodd-Frank restrictions on Fed lending were motivated by public opposition to financial rescues, or, to use the popular and pejorative term, to "bailouts" of financial institutions. Bernie Sanders captured the sentiment of many people when he called such rescues "socialism for the rich" – transfers of public funds to Wall Street firms that have made risky bets and lost. In this view, bailouts have costs that are unfairly borne by US taxpayers.[5]

This view is misguided. Many so-called bailouts – including, certainly, the liquidity assistance that Lehman Brothers needed – are short-term loans from the Fed that are very likely to be repaid with interest. Even if a borrower like Lehman were to default, the collateral posted for the loan would protect the Fed and taxpayers from significant losses. Most important, Fed assistance can prevent a run from quickly destroying a financial institution, so the firm can either survive or be wound down in a controlled way that minimizes the damage to the economy. Such interventions by the Fed can prevent or mitigate recessions, and more people can keep their jobs.

An accurate understanding of what happened to Lehman Brothers may lead to better economic policies. If the public and Congress learn the right lessons, perhaps the dangerous restrictions on Fed lending in Dodd-Frank will be eliminated, and the Fed will be able to serve the economy effectively as the lender of last resort.

There is, however, a more fundamental reason we need to understand the Lehman bankruptcy: The record of momentous historical events should be accurate. From shortly after the bankruptcy until today, the Fed's leaders in 2008 have given an account of the episode that absolves themselves of the blame for Lehman's disastrous failure. Everyone should understand that this version of history is not rooted in reality.

Notes

Many of the documents discussed in this book are cited in the footnotes of the Bankruptcy Examiner (Valukas) Report or the endnotes of the Financial Crisis Inquiry Commission (FCIC) Report. Documents cited in the Valukas footnotes can be accessed through hyperlinks in the footnotes. Documents cited in the FCIC endnotes can be accessed by searching by endnote number in the Archives on the FCIC website.

PREFACE

1. "Current Economic and Financial Conditions," background document for September 16, 2008 meeting of the Federal Open Market Committee, pp. 1–16, website of the Board of Governors of the Federal Reserve System.
2. See, for example, Greenspan, 2008, and Baker, 2011.
3. Blinder, 2013, p. 3.
4. Krugman, 2009; Paulson, 2010, p. 436.
5. Baker and Hassett, 2012, describe "The Human Disaster of Unemployment."
6. Bernanke, Testimony at Financial Crisis Inquiry Commission hearing on "Too Big to Fail," September 2, 2010, pp. 75–76 of transcript.
7. Cline and Gagnon, 2013; Avent, 2014.
8. Bordo, 1990.
9. Friedman and Schwartz, 1963; Bernanke, 1983.
10. See, for example, Bernanke's 2012 lecture at George Washington University, "The Fed's Response to the Financial Crisis."
11. Blinder, 2013; Wessel, 2009; Wolf, 2014.

I INTRODUCTION

1. Bernanke, "Reflections on a Year of Crisis," Speech at the Federal Reserve Bank of Kansas City's Annual Economic Symposium, Jackson Hole, Wyoming, August 29, 2009, www.federalreserve.gov.

2. Bernanke, Testimony at Financial Crisis Inquiry Commission hearing on "Too Big to Fail," September 2, 2010, pp. 75–76 of transcript, www.fcic.law .stanford.edu.

3. Bernanke, *The Courage to Act*, p. 288.

4. Detailed citations for all facts and quotations in this section are provided in later chapters of this book.

5. FCIC Report, p. 340.

2 THE CRISIS OF 2008

1. These percentages are calculated from the assets and equity reported on the 2007 Form 10-K's filed with the SEC by Goldman Sachs (p. 110), Morgan Stanley (pp. 101–102), Merrill Lynch (p. 19), Lehman Brothers (p. 29), and Bear Stearns (p. 82).

2. FCIC, Lehman Chronology, Tab 14. This chronology is a background document for the FCIC hearing on "Too Big to Fail," September 1–2, 2010.

3. Copeland et al., 2010.

4. Diamond and Dybvig, 1983.

5. Since the 2008 crisis, the mechanics of tri-party repos have been modified to greatly decrease the amount of intraday credit provided by clearing banks. See the New York Fed's "Update on Tri-Party Infrastructure Reform," February 13, 2014.

6. This section draws on chapters 12, 15, and 16 of the FCIC report.

7. FCIC, p. 286.

8. FCIC, pp. 288–289.

9. FCIC, p. 293.

10. Duffie, 2010; Copeland et al., 2010.

11. FCIC Lehman chronology, Tab 40.

12. Duffie, 2010, p. 30.

13. FCIC staff interview of Ben Bernanke, November 17, 2009, pp. 21–22.

14. Compare the "PDCF Collateral Margins Table" in the "Credit and Liquidity Programs" section of the Board of Governors website to the market haircuts from the FCIC Lehman Chronology, Tab 14.

15. FCIC, note 16.15.

16. Valukas, note 5340.

17. Valukas, pp. 58–163.

18. Valukas, note 248.

19. LBHI, Form 10-K for 2007, p. 33.

20. Valukas, Appendix 13, note 16.

21. FCIC, p. 327.

22. Valukas, Appendix 13, pp. 7–9.

23. Levisohn, 2008.

24. FCIC, p. 328.

25. Valukas, note 6341.

26. Valukas, pp. 609–726 and Appendix 13.

27. Valukas note 750.

28. Valukas, Appendix 13.

29. Valukas, Appendix 15; FCIC Lehman Chronology, background document for hearing on "Too Big to Fail," September 1–2, 2010.

30. Valukas, Appendix 15, note 89.

31. Valukas, note 5438.

32. Valukas, Appendix 15, note 117.

33. FCIC, p. 332.

34. Valukas, p. 698.

35. Valukas, Appendix 15, note 167.

36. Robert Diamond FCIC interview, c. 32:00 in the audio recording.

37. Valukas, Appendix 15, note 283.

38. FCIC, pp. 335–336 and note 18.85.

39. Valukas, Appendix 13, p. 57.

40. Sorkin, pp. 361–362.

41. Board of Governors of the Federal Reserve System, press release, September 14, 2008.

42. See Chapter 10, pp. 178–179.

43. William Dudley, FCIC interview, c. 31:00 in the audio recording.

44. Thomas Baxter, written testimony for FCIC hearing on "Too Big to Fail," September 1, 2010, p. 11.

45. Haircuts for LBI's collateral are given in the "September 14, 2008 Burke letter," a background document for the FCIC hearing on "Too Big to Fail," September 1, 2010.

46. Valukas, note 5992.

47. Valukas, p. 2165.

48. FCIC, note 19.26.

49. Quoted in LaCapra, 2009.

50. Congressional Oversight Panel on TARP, pp. 52–55.

51. FCIC, pp. 356–360.

52. FCIC, p. 360.

53. FCIC, p. 362.

54. Bloomberg News website, "Bloomberg Uncovers the Fed's Secret Liquidity Lifelines."

55. FCIC, note 20.55.

56. For estimates of the long-term damage from the Great Recession, see Reifschneider et al., 2013; Ball, 2014; and Mason, 2017.

3   THE LEGAL CRITERIA FOR FED ASSISTANCE

1. The website of the Board of Governors describes these actions in its section on "Credit and Liquidity Programs and the Balance Sheet."

2. Bagehot, 1873, Chapter 7.

3. For example, in a 2009 article that is widely quoted, Paul Tucker of the Bank of England says that "Bagehot's dictum" for central banks is to lend "to solvent firms against good collateral." For more on interpreting Bagehot, see Goodhart, 1999.

4. See Todd, 1993, for the history of Section 13(3).

5. FCIC, note 18.135.

6. Alvarez mentions the memos on 13(3) authorizations in his interview with the FCIC staff (approximately 1:15 in the audio recording). It is not clear why the CPFF memo has been released and others have not. I sought the memos on Maiden Lane and AIG in an unsuccessful Freedom of Information Act request to the Board of Governors (see Chapter 10, pp. 188–189).

7. Scott Alvarez, FCIC interview, c. 1:17 in the audio recording.

8. Valukas, pp. 1503–1504.

4   LEHMAN'S BALANCE SHEET AND SOLVENCY

1. Valukas, note 7362.

2. Valukas, pp. 1551–1553.

3. Valukas, note 750.

4. A major finding of the Valukas Report (Volume 3 and Appendix 17) is that Lehman's balance sheet was distorted by an accounting trick called "Repo 105." Under normal accounting rules, a firm's repos are treated as collateralized borrowings, and the collateral used to secure the repos is included in the firm's assets. Under Repo 105, some repos were counted as sales of the assets being used as collateral, thus removing the assets from Lehman's balance sheet. The purpose of this maneuver was to reduce the

firm's reported ratio of assets to equity (its leverage ratio), a widely watched indicator of its financial health. On May 31, Lehman used Repo 105 to reduce its measured assets by $44.5 billion.

The Valukas Report argues that the use of Repo 105 "materially misrepresented Lehman's true financial condition" (p. 747). Yet Repo 105 is not important for the issues examined in this book. The assets removed from the balance sheet were safe and liquid: 91 percent were Treasury and agency securities, and over 99 percent were investment grade (Valukas Appendix 17, pp. 12–14). If we put those assets back on the balance sheet, along with the corresponding liabilities to repo counterparties, this adjustment does not significantly affect this analysis of Lehman's solvency, its liquidity needs, or whether it had adequate collateral for a Fed loan.

5. The 10-Q reports that $43 billion of these assets are "pledged as collateral." This figure is determined by complex accounting rules that count some but not all of the collateral for Lehman's repos (see King, 2008).

6. LBHI Form 10-Q for 2008 Q2, p. 38.

7. LBHI Form 10-Q for 2008 Q2, p. 38.

8. LBHI press release, p. 2, in Valukas note 750.

9. LBHI press release, p. 1, in Valukas note 750.

10. Valukas, p. 1570.

11. Adrian et al., 2013.

12. See Exhibit 4.4.

13. LBHI, Form 10-Q for 2008 Q2, p. 27.

14. LBHI, Form 10-Q for 2008 Q2, pp. 27–29.

15. LBHI, Form 10-Q for 2008 Q2, p. 29.

16. LBHI, Form 10-Q for 2008 Q2, p. 29.

17. Valukas, note 7788.

18. The memo says, "Analysis on Leveraged & Corporate Lending and Muni portfolios are still in progress and excluded from current write-down estimate." These types of assets were not among those that Barclays refused to take in its tentative deal with LBHI, so I presume they were not significantly overvalued.

19. Valukas, note 4875.

20. Paulson, p. 206.

21. FCIC, p. 335.

22. Paulson, p. 199.
23. Valukas, note 2195.
24. Valukas, pp. 203–609 and Appendices 12, 14, and 16.
25. Valukas, p. 214.
26. Valukas, pp. 285–355.
27. Valukas, pp. 484–492.
28. Valukas, pp. 1570–1587 and Appendix 21.
29. Duff and Phelps's reasoning, somewhat simplified, is the following. They assume (1) a firm is solvent if the market value of its assets exceeds the book value of its liabilities; and (2) the market value of assets equals the market value of equity plus the market value of liabilities. These two assumptions imply the solvency condition stated above. Assumption (2) is not valid if the risk of bankruptcy depresses the prices of the firm's debt and equity. The Valukas Report (p. 1579) cites a finance textbook, Pratt (2008), as the source of assumption (2), but Pratt does not actually suggest that assumption anywhere.
30. Bernanke, 2015, p. 264.
31. In 2014, the *New York Times* published an article about Lehman based on interviews with unnamed staff at the New York Fed (Stewart and Eavis, 2014). These sources say they analyzed Lehman's finances in its final days, and their "preliminary finding" was that the firm was solvent. Senior policymakers were unaware of this analysis, according to the *Times*.
32. FCIC, hearing on "Too Big to Fail," September 1, 2010, p. 253 of transcript.
33. FCIC, hearing on "Too Big to Fail," September 1, 2010, pp. 253–255.
34. Pirro, 2013.
35. FCIC, follow up documents for hearing on "Too Big to Fail," September 1–2, 2010.
36. FCIC, hearing on "Too Big to Fail," September 1, 2010, p. 145.
37. Cline and Gagnon, 2013, also argue that Lehman was insolvent at the time of its bankruptcy. They cite the deep insolvency of the LBHI estate after the bankruptcy and suggest that value destruction cannot fully explain the estate's condition.
38. Fleming and Sarkar, 2014.
39. Miller and Horwitz, 2013.
40. Fleming and Sarkar, 2014.

41. National Organization of Life and Health Insurance Guaranty Associations, 2013.

42. McCracken, 2009. For more on this topic, see Duffie, 2010, and Roe and Adams, 2014.

43. Valukas, p. 2193.

44. Crapo, 2008.

45. Giddens, 2014.

46. Crapo, 2008.

47. Harvey Miller, testimony at FCIC hearing on "Too Big to Fail," September 1, 2010, p. 271 of transcript and p. 13 of written testimony.

5 LEHMAN'S LIQUIDITY CRISIS

1. See, for example, Lehman's presentations to Standard and Poor's and to the Fed in May 2008 (Valukas, notes 6250 and 6251).

2. LBHI Form 10-Q for 2008 Q2, p. 81.

3. LBHI memo on "Liquidity Management," June 2008, Valukas, note 6312.

4. LBHI Form 10-Q for 2008 Q2, p. 81.

5. Valukas, note 5422.

6. LBHI Form 10-Q for 2008 Q2, pp. 80–81.

7. LBHI memo on "Liquidity of Lehman Brothers," October 7, 2008, Valukas, note 6341.

8. The figure of $188 billion appears in the discussion of liquidity management in LBHI's 10-Q for 2008 Q2 (p. 84). The balance sheet in the same 10-Q reports only $128 billion in repos (see Exhibit 4.2). The balance sheet may omit some repos because they are netted with reverse repos in the same securities.

9. See, for example, LBHI 10-Q for 2008 Q2, pp. 84–85, and Valukas, note 6251.

10. LBHI memo on "Funding Lehman Brothers," September 10, 2008, Valukas, note 6259.

11. Valukas, note 6251.

12. Valukas, note 6329.

13. Valukas, notes 6331 and 6334.

14. Quoted in Lehman presentation to the Chicago Mercantile Exchange, Valukas, note 6312.

15. Valukas, Appendix 13, note 16.

16. Valukas, pp. 1665–1687.

17. Valukas, note 6259.

18. Valukas, note 6341.

19. LBHI press release, p. 2, in Valukas, note 750.

20. The September 10 memo reports that Lehman lost $10 billion of repos from May 31 through August 31, with no change in overfunding. The October 7 memo says that Lehman's liquidity position, including its repos, was "relatively stable" from August 31 through September 9.

21. Valukas, pp. 1084ff.

22. See Chapter 2, pp. 34–35, for more on the events of September 9 and 10.

23. Valukas, note 5604.

24. Valukas, Appendix 13, note 350.

25. Aubin, 2008.

26. Sorkin, pp. 366–369; FCIC, hearing on "Too Big to Fail," September 1, 2010, written testimony of Harvey Miller, pp. 9–10.

27. Valukas, Appendix 15, p. 61.

6   LEHMAN'S COLLATERAL AND THE FEASIBILITY OF LIQUIDITY SUPPORT

1. For example, Tarullo, 2014.

2. Basel Committee, 2014; Board of Governors of the Federal Reserve System, press release, May 3, 2016.

3. Exhibit 4.3 presents part of Lehman's financial statement for August 31, 2008. The statement reports that the firm had equity of $28 billion and "total long-term capital" of $143 billion. Total long-term capital is defined as equity plus long-term debt (p. 11 of the statement, Valukas, note 750). These figures imply that long-term debt is $115 billion ($143 billion minus $28 billion).

4. My analysis assumes that all of Lehman's assets could have served as collateral, which the Fed could have seized if the firm defaulted on a loan. Arguably, intangible assets and goodwill could not have served as collateral. However, these items accounted for only $4 billion of Lehman's assets, so excluding them does not change my calculations substantially.

5. We can reduce this upper bound substantially by making the worst case scenario a bit more realistic, in particular, by accounting for the $273 billion of reverse repos and securities borrows on the asset side of Lehman's August 31 balance sheet. These items were effectively short-

term loans of cash from Lehman to its customers, which Lehman could have refused to roll over to offset its cash losses. If Lehman had to pay off all its short-term liabilities but terminated its reverse repos and securities borrows, it would need a loan of only $184 billion ($457 billion minus $273 billion) from the Fed.

6. LBI's collateral in repos maturing on September 15 included $54.6 billion of Treasury and agency securities, and that day it pledged only $6.6 billion of Treasuries and agencies to the PDCF. These figures imply that LBI pledged $48.0 billion of Treasuries and agencies to private counterparties on September 15. See Chase Triparty Haircut Summary, Valukas note 7810, and the data on PDCF lending on the Board of Governors website.

7. Valukas, Appendix 13, note 350.

8. This assumption is not essential. If JPMC refused to clear Lehman's repos, the Fed could have bypassed the tri-party market and lent to Lehman directly. This strategy was proposed in a July 2008 analysis at the New York Fed (see Chapter 7, p. 116).

9. Valukas, notes 5604, 6259, 6331, 6334, 6341, and Appendix 13, note 350.

10. See Chapter 5, p. 91.

11. Valukas, note 7807.

12. Lehman's commercial paper outstanding was approximately $4 billion on August 31 and fell by $2 billion between then and September 12, leaving $2 billion at the time of the bankruptcy. Memo on "Liquidity of Lehman Brothers," Valukas, note 6341.

13. Lehman limited its long-term debt maturing within any quarterly interval to 7.5 percent of its total long-term debt. On August 31, this limit was $8.5 billion. Memo on "Funding Lehman Brothers," Valukas, note 6259.

14. FCIC Lehman chronology, Tab 40.

15. The New York Fed stress test in June lists liquidity losses related to "operating cash flows," which include the $9 billion of collateral calls listed in a previous bullet point and two other items: $2 billion for "prime brokerage" and $2 billion for "derivatives/margins payment mismatches." I conjecture that these two items are part of the operational friction discussed in Lehman memos, and do not count them as additional liquidity drains.

16. See Chapter 2, pp. 40–41.

17. Leising, 2011. Bloomberg obtained these data through a lawsuit against the Fed under the Freedom of Information Act.

18. Data on PDCF lending in section on Credit and Liquidity Programs and the Balance Sheet, website of the Board of Governors of the Federal Reserve System.

19. Wachtell et al., 2011.

20. Geithner, pp. 187–188.

21. See Chapter 2, pp. 27–28 and 40–41.

22. Valukas, p. 1659.

23. Valukas, note 5349.

24. See Chapter 5, pp. 87 and 89.

25. Valukas, pp. 584 and 596 and note 6255 (Lehman's Global Liquidity MIS).

26. Valukas, notes 750 and 2065.

27. The balance sheet footnote from which I take other figures lists $55.0 billion of mortgages and asset-backed securities. However, this figure includes $9.2 billion of mortgages which were serving as collateral for securities that Lehman had issued, and which therefore could not be pledged to the PDCF. (The relevant accounting issues are discussed in Lehman's 10-Q for 2008 Q2, p. 29, note (1).)

28. Valukas, note 5601.

29. September 14, 2008 Burke letter, background document for FCIC hearing on "Too Big to Fail," September 1, 2010.

30. Valukas, note 4293.

31. PDCF Collateral Margins Table, in section on Credit and Liquidity Programs, website of the Board of Governors.

32. Thomas Baxter, follow-up letter after FCIC hearing on "Too Big to Fail," September 1, 2010.

33. Transcript of Federal Open Market Committee meeting, September 16, 2008, p. 7.

34. Valukas, note 7807.

35. Over September 16 and 17, this total grew to $36 billion ($20 billion from the PDCF and $16 billion from Barclays). I have not found precise figures for repos maturing on the 16th and 17th, so it is more difficult to determine LBI's liquidity needs on those days.

36. This figure is an estimate based on the fact that LBI pledged $6.6 billion of Treasury and agency securities as PDCF collateral on September 15, and on the range of PDCF haircuts on various types of Treasuries and agencies. As discussed in note 6, most of LBI's Treasury and agency repos with the private sector rolled over on September 15.

37. Valukas, note 7810.
38. Valukas, note 7807.
39. Valukas, note 5604.
40. James Giddens, LBI Trustee Preliminary Investigation Report, pp. 74–75.
41. See Exhibit 5.1, which shows that collateral calls on derivatives ("derivative margins") during the week of September 8 occurred at LBHI, not LBI or LBIE.

7 FED DISCUSSIONS OF COLLATERAL AND LIQUIDITY SUPPORT

1. Valukas, note 6331.
2. Valukas, note 6334.
3. FCIC Lehman Chronology, background document for hearing on "Too Big to Fail," September 1–2, 2010, Tabs 14–17.
4. FCIC Lehman Chronology, Tab 18.
5. FCIC Lehman Chronology, Tab 36.
6. FCIC Lehman Chronology, Tab 37.
7. There is a small mistake here: it is the Board of Governors, not the FOMC, that approves lending facilities under Section 13(3).
8. FCIC Lehman Chronology, Tab 50.
9. FCIC Lehman Chronology, Tab 53.
10. Section 10(b) of the Federal Reserve Act concerns discount loans to depository institutions. It is relevant here because the March 14 loan to Bear, which was not a depository institution, was channeled through JPMorgan Chase, which was.
11. FCIC Lehman Chronology, Tab 61.
12. All of Bernanke's Congressional testimony and speeches as Fed Chair are available on the website of the Fed's Board of Governors.
13. FCIC hearing on "Too Big to Fail," September 2, 2010, p. 19 of transcript.
14. FCIC hearing on "Too Big to Fail," pp. 24–25.
15. FCIC hearing on "Too Big to Fail," pp. 76–77.
16. FCIC Report, p. 340.
17. Bernanke, 2015, p. 289.
18. Henry Paulson also suggested initially that the failure of Lehman was a policy choice, and later said that the Fed and the government had no legal means to rescue the firm. In a 2013 update of his memoir, Paulson gives the same explanation as Bernanke for an initial lack of candor. Speaking of

his press conference on September 16, Paulson says (p. xxi): "When asked why we didn't save Lehman, I wouldn't publicly admit that the U.S. couldn't find a single authority to rescue a failing investment bank. I believed that if I acknowledged as much, Morgan Stanley, which was also on the ropes, would have gone down within a few days."

19. Bernanke interview with FCIC staff, November 17, 2009, p. 30.
20. Bernanke interview with FCIC staff, pp. 25–26.
21. Valukas, pp. 1503–1504.
22. Bernanke, "The Federal Reserve's Response to the Financial Crisis," lecture at George Washington University, March 27, 2012.
23. Bernanke, pp. 287–288.
24. Bernanke, pp. 267–268.
25. Geithner, p. 186.
26. Geithner, p. 187.
27. FCIC hearing on "Too Big to Fail," September 2, 2010, pp. 18–21 of transcript.
28. FCIC hearing on "Too Big to Fail," pp. 22–23.
29. FCIC hearing on "Too Big to Fail," pp. 25–27.
30. FCIC hearing on "Too Big to Fail," pp. 80–84.
31. FCIC hearing on "Too Big to Fail," pp. 87–88 and p. 89.
32. Geithner, p. 182.
33. Bernanke, reply to follow-up letter from FCIC after hearing on "Too Big to Fail," November 4, 2010, pp. 11–14.
34. See Chapter 4, pp. 74–76.
35. FCIC Lehman chronology, Tab 40.
36. Thomas Baxter, written testimony for FCIC hearing on "Too Big to Fail," September 1, 2010, p. 9.
37. FCIC hearing on "Too Big to Fail," September 1, 2010, pp. 185–186 of transcript.
38. FCIC hearing on "Too Big to Fail," pp. 165–166.
39. The OMOs counted here were repos of Treasury securities from Lehman to the New York Fed, which the latter initiated as part of its implementation of monetary policy.
40. Harvey Miller, written testimony for FCIC hearing on "Too Big to Fail," September 1, 2010, p. 18.
41. The source of Miller's figure is not clear. If he is suggesting that a wind down would have cost the government $40–50 billion, then I disagree.

The only necessary public assistance would have been Fed liquidity support during the wind down, which could have been well secured (see Chapter 9, pp. 173–176).

42. FCIC hearing on "Too Big to Fail," pp. 161–163. In the transcript, the sentence quoted here includes the word "can" rather than "can't," but that appears to be a typo.
43. FCIC hearing on "Too Big to Fail," pp. 163–164.
44. FCIC hearing on "Too Big to Fail," p. 253.
45. FCIC hearing on "Too Big to Fail," p. 254.
46. FCIC hearing on "Too Big to Fail," pp. 174 and 253.
47. Thomas Baxter, reply to follow-up letter from FCIC after hearing on "Too Big to Fail," October 15, 2010, p. 5.
48. FCIC hearing on "Too Big to Fail," p. 41.
49. FCIC hearing on "Too Big to Fail," pp. 43–44.
50. Scott Alvarez interview with FCIC staff, July 29, 2010, around 1:21 in the audio recording.
51. See, for example, Paulson, p. 189.
52. See Chapter 4, pp. 72–73.
53. Statement by the UK Financial Services Authority, Valukas, note 5918.
54. Thomas Baxter, written testimony for FCIC hearing on "Too Big to Fail," September 1, 2010, pp. 8–9.
55. FCIC hearing on "Too Big to Fail," pp. 151–152.
56. FCIC hearing on "Too Big to Fail," p. 164.
57. FCIC hearing on "Too Big to Fail," p. 166.
58. Scott Alvarez, interview with FCIC staff, around 1:23 in the audio recording.

8   FED ACTIONS THAT ENSURED LEHMAN'S BANKRUPTCY

1. Valukas, Appendix 15, p. 58.
2. Harvey Miller, written testimony for FCIC hearing on "Too Big to Fail," September 1, 2010, pp. 7–9.
3. Sorkin, pp. 356–359.
4. Harvey Miller, written testimony, pp. 9–10.
5. Paulson, p. 220.
6. Valukas, note 2829.
7. FCIC hearing on "Too Big to Fail," September 1, 2010, pp. 147–148 of transcript.
8. FCIC hearing on "Too Big to Fail," pp. 159–160.

9. FCIC hearing on "Too Big to Fail," p. 178.

10. Bart McDade, interview with FCIC staff, August 9, 2010, around 54:00 in the audio recording.

11. Ian Lowitt, interview with FCIC staff, August 25, 2010, around 37:00.

12. FCIC hearing on "Too Big to Fail," September 1, 2010, p. 166 of transcript.

13. FCIC hearing on "Too Big to Fail," p. 177.

14. FCIC hearing on "Too Big to Fail," pp. 183–184.

15. FCIC hearing on "Too Big to Fail," pp. 180–181.

16. Thomas Baxter, follow-up letter after FCIC hearing on "Too Big to Fail," footnote 8.

17. Valukas, note 5978.

18. Federal Open Market Committee meeting, September 16, 2008, p. 7 of transcript.

19. FCIC, p. 337.

20. Thomas Baxter, follow-up letter after FCIC hearing on "Too Big to Fail," p. 4.

21. Thomas Baxter, follow-up letter, Exhibit 7.

22. Other parts of the record add more confusion. The minutes of the September 14 Lehman board meeting (p. 2) state: "Mr. Russo [Lehman's General Counsel] described the Fed's emergency order allowing non-investment grade securities to be used as collateral at the Fed window and the Firm's need for the Fed to accept a broader range of collateral, but that the Fed's position is that the expanded window would only apply to tri-party repos of securities." Also on September 14, Board Vice Chair Kohn wrote to Ben Bernanke that "LEH heard about the pdcf enlargement and thought it was a lifeline, but they didn't understand it was limited to triparty" (FCIC Lehman Chronology, Tab 66). The FCIC final Report (p. 337) interprets Russo to mean that Lehman asked to borrow against an even broader range of collateral than that accepted by the expanded PDCF, which accepted assets that "closely matched" the collateral in tri-party repos. The Kohn remark can be interpreted the same way. Most evidence, however, suggests that Lehman only sought to borrow against the expanded PDCF collateral.

23. Valukas, note 2829.

24. FCIC, note 18.98.

25. Data on PDCF lending in section on "Credit and Liquidity Programs and the Balance Sheet," website of Board of Governors of the Federal Reserve System.

26. LBHI, Form 10-Q for 2008 Q2, p. 48.

27. Valukas, pp. 1550–1554.

28. James Giddens, LBI Trustee Preliminary Investigation Report, p. 53.

29. Joint Administrators of LBIE, First Progress Report, p. 51.

30. Giddens, Preliminary Investigation Report, p. 74.

31. Giddens, Preliminary Investigation Report, Exhibit C, p. 10. The Report does not cite the original source of this information.

32. Valukas, pp. 584 and 596.

33. Valukas, pp. 1532–1533.

34. Thomas Baxter, follow-up letter after FCIC hearing on "Too Big to Fail," p. 2.

35. Alex Kirk, interview with FCIC staff, August 16, 2010, around 1:05 in the audio recording.

36. Alex Kirk interview, around 1:11.

37. Valukas, note 5995.

38. FCIC hearing on "Too Big to Fail," September 2, 2010, p. 26 of transcript.

39. Thomas Baxter, follow-up letter after FCIC hearing on "Too Big to Fail," p. 2.

40. United States Code, Section 547.

41. United States Code, Section 548.

9   POSSIBLE LONG-TERM OUTCOMES FOR LEHMAN

1. I do not consider the possibility of a capital injection from the Troubled Asset Relief Program. If Lehman had survived, the financial crisis would have been less severe, and Congress might not have decided to create the TARP.

2. See Chapter 2, pp. 38–39.

3. See Chapter 2, p. 39.

4. Paulson, pp. 210–211.

5. FSA Statement to Bankruptcy Examiner, pp. 6–10, FCIC note 18.98.

6. Bernanke, p. 254.

7. Valukas, note 5816.

8. FCIC Lehman Chronology, background document for hearing on "Too Big to Fail," September 1, 2010, Tab 17.

9. Valukas, note 5816.
10. FCIC Lehman Chronology, Tab 36.
11. FCIC Lehman Chronology, Tab 37.
12. Valukas, note 5896.
13. Valukas, Appendix 13.
14. Valukas, Appendix 15, note 79.
15. Valukas, Appendix 15, p. 18.
16. Valukas, Appendix 13, p. 12; FCIC, p. 328.
17. See Scott, 2016, for estimates of recovery rates for Lehman's creditors.
18. Thomas Baxter, written testimony for FCIC hearing on "Too Big to Fail," p. 11.
19. Alex Kirk, interview with FCIC staff, August 16, 2010, around 31:00 in the audio recording.
20. Valukas, Appendix 15, pp. 55–56.

10 HOW RISKY WERE THE FED'S RESCUES OF OTHER FIRMS?

1. Data on PDCF lending in section on Credit and Liquidity Programs and the Balance Sheet, website of Board of Governors of the Federal Reserve System.
2. Compare the haircuts for LBI in Christopher Burke's letter to Lehman (background document for FCIC hearing on "Too Big to Fail"); the market haircuts on September 12 reported by JPMorgan Chase (Valukas, note 7810); and the normal PDCF haircuts on the Board of Governors website (PDCF Collateral Margins Table in the Credit and Liquidity Programs section).
3. See Chapter 2, p. 25 for details of the March 14 loan.
4. FCIC, note 15.80.
5. Section on Maiden Lane Transactions, website of the Federal Reserve Bank of New York.
6. PDCF Collateral Margins Table, section on Credit and Liquidity Programs and the Balance Sheet, website of the Board of Governors.
7. Alloway, 2010.
8. See Publication H.4.1 on the Board of Governors website.
9. For a detailed review of the Fed's assistance to AIG, see Congressional Oversight Panel for TARP, 2010, pp. 46–82.
10. Congressional Oversight Panel, p. 57.

11. FCIC hearing on "Too Big to Fail," September 2, 2010, p. 37 of transcript.

12. FCIC hearing on "Too Big to Fail," September 2, 2010, pp. 60–61.

13. Thomas Baxter, written testimony for FCIC hearing on "Too Big to Fail," September 1, 2010, p. 10.

14. Geithner, p. 193.

15. Geithner, pp. 194 and 197.

16. Quoted in Stewart, 2014.

17. Bernanke, p. 281.

18. Bernanke, pp. 282–283.

19. Secured Credit Facility Authorized for American International Group, Inc, in Reports Pursuant to Section 129 of the Emergency Economic Stabilization Act of 2008, website of the Board of Governors, p. 7.

20. Secured Credit Facility Authorized for American International Group, Inc, p. 7.

21. *Ball v. Board of Governors of the Federal Reserve System*, D.D.C. No. 13-cv-0603, 2015.

22. My FOIA request also included memos by the Board's General Counsel about the legal justifications for the Maiden Lane and AIG loans. This part of my request was also denied, and the denial was upheld by the court. Despite these outcomes, I am grateful for the outstanding work on my case by PCLG attorneys, especially Jehan Patterson.

23. Office of the Special Inspector General for the Troubled Asset Relief Program, Factors Affecting Efforts to Limit Payments to AIG Counterparties, SIGTARP-10–003, November 17, 2009, p. 8.

24. Congressional Oversight Panel on the Troubled Asset Relief Program, The AIG Rescue, Its Impact on Markets, and the Government's Exit Strategy, June 10, 2010, note 246.

25. Congressional Oversight Panel, pp. 54–55.

26. FCIC, note 19.38.

27. See Congressional Oversight Panel, pp. 68–82.

28. See Publication H.4.1 on the Board of Governors website.

29. FCIC note 18.135.

30. FCIC note 18.135 (Alvarez memo, p. 3).

31. Kacperczyk and Schnabl, 2010.

32. Adrian et al., 2011.

33. FCIC note 18.135 (Alvarez memo, p. 8).

34. Kacperczyk and Schnabl, 2010.

11 WHO DECIDED THAT LEHMAN SHOULD FAIL?

1. Geithner, p. 154.

2. Paulson, pp. 100–116; Geithner, pp. 147–158; Wessel, pp. 157–171.

3. Geithner, p. 156.

4. Paulson, pp. 136–137.

5. Geithner, p. 178.

6. Paulson, p. 186.

7. Geithner, p. 179.

8. Sorkin, pp. 282–283.

9. Sorkin, p. 295.

10. Quoted by Geithner, p. 179.

11. In his memoir, Paulson says he would have changed his position and agreed for the Fed to finance some of Lehman's assets if doing so would have facilitated an acquisition of the firm. He says of himself and Geithner, "we both knew that if a Bear Stearns-style rescue was the only option, we would take it" (p. 181). The Fed financed some of Bear's assets as part of the deal with JPMorgan Chase. According to Paulson, it was the absence of an acquirer that made a Lehman rescue impossible.

12. Paulson, pp. 187–190.

13. Thomas Baxter, written testimony for FCIC hearing on "Too Big to Fail," September 1, 2010, p. 6.

14. Wessel, p. 16.

15. Paulson says that "Tim opened the meeting" and then "handed the meeting over to me" (p. 191). However, Geithner, Baxter, Sorkin, and Wessel all report that Paulson spoke first. Paulson confirms that he said "there could be no government money involved in any rescue" (p. 192).

16. Geithner, pp. 181–182.

17. Paulson, pp. 194–206.

18. Paulson, p. 206.

19. See Chapter 2, p. 39.

20. Paulson, p. 211; Sorkin, p. 349.

21. Paulson, p. 212.

22. See Chapter 8, pp. 151–153.

23. Sorkin, p. 355.

24. Paulson, p. 225.

25. FCIC, note 18.101.

26. Paulson, p. 209.

27. Bernanke, p. 263.

28. Bernanke, pp. 263–269; Paulson, pp. 186–221; Geithner, pp. 180–190; Sorkin, pp. 297–372; FCIC Lehman Chronology, background document for hearing on "Too Big to Fail," September 1, 2010.

29. Bernanke, p. 263.

30. FCIC Lehman Chronology, Tab 58.

31. Sorkin, pp. 350–351.

32. Bernanke, pp. 267–268.

33. Paulson, p. 218.

34. Wessel, p. 13.

35. Bernanke, p. 263.

36. FCIC Lehman Chronology, Tabs 66–67.

37. FCIC Lehman Chronology, Tab 66. Kohn's remark that the PDCF expansion "was limited to triparty" is puzzling and is discussed in Chapter 8 note 22.

38. Bernanke, p. 289.

39. Geithner, p. 178.

40. Wessel, p. 12; Sorkin, pp. 41 and 44.

41. Ball, 2016.

42. Appelbaum, 2014.

43. Davidson, 2009.

44. Blinder, 2013, p. 98.

45. Geithner, p. 154.

46. Sorkin, p. 366.

47. Geithner, p. 189.

48. Paulson describes the same conversation on pp. 219–220 of his memoir. In Paulson's account, his language is more polite, but the message is the same. He says, "I finally walked into Chris's office around 7:15 PM and urged him to move quickly to execute the SEC's plan" [for bankruptcy]. Paulson quotes himself as telling Cox, "It is essential that you call the company now."

12   EXPLAINING THE LEHMAN DECISION

1. Sorkin, pp. 38 and 78.
2. Paul Volcker, speech at Economic Club of New York, April 8, 2008.
3. Vincent Reinhart, speech at American Enterprise Institute, April 28, 2008.
4. Geithner, pp. 159–160.
5. Geithner, p. 175.
6. Sender, 2008.
7. Paulson, p. 212.
8. Bernanke, p. 261.
9. Schuman, 2008.
10. Quoted in Geithner, p. 190.
11. Wessel, p. 14; Sorkin, p. 282; Geithner p. 179; Paulson, p. 186.
12. Sorkin, p. 239.
13. Sorkin, p. 302.
14. FCIC Lehman Chronology, background document for hearing on "Too Big to Fail," September 1, 2010, Tab 32.
15. Wessel, p. 274.
16. See Chapter 7, pp. 121–123.
17. Bernanke, interview with FCIC staff, November 17, 2009, pp. 25–26 of transcript.
18. FCIC hearing on "Too Big to Fail," September 2, 2010, p. 22 of transcript.
19. Bernanke, p. 268.
20. Paulson, p. 225; Geithner, p. 187.
21. Scott Alvarez, interview with FCIC staff, July 29, 2010, around 44:00 in the audio recording.
22. Paulson, p. 187.
23. Wessel, p. 11.
24. Sorkin, pp. 357–359; Harvey Miller, written testimony for FCIC hearing on "Too Big to Fail," September 1, 2010, pp. 8–9.
25. FOMC meeting, September 16, 2008, p. 3 of transcript.
26. FOMC meeting, pp. 3–6.
27. FOMC meeting, p. 51.
28. FOMC meeting, p. 51.
29. FOMC meeting, pp. 61–62.
30. FOMC meeting, p. 71.
31. President Rosengren of Boston advocates a quarter-point cut in the funds rate, but he is not a voting member of the Committee.

32. Geithner, p. 176.
33. Congressional Oversight Panel for the Troubled Asset Relief Program, 2010, p. 52.
34. Sorkin, pp. 383 and 388.
35. Geithner, p. 193.
36. Quoted in Sorkin, p. 386.
37. Sorkin, p. 396.
38. Sorkin, p. 295.
39. Bernanke, interview with FCIC staff, p. 25; Paulson testimony to House Committee on Oversight and Government Reform, January 27, 2010; Geithner, p. 194.
40. Paulson, p. 228; Blinder, p. 129.
41. Paulson, pp. 227–228 and 230.
42. Geithner, p. 184.
43. Congressional Oversight Panel, note 252.
44. See Chapter 7, pp. 121–122.
45. Nocera, 2009.
46. For example, Ickes, 2009.
47. Bernanke, p. 291.

13   CONCLUSION

1. Bernanke, p. 291.
2. Bernanke, p. 288.
3. Bernanke, "The Federal Reserve: Looking Back, Looking Forward," January 3, 2014.
4. See Chapter 3, pp. 50–51 for more on the Dodd-Frank revisions to Section 13(3). Scott, 2016, Chapter 9 gives a detailed analysis.
5. Sanders is quoted in Solman, 2012.

References

Adrian, Tobias et al., "The Federal Reserve's Commercial Paper Funding Facility," *Federal Reserve Bank of New York Economic Policy Review*, May 2011.

Adrian, Tobias et al., "Repo and Securities Lending," *Federal Reserve Bank of New York Staff Reports*, February 2013.

Alloway, Tracy, "The Illustrative Maiden Lane I Portfolio," *FT Alphaville*, April 9, 2010.

Appelbaum, Binyamin, "Fed Misread Crisis in 2008, Records Show," *New York Times*, February 21, 2014.

Aubin, Dena, "Major Credit Rating Agencies May Cut Lehman Ratings," Reuters, September 10, 2008.

Avent, Ryan, "They Let It Happen," *The Economist*, Free Exchange blog, September 30, 2014.

Bagehot, Walter, *Lombard Street: A Description of the Money Market*, 1873.

Baker, Dean, "Lehman Three Years Later: What We Haven't Learned," *The Guardian Unlimited*, September 12, 2011.

Baker, Dean, and Kevin Hassett, "The Human Disaster of Unemployment," *New York Times*, May 12, 2012.

Ball, Laurence, "Long-Term Damage from the Great Recession in OECD Countries," NBER Working Paper 20185, May 2014.

Ball v. Board of Governors of the Federal Reserve System, District Court for the District of Columbia, No. 13-cv-0603, 2015.

Ball, Laurence, "Ben Bernanke and the Zero Bound," *Contemporary Economic Policy*, January 2016.

Basel Committee on Banking Supervision, "Basel III: The Net Stable Funding Ratio," Bank for International Settlements, October 2014.

Bernanke, Ben, Nonmonetary Effects of the Financial Crisis in the Propagation of the Great Depression, *American Economic Review*, June 1983.

Bernanke, Ben, Various speeches and Congressional testimony, 2008–2014, www.federalreserve.gov.

Bernanke, Ben, *The Courage to Act: A Memoir of a Crisis and Its Aftermath*, W. W. Norton & Company, 2015.

Blinder, Alan, *After the Music Stopped: The Financial Crisis, the Response, and the Work Ahead*, Penguin Press, 2013.

Bloomberg News, data from FOIA request No. 2008–356, http://documents .theblackvault.com/documents/financial/bloomberg/

Board of Governors of the Federal Reserve System, various press releases, 2008, www.federalreserve.gov.

Board of Governors of the Federal Reserve System, publication H.4.1, various months, 2008–2009, www.federalreserve.gov.

Board of Governors of the Federal Reserve System, "Report Pursuant to Section 129 of the Emergency Economic Stabilization Act of 2008: Secured Credit Facility Authorized for American International Group, Inc. on September 16, 2008," www.federalreserve.gov.

Board of Governors of the Federal Reserve System, "Credit and Liquidity Programs and the Balance Sheet," www.federalreserve.gov.

Bordo, Michael D., "The Lender of Last Resort: Alternative Views and Historical Experience," *Federal Reserve Bank of Richmond Economic Review*, January/February 1990.

Cline, William R., and Joseph E. Gagnon, "Lehman Died, Bagehot Lives: Why Did the Fed and Treasury Let a Major Wall Street Bank Fail?," Policy Brief PB13-21, Peterson Institute for International Economics, September 2013.

Congressional Oversight Panel for TARP, *The AIG Rescue, Its Impact on Markets, and the Government's Exit Strategy*, US Government Printing Office, June 2010.

Copeland, Adam, Antoine Martin, and Michael Walker, "The Tri-Party Repo Market before the 2010 Reforms," *Federal Reserve Bank of New York Staff Reports* 477, November 2010.

Cox, Christopher, "Testimony Concerning Recent Events in the Credit Markets," Senate Banking Committee, April 3, 2008.

Crapo, David, "Lehman Brothers Dismantles in Bankruptcy," *Pratt's Journal of Bankruptcy Law*, November/December 2008.

Davidson, Adam, "Inside the Meltdown," *National Public Radio Frontline*, February 17, 2009, www.pbs.org.

Diamond, Douglas, and Philip Dybvig, "Bank Runs, Deposit Insurance, and Liquidity," *Journal of Political Economy*, June 1983.

Duffie, Darrell, *How Big Banks Fail and What to Do about It*, Princeton University Press, 2010.

Federal Reserve Bank of New York, financial statement for Maiden Lane LLC on 12/31/2008, released 2010, newyorkfed.org.

Federal Reserve Bank of New York, "Update on Tri-Party Repo Infrastructure Reform," June 24, 2015, newyorkfed.org.

Federal Open Market Committee, meeting transcript and background documents, September 16, 2008, www.federalreserve.gov.

Financial Crisis Inquiry Commission, *Report*, with supporting documents, 2011, fcic.law.stanford.edu.

Fleming, Michael J., and Asani Sarkar, "The Failure Resolution of Lehman Brothers," *Federal Reserve Bank of New York Economic Policy Review*, December 2014.

Friedman, Milton, and Anna J. Schwartz, *A Monetary History of the United States, 1867–1960*, Princeton University Press, 1963.

Geithner, Timothy F., *Stress Test: Reflections on Financial Crises*, Crown Publishers, 2014.

Giddens, James W., *LBI Trustee's Preliminary Investigation Report*, August 2010, http://dm.epiq11.com/LBI/Project#

Giddens, James W., *LBI Trustee's Preliminary Realization Report*, February 2015, http://dm.epiq11.com/LBI/Project#

Goodhart, Charles A. E., "Myths about the Lender of Last Resort," *International Finance*, November 1999.

Greenspan, Alan, Testimony before the House Committee on Oversight and Government Reform, October 23, 2008.

Ickes, Barry, "Lehman and Pearl Harbor," September 12, 2009, ickmansblog .blogspot.com.

Joint Administrators of Lehman Brothers International (Europe), *First Progress Report*, April 14, 2009, pwc.co.uk.

Kacperczyk, Marcin, and Philipp Schnabl, "When Safe Proved Risky: Commercial Paper during the Financial Crisis of 2007–2009," *Journal of Economic Perspectives*, Winter 2010.

King, Matt, "Are the Brokers Broken?," Citi research note, September 5, 2008.

Krugman, Paul, "Fighting Off Depression," *New York Times*, January 4, 2009.

LaCapra, Lauren Tara, "AIG Ex-CEO Breaks Down the Final Days," *The Street*, September 25, 2009.

Lehman Brothers Holdings Inc., various forms 10-K and 10-Q, 2007–2008, www.sec .gov.

Leising, Matthew, "Fed Let Brokers Turn Junk to Cash at Height of Financial Crisis," *Bloomberg Business*, April 1, 2011.

Levisohn, Ben, "Lehman: Independent for How Long?," *Bloomberg Business*, June 11, 2008.

Mason, J. W., "What Recovery? The Case for Continued Expansionary Policy at the Fed," Roosevelt Institute, July 25, 2017.

McCracken, Jeffrey, "Lehman's Chaotic Bankruptcy Filing Destroyed Billions in Value," *Wall Street Journal*, December 29, 2008.

Miller, Harvey R., and Maurice Horwitz, "Resolution Authority: Lessons from the Lehman Experience," Presentation at NYU Stern School of Business, April 11, 2013.

National Organization of Life and Health Insurance Guarantee Associations, "Conversation with Bryan Marsal," *NOLHGA Journal*, 2013.

Nocera, Joe, "Lehman Had to Die So Global Finance Could Live," *New York Times*, September 11, 2009.

Paulson, Henry M., Jr., *On the Brink: Inside the Race to Stop the Collapse of the Global Financial System*, Business Plus, 2010 and update in 2013.

Paulson, Henry M., Jr., Testimony before the House Committee on Oversight and Government Reform, January 27, 2010.

Pirro, Christine, "Cash Flow vs. Balance Sheet Insolvency in Chapter 11: Who Cares?," Weil Bankruptcy Blog, August 13, 2013.

Pratt, Shannon P., *Valuing a Business: The Analysis and Appraisal of Closely Held Companies*, fifth edition, McGraw Hill, 2008.

Reifschneider, Dave, William Wascher, and David Wilcox, "Aggregate Supply in the United States: Recent Developments and Implications for the Conduct of Monetary Policy," FEDS Working Paper 2013–77.

Reinhart, Vincent, Remarks at American Enterprise Institute, April 28, 2008.

Roe, Mark J., and Stephen Adams, "Restructuring Failed Financial Firms in Bankruptcy: Selling Lehman's Derivatives Portfolio," *Yale Journal on Regulation*, Summer 2015.

Schuman, Joseph, "The Morning Brief: It's a Decisive Weekend for Lehman," *WSJ Online Edition*, September 12, 2008.

Scott, Hal S., *Connectedness and Contagion: Protecting the Financial System from Panics*, MIT Press, 2016.

Sender, Henry et al., "Clock Ticking for Lehman Rescue," *Financial Times*, September 13, 2008.

Solman, Paul, "Trillions of Dollars in Bank Bailouts: Socialism for the Rich?," *PBS Newshour Making Sense*, September 19, 2012.

Sorkin, Andrew Ross, *Too Big to Fail: The Inside Story of How Wall Street and Washington Fought to Save the Financial System – and Themselves*, Viking Press, 2009.

Special Inspector General for the Troubled Asset Relief Program, "Factors Affecting Efforts to Limit Payments to AIG Counterparties," SIGTARP-10–003, November 2009.

Stewart, James B., "Solvency, Lost in the Fog at the Fed," *New York Times*, November 7, 2014.

Stewart, James B., and Peter Eavis, "Revisiting the Lehman Brothers Bailout That Never Was," *New York Times*, September 29, 2014.

Tarullo, Daniel K., "Liquidity Regulation," Speech at the Clearing House Annual Conference, November 20, 2014, www.federalreserve.gov.

Todd, Walker F., "FDICIA's Emergency Liquidity Provisions," *Federal Reserve Bank of Cleveland Economic Review*, July 1993.

Tucker, Paul, "The Repertoire of Official Sector Interventions in the Financial System: Last Resort Lending, Market-Making, and Capital," speech at the Bank of Japan, May 28, 2009.

Valukas, Anton, *Lehman Brothers Holdings Inc. Chapter 11 Proceedings Examiner Report*, with supporting documents, 2010, jenner.com/lehman.

Volcker, Paul, Speech at the Economic Club of New York, April 8, 2008.

Wachtell, Lipton, Rosen, and Katz, Amended Counterclaims of JPMorgan Chase Bank N.A., United States Bankruptcy Court for the Southern District of New York, No. 10–03266 Doc 79–1, February 7, 2011.

Wessel, David, *In Fed We Trust: Ben Bernanke's War on the Great Panic*, Three Rivers Press, 2009.

Wolf, Martin, *The Shift and the Shocks: What We've Learned – and Still Have to Learn – From the Financial Crisis*, Penguin Press, 2014.

Index

Michael D. Bordo, *The Gold Standard and Related Regimes: Collected Essays* (1999)

Michele Fratianni and Franco Spinelli, *A Monetary History of Italy* (1997)

Mark Toma, *Competition and Monopoly in the Federal Reserve System, 1914–1951* (1997)

Barry Eichengreen, Editor, *Europe's Postwar Recovery* (1996)

Lawrence H. Officer, *Between the Dollar-Sterling Gold Points: Exchange Rates, Parity and Market Behavior* (1996)

Elmus Wicker, *Banking Panics of the Great Depression* (1996)

Norio Tamaki, *Japanese Banking: A History, 1859–1959* (1995)

Barry Eichengreen, *Elusive Stability: Essays in the History of International Finance, 1919–1939* (1993)

Michael D. Bordo and Forrest Capie, Editors, *Monetary Regimes in Transition* (1993)

Larry Neal, *The Rise of Financial Capitalism: International Capital Markets in the Age of Reason* (1993)

S. N. Broadberry and N. F. R. Crafts, Editors, *Britain in the International Economy, 1870–1939* (1992)

Aurel Schubert, *The Credit-Anstalt Crisis of 1931* (1992)

Trevor J. O. Dick and John E. Floyd, *Canada and the Gold Standard: Balance of Payments Adjustment under Fixed Exchange Rates, 1871–1913* (1992)

Kenneth Mouré, *Managing the Franc Poincaré: Economic Understanding and Political Constraint in French Monetary Policy, 1928–1936* (1991)

David C. Wheelock, *The Strategy and Consistency of Federal Reserve Monetary Policy, 1924–1933* (1991)